WELLS FARGO

the American Frontier

BY EDWARD HUNGERFORD

BONANZA BOOKS · NEW YORK

WELLS FARGO

Advancing the American Frontier

This is the stout, iron-bound, green box in which Wells Fargo carried untold millions of gold over the wild and lonely roads of frontier America. It was the objective of every stage robber in the Sierras.

Acknowledgments

Mr. Hungerford died shortly after finishing the manuscript of this book and before he was able to complete the list of those to whom he was indebted for information, research and old records of the Wells Fargo Company. He had planned to write such a history for years before he actually began it, and had been accumulating material during all that time. He made many trips across the country, visiting Wells Fargo men, libraries, studying old records and other sources.

Among authorities which his records show to have been consulted, and to whom he would wish to express his thanks, are the following:

Miss Marcia Fee of San Francisco, who helped the author in his research and who contributed greatly by her knowledge of sources. To Miss Fee the publishers are indebted for certain of the names which follow and also for many entries in the bibliography at the end of the book, indicating authorities consulted in its preparation.

The Henry E. Huntington Library and Art Gallery, San Marino, Calif.

The Bancroft Library, University of California, Berkeley, Calif.; Mrs. Eleanor Bancroft, Assistant Director, Mrs. Elizabeth Euphrat and Mrs. Violet Homem.

California Historical Society, Inc.; Mrs. Rogers Parratt.

Mechanics Library, San Francisco; Mr. John Stump.

San Francisco Public Library, History Room staff.

Miss Catherine Harroun, Wells Fargo Bank & Union Trust Company, San Francisco; and Miss Irene Simpson, Curator, Wells Fargo Bank History Room.

Mr. G. W. Wickland, Vice-President, Wells Fargo Bank & Union Trust Company, San Francisco, who established the Bank's History Room.

Mr. Frederick L. Lipman, Former President and Chairman of the Board, Wells Fargo Bank & Union Trust Company, San Francisco, for first-hand recollections of his long career with Wells Fargo.

Mr. Gilbert H. Kneiss of Berkeley, Calif., Assistant to the President of the Western Pacific Railroad.

Mr. F. Q. Treadway, General Advertising Manager, Southern Pacific Company, and Mr. Earle Heath, Editor, Southern Pacific News Bureau.

Mr. Elmer Ray Jones, President of Wells, Fargo and Company, New York.

Mr. James O. Ellis, Vice-President of Wells, Fargo and Company, New York.

There were many others whose names do not appear in Mr. Hungerford's records whom he would want to thank and the publishers do so now in his behalf.

The publishers should also like to thank those who assisted in the preparation of this manuscript for publication, including the following:

Mr. James T. Babb, Director of the Yale University Library, and Miss Dorothy Bridgewater of that library, who kindly made available material in the Coe Collection of Western Americana.

The Columbia University Library.

The staff of the American History Room at the N. Y. Public Library.

Mr. Arthur B. Carlson of the New-York Historical Society, the latter for help in the selection of illustrations.

The publishers also wish to thank Mrs. Hungerford Devereaux, the author's daughter; and Miss Eunice Boehle, who was the author's secretary for several years.

Special acknowledgment is made to authors and publishers for permission to quote from certain books listed on the copyright page and in the bibliography at the back.

Table of Contents

Illustrations

Maps

xiv

Introduction

BY ELMER RAY JONES

In a Pan-American airplane flying over the Gulf of Mexico
en route from Mexico to Havana, Cuba, my mind has wandered to a recent visit in Mexico City with the author of this
book, my dear friend Ed Hungerford, who was recently called
to the great beyond before its publication. The writing of this
story was his last and greatest love. It was Ed's request both
personally and by cable that I should write the Foreword.

Little did I realize that this short expression of approval of his work and deep affection for my friend of thirty and seven years would be written high up in the Heavens in an airplane and thousands of miles from the lonely hospital room from which his spirit took its flight.

The writing of this history of the greatest pioneer company of our Republic was a joy and a fulfillment of a long-standing ambition of Ed Hungerford. He has done a fine job. The subject is too large and the history too long and romantic to be amply portrayed in any one volume, but those things herein recorded will, I hope, be sympathetically received by the reader. Ed Hungerford has devotedly tried to give us a true picture of one of America's most daring and romantic organizations, Wells, Fargo and Company, with its Pony Express, stage coaches, highway robberies, together with the experiences of those men who from the beginning, almost one hundred years ago, to the present day have so faithfully endeavored to render a valuable and useful service to this, our beloved country.

WELLS FARGO

Advancing the American Frontier

I Gold!

Gold started it and gold continued to be the chief concern of Wells, Fargo and Company* for many decades; indeed the transfer of gold remains today an important aspect of its many-sided business. As express messengers to a frontier nation, the Wells Fargo men were intimately tied up with the most roman-

---

*The official form of the name from the time of first incorporation to 1866 was Wells, Fargo & Company. After that it was Wells, Fargo and Company. The tendency at present is to omit the comma. However, to avoid confusion, the form used in the text above has been followed consistently throughout except in quotations. In these the verbatim form has been followed.—The Editor.

tic and stirring chapters of the opening of the West. It was all in the day's work to them, but it was a part of the "manifest destiny" which made the vast territory west of the Mississippi part of a unified nation.

In the business of transporting treasure the Wells Fargo people knew violence and death, Indian raids, stage robberies, financial panic, blizzards in the mountain passes, blinding heat and thirst on the desert, train robberies, titanic financial battles. They organized a stagecoach empire, they operated over the world-famous Pony Express, they fought the United States Government for the privilege of carrying the mails and their shotgun messengers are a legend in the epic of the West.

It all started with the discovery of gold in California on January 24, 1848. Things did not move as swiftly then as they do today. Even the San Francisco newspapers were slow to recognize the significance of James Marshall's find near Sutter's Mill. But when they did take it in, the papers stopped publication because there was no one there to set type, run the presses, write the news. They had all gone to the diggings. Nor did it stop there, for the gold madness seized the nation. From New England to the Mississippi clerks closed their ledgers, not to reopen them again; men deserted their looms and their lathes, or their places behind store counters; physicians left their patients and lawyers their clients. It seemed that half the United States was seeking the best path for the arduous journey to the western rim of the sprawling nation. In a single year, seventy-five thousand restless men made the unspeakably hard journey from the Eastern United States to California. It was, of course, the news story of the century and the Eastern papers made the most of it. The rush suddenly peopled the lonely pine-clad slopes of the Sierras with gold-seekers and changed San Francisco from a quiet little Spanish seaport on the sand dunes beside the Golden Gate to a seething, hectic, money-mad city. It was gold that brought the artisan, ill at ease in the habiliments of the miner: that brought in his train, the blackleg, the gambler, the thief. It was the lust for gold by the corrupt elements which brought about the organization of the Vigilantes.

The gold rush was given great impetus by President Polk's

annual message to Congress, delivered on December 5, 1848, in which he said: "The accounts of the abundance of gold in that territory are of such extraordinary character as would scarcely command belief were they not corroborated by the authentic reports of officers in the public service, who have visited the mineral district, and derived the facts which they detail from personal observation." By 1850 at least 100,000 immigrants had come to California. By 1851 there were more than 300,000 newcomers.

Back in New York State two men who had had some experience in organizing the carrying of parcels on the growing network of Eastern railroads read of the excitement and watched their friends depart for the gold fields. They read of the admission of California to statehood in 1850. They were in no hurry. Two years later they met in the back room of a bookstore in Syracuse and made their plans. They were Henry Wells of Auburn and William G. Fargo of Pompey Hill back of Syracuse. They and the others who founded Wells Fargo were closely connected with the earliest beginnings of the express business in this country. In 1841, Henry Wells, with George Pomeroy and Crawford Livingston formed the express firm of Livingston, Wells & Pomeroy Company to operate between Albany and Buffalo, New York. In 1845, Henry Wells organized another firm, Wells & Company, which operated west of Buffalo to Cincinnati, St. Louis and Chicago.

In 1849, John Butterfield, one of the outstanding men in the field, formed Butterfield, Wasson and Company, which operated on the New York Central Railroad. Finally, in 1850, Wells, William Fargo, John Butterfield as well as several others, organized the American Express Company. The men who founded the American Express were shrewd; they had plenty of capital, and they knew their business.

They watched the development of the gold rush for several years and, on March 18, 1852, at the historic Astor House in New York City, formed the firm of Wells, Fargo and Company. They proposed to compete in California with Adams and other expresses on a new and strange ground where stagecoaches and highroads took the place of the steel tracks of the

5

eastern railroads, where expressmen, armed with shotguns, rode behind six horses, where for a time gold dust was the most important commodity. And they proposed to fill a need and to make money at it. They did both.

Wells Fargo was formed as a "joint stock association express company" with a capitalization of $300,000, divided into 3,000 shares with a par value of $100 per share. Its first public announcement was made on May 20, 1852, in the *New York Times*:

WELLS, FARGO & CO. CALIFORNIA EXPRESS

CAPITAL $300,000

A joint stock company.   Office 16 Wall Street

Directors

Henry Wells, Johnston Livingston, Elijah P. Williams, Edwin B. Morgan, Wm. G. Fargo, Jas. McKay, Alpheus Reynolds, Alex M. C. Smith, Henry D. Rice.

Edwin B. Morgan, *President*

James McKay, *Secretary*

This company having completed its organisation as above is now ready to undertake the general forwarding agency and commission business; the purchase and sale of gold dust, bullion and specie, also packages, parcels and freight of all description in and between the City of New York and the City of San Francisco, and the principal cities and towns in California, connecting at New York with the lines of the American Express Company, the Harnden Express, Pullen, Virgil & Co. European Express.

They have established offices and faithful agents in all the principal cities and towns throughout the eastern, middle and western states, energetic and faithful messengers furnished with iron chests for the security of treasure and other valuable packages accompany each express upon all their lines as well as in California and in the Atlantic States.

Samuel P. Carter for many years connected with the American Express, and R. W. Washburn, late of the bank of Syracuse, have been appointed principal agents in California.

6

Carter arrived in San Francisco on June 27, 1852, on the *S. S. Oregon* and two weeks later, on July 11th, Reuben Washburn arrived on the *Tennessee*. Carter came to run the express business, and Washburn, the banking end.

Even before Wells Fargo's office was opened or Washburn and Carter had arrived in San Francisco, the following notice appeared in the *Alta California*:

> Wells, Fargo & Co's Atlantic and Pacific Express, a joint stock company . . . is now ready to undertake a general Express Forwarding Agency and Commission Business; the purchase and sale of Gold Dust, Bullion and Bills of Exchange; the payment and collection of Notes, Bills and Accounts; the forwarding of Gold Dust, Bullion and Specie; also, Packages, Parcels and Freight of all descriptions, and between the city of New York and the city of San Francisco, and the principal cities and towns in California . . . energetic and faithful messengers furnished with iron chests for the security of treasure and other valuable packages accompanying each Express upon all their lines, as well in California as in the Atlantic states.
>
> They will immediately establish offices at all the principal towns in California, and run messengers on their own account for the purpose of doing a general Express business. As soon as arrangements are completed, notice will be given.

Prospective New York customers were more interested in the "joint stock company," while the California miners would have been impressed with the "messengers furnished with iron chests." Wells Fargo was to prove itself quickly able to adapt its operations to the strenuous conditions in California.

The promise of offices and messengers was quickly kept. By August, 1852, three branches were opened for business in Placer County, others in Sacramento, Benicia, Monterey and San Diego. Before the close of 1852 Wells Fargo had twelve offices in operation. From the beginning the firm was enterprising.

In the late autumn of '52 Henry Wells decided to go out west and see for himself how the "arrangements" had been made. It was the only trip he ever had to make to California for the company. He traveled by way of the Isthmus of Panama.

7

When he reached Panama he wrote back to New York, "Thank God the Isthmus is passed and I am alive and kicking but awful sore and tired. It was a dangerous and difficult trip." Wells paid $30 for the doubtful pleasure of riding a mule from Cruces to Panama. The same letter added:

> Give me credit of being the first man across the Isthmus in a race of six hundred and all or nearly all young men and very many are not in now and will not be for 24 hours yet. I passed everything on the road.

Passing everything on the road was a habit of Henry Wells. A "broadside" published in 1849, now in the Coe Collection of Western Americana at Yale University Library, provides interesting information about the hazards of the trip across the Isthmus:

> ... The journey to Panama [from Chagres, the Caribbean port] is made by taking small canoes (or a steamboat which has now gone there) to the town of Cruces or Gorgona, a distant of about 33 miles, and from there to Panama, about 24 miles by land. The river part of the route formerly cost from one to four doubloons (16 dollars each) but when the steamboat is there the expense will probably be less. The stagnant waters, reptiles, &c. in the vicinity of the river, render walking across next to impossible. Gorgona, the first landing place, is a small village, situated on a small plain on the banks of the river. Cruces, the other landing, is a few miles further up, from both . . . are roads leading to Panama, about the same distance, and which unite about nine miles from that city. This 24 miles of land route is usually performed on horse or mules, with another mule to carry baggage & a Muleteer to act as guide. Owing to rains and the face of the country, the progress is slow, as the road is merely a bridle path, and the journey occupies 10 to 12 hours before reaching the city of Panama.

Neither Henry Wells nor his partners were unprepared for the competition their new company faced. Rather than rush in blindly they had waited until the seething territory had become a state and until they were prepared to meet the rough-and-tumble competition of the expresses that mushroomed in the gold regions.

8

Ernest Wiltsee's book, *The Pioneer Miner and the Pack Mule Express,* lists scores of these early express companies. Cady's Express, which was "short-lived but historic" was the only one to serve California before the gold rush. C. L. Cady announced his express in *The Californian* as early as April 24, 1847. He provided weekly service between San Francisco and Sutter's Fort.

Alexander Todd, one of the great early expressmen, reached San Francisco by sea in June, 1849. He came to prospect for gold and headed for the Mother Lode, as the gold-mining region was called. But Todd wasn't strong enough for the difficult physical work of mining and he soon gave it up. As a miner, though, he quickly saw the crying need for an express service. The men in the isolated gold fields wanted mail and parcels. He therefore rode on horseback through Columbia, Sonoro and other towns in the southern Mother Lode region, recording the names, at a dollar a head, of the men who wanted their mail brought up from San Francisco. In addition to this charge, he collected an ounce of gold for each letter delivered. Men gave their names and their dollars readily and, shortly after he started, Todd was an expressman with more than two thousand customers. His business was booming. Todd, as quoted by Wiltsee, tells of his first trip down to "the Bay" from the gold fields:

> When I had collected a long list of names, and was making my arrangements for my first trip to San Francisco, on reaching Stockton, some merchants there asked me when I was going to start my express, and I told them the next morning, and they said they had something to send, and I went into Bell's store to see what it was. He had a lot of gold dust in boxes and he gave it to me to bring down. I put it in a butter keg, in different packages, and I delivered it to the firm of Lord & Co. here, one of the oldest firms in San Francisco. My express matter was pretty heavy. I suppose I had at least two hundred thousand dollars worth of dust with me. We landed at the corner of Clay and Sansome Streets, where the old *Niantic* was lying. There was a wooden staging along the side, to walk up from the water, and I had to roll my keg of gold dust, which contained

probably a hundred and fifty thousand dollars, along this place, and it cracked and creaked, and I felt uneasy until it was delivered. I charged five per cent on the dust for bringing it down. . . . After getting my letters, I bought a rowboat to go back to Stockton, and took up sixteen passengers, who paid me an ounce apiece for passage, and "eat themselves." I was the Captain, and though I did not know anything of the river, I sat in the stern and steered, and they rowed. We got there in about twenty-four hours, and that gave me a reputation. I paid $300 for my boat, and sold her for $500 in Stockton, and had made a handsome turn with the passengers and freight I carried up.

Todd's account goes on to explain how rapidly his business expanded. It wasn't long before he not only carried express but also served as banker for the miners:

. . . we were obliged to have safes at our different offices, and our express business soon merged into a banking business. We charged them [the miners] for taking care of their dust one-half per cent a month, and they gave us the privilege of using it also. That was termed a general deposit. A special deposit was when a miner would bring in his dust, and put his name on it, and put a seal on it, and for keeping such deposits in our safe, we charged them one per cent a month.

For a time Todd shared offices in Stockton with Adams and Company. In the fall of 1851 he sold his interests to Newell and Company who shortly thereafter became the agents in Stockton for Adams. Later Todd helped establish the Reynold's, Todd and Company Express which was absorbed by Wells Fargo in 1853.

The early days were exciting and profitable ones for the expressmen. The highwaymen had not yet begun to hold up the stages carrying great quantities of gold. Todd's personal account tells about some of the problems they faced:

An expressman on the road was almost exempt from interference because everybody was interested, and if an expressman had been attacked, and his assailant discovered, punishment would have been very speedy. I don't know that people were any more honest then than now, but . . . an expressman, though carrying large sums of money, bore almost a charmed life in those days. We were robbed by our clerks. One of our confidential clerks in 1852 robbed us of $70,000 in Stockton; another of $50,000 in Mariposa, and another of $40,000 at Mokelumne Hill. In the latter case the thing came to our knowledge when we came to settle up, and he committed suicide.

I have been burned out nine times in different parts of the country since I have been here. In the first days there was no insurance, and the only safety was to jump and run. In the May fire of 1850, I wrote to my partner at another point after I was burned out, saying how I had escaped, and had no clothing, and asked him to send me some money. He wrote back, saying that he could sympathize with me as the night before he had to jump out of the window to save his life, on account of the fire which burned him out, and he could do nothing for me.

The Adams Express Company sent Daniel Hale Haskell to California to establish its express service there. He arrived in San Francisco on October 31, 1849, and by November 8th, only nine days later, he had leased a small wooden building and placed an announcement of express services in the *Alta California*. By early 1852 Adams in California covered the whole state and, by 1854, it was the leading express concern on the coast. Adams had bought out smaller concerns, proved enterprising by establishing a pony express service in some parts of the state and, in general, making itself a vital cog in the development of the whole region. It was the only concern, before Wells Fargo, to provide a messenger with its regular shipments of express by water from San Francisco to New York.

Thus, while Wells Fargo was not the first express company in California, it became the greatest and most powerful of them all within a few years after its arrival in 1852. By careful planning and with its influential backer in the East, the American Express Company, to help it along, it grew rapidly. Wells Fargo opened office after office in the Mother Lode and each of these was as fully equipped for service as its headquarters on Montgomery Street in San Francisco.

The miner took his nuggets or dust to the nearest Wells Fargo office, and a short while after the company came to

California there was never one far away. The Wells Fargo agents weighed the gold on the delicate scales kept for the purpose and gave the miner a receipt. The process was simple and the miners liked it. Whether the company shipped parcels or acted as banker its watchwords were responsibility and reliability.

Wells Fargo eventually bought the great stagecoach lines on which it first rode as messenger and, by the middle of the 1860's, owned the greatest staging empire in the world. Its mails rode the Pony Express. The company expanded into the Comstock Lode country when that field was developed, fanned out into Oregon, Montana, Idaho and the great Southwest. For years it carried mail in addition to its express cargoes. It developed its own police system to combat the bandits who early began to covet its rich cargoes.

When the railroad replaced the six-horse stage, Wells Fargo continued to expand. In addition to bullion it carried merchandise of all kinds by rail. The name Wells Fargo became synonymous with the West. It is irretrievably linked with the expansion of the American frontier—with gold and bandits, Indians and adventure.

In 1852 John Parrott completed the first stone building in all San Francisco, at a cost of $117,000. It was located at the northwest corner of Montgomery and California Streets and, when it was completed, Daniel Haskell's Adams Express moved in. The building was large enough for two firms and so Page, Bacon and Company, bankers, shared the building with Adams. There is an interesting story about the erection of that building.

Parrott's castle, which stood until the late 1920's, was made of large stones imported in sailing ships from China. Each stone was hand cut and numbered. However, the marks were indecipherable to the Americans and when Chinese masons of San Francisco, who supposedly would understand what the markings meant were brought to assemble the building, they took one look and refused to work. The key to the puzzle apparently had been left in China.

For once Yankee ingenuity was sadly lacking. Parrott and

the contractors were both puzzled and helpless. Finally, in desperation, Parrott sent to China for the man who had designed the building and supervised the cutting of the stones.

When he arrived, the small, wizened Chinese first asked to be shown the site for the building. He went over it with foot rule and compass and, when he had finished his careful inspection, he slowly shook his head and said:

"You are placing your building on the wrong corner of the street. It should be erected on the opposite side. The stones are all cut and marked for the other corner where no evil influences are to be encountered, as will be found here."

Parrott protested that he had already purchased the land on the northwest corner. The Chinese continued to shake his head. It would not do. Chinese tradition was a powerful thing and no building might be erected that defied it. The gods might wreak vengeance upon such a building.

There was almost nothing that Parrott could do but defy tradition. He proceeded with the building and, finally, managed to get the stones together. The Chinese of San Francisco were horrified. Yet, according to Alexander McLeod's *Pigtails and Gold Dust*, they finally proposed that the building be exorcised and purified. This was to be done by a series of rites which involved burning of yellow papers upon a tray and drenching them with rice and three cups of tea. By doing this the evil spirits would be driven away and the good ones would be appeased.

The contractors had promised to perform the rites, but when the building was finished they refused to permit the ceremony to be held. No Chinese would enter the building. Instead they all went to the new red brick building across the street which Sam Brannan, the Mormon, had just built for the firm of Wells, Fargo and Company. More than that, the Chinese prayed for the success of Wells Fargo and gave the newcomer their business.

When Henry Wells arrived in San Francisco in February of 1853, Wells Fargo was doing business in the red brick building on Montgomery Street, opposite John Parrott's stone building. Washburn and Carter, as we have seen, had been there for six months and Wells found the office in ship-shape condition. The company's new sign was polished and bright green shutters, made of cast iron imported from South Brooklyn by way of the Horn, were hung. These green shutters were put at the windows of every Wells Fargo building. They looked substantial and they were. They became a kind of trade-mark, and the company was so proud of them that it gladly paid the freight on their not inconsiderable weight all the way from South Brooklyn right up to the latest boom town in the gold fields.

Inside the tidy counting room Henry Wells could see a long line of shiny, brass balance scales at which tellers weighed, to the smallest fraction of an ounce, the chief commodity—gold. Wells Fargo was already a well-established firm with a high standing in the region. Henry Wells was pleased. He wrote, on February 15th, to his close friend and associate, Colonel Edwin B. Morgan at Aurora, New York, saying that his first day in San Francisco had not lessened his high hopes for the California enterprise:

> It cannot fail of being the most profitable part of our business. Our Internal Express here is one of the most profitable that I ever knew for its age & is constantly growing . . . After the *Golden Gate* comes in I will go up to all our offices. If Pardee or someone else comes he will go along with Carter & me. If by any possibility no one has started, for Heaven's Sake do not lose any time in sending a man here for Carter will go home, at any rate I am perfectly satisfied with all Carter's Arrangements. They have been Judicious and well timed, liberal but not extravagant & such as have given him the confidence of the best men of the Town.
>
> You may recollect Brigham of the Harnden Express was spoken of & he has kindly offered to take charge of our interests here in connection with the Vanderbilt line of steamers at the moderate salary of Ten Thousand a Year. Carter is worth Two of him. In fact he is the man for the position and were it not that he wants to go home I should rest content with his Management of our External Arrangements but he will come back & remain here. . . .
>
> This is a great Country & a greater people. Our Express

14

is just in from Sacramento & the mines & our Way-bill for New York will amount to nearly $3000. The amt. going forward by this Steamer as you will see is the largest ever shipped from this Port. Had the express got in from the Southern mines we should have had some Two Hundred Ounces more to add to our amount. But it will come next time.

Colonel William Pardee didn't arrive in San Francisco to replace Samuel Carter until July 7, 1853. Henry Wells returned to New York in the spring before Pardee arrived. Even at that time he was not in good health. He spent less and less time in the business of the firm, and finally retired to his home in Aurora, New York, where, in 1868, he founded the woman's college that bears his name.

In October, 1853, Edwin B. Morgan was succeeded as president of Wells Fargo by D. N. Barney of Watertown, New York. Young Barney had already made a name for himself as a banker in New York City.

Although Wells Fargo came to California four years after gold was discovered, and other express companies were established, it prospered and began to outdistance its competitors. One of the major factors in its early growth was its custom of buying out its competitors. As early as November, 1852, Wells Fargo bought Gregory and Company's Express. This was the first of three major acquisitions. Almost a year later, in September, 1853, Todd's express was bought out. The next major purchase was made in July, 1854, when Hunter and Company's Express was taken over. Wells Fargo now owned expresses operating over a string of lines blanketing California. The company had come a long way in two years. Competition pretty much narrowed down to a battle between Adams and Wells Fargo. Page, Bacon and Company, which shared Parrott's great stone building with Adams, were bankers handling a good deal of gold in San Francisco but they were never in the general express business.

Along with the men who came to dig for gold, came the gamblers, the riffraff and the prostitutes. Horace Greeley, in his book *An Overland Journey*, shows by indirection why the harlots were so popular:

15

The Census of 1850* made the total population of California (Indians not counted) ninety-two thousand five hundred and ninety-seven; but there were some counties from which no returns were received, which, it was estimated, would increase the aggregate to one hundred and seventeen thousand five hundred and thirty-eight. Only two years thereafter, a state census was taken, which increased the number to two hundred and sixty-four thousand four hundred and thirty-five—it having more than doubled (by immigration) in two years. Of this number, only twenty-two thousand one hundred and ninety-three were females—less than one-tenth of the whole; while the great majority were men in the vigorous prime of life. The state of public morals among a population so disproportioned, in a land far removed from the restraining influences of home and kindred, were better imagined than described.

Neither San Francisco nor any other part of California could handle the avalanche of people. There was insufficient food, clothes and housing. Prices of almost every commodity skyrocketed. Many of the men who went into the hills to find gold weren't equipped with either the physique or the knowhow. They failed to find riches and so they wandered back to San Francisco.

Frederick Johnson's old book, *Sights in the Gold Region and Scenes on the Way*, which he wrote after making a trip to California at the time, gives a fine picture of San Francisco in the gold-rush days:

> Discharged convicts from New South Wales, Mexicans, Kanakas, Peruvians, Chileans, representatives of all the European nations, with here and there the dangling cue of the Chinaman, were intermixed like stray cattle in a pound . . .
>
> We found the streets, or properly the roads, laid out quite regularly, those parallel with the water being a succession of terraces . . . Except a portion of the street fronting upon the cove they are all hard-beaten, sandy clay and as solid as if Macadamized. About three hundred houses, stores, shanties and sheds, with a great many tents, composed the town at that period. The houses were mostly built of rough boards and unpainted; brown cottons or calico nailed against the beams and

* These figures are conservative.

MAP OF THE GOLD REGION

Published by the NEW-YORK COMMERCIAL ADVERTISER July 26, 1849

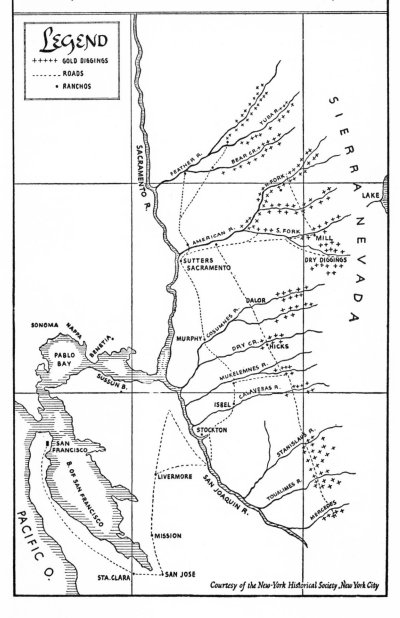

LEGEND
+++++ GOLD DIGGINGS
------- ROADS
• RANCHOS

Courtesy of the New-York Historical Society, New York City

joists answered for wall and ceiling of the better class of tene-
ments . . . the establishments of the commercial houses of
which we heard so much, were inferior to the outhouses of the
country seats on the Hudson.

Of those who did find gold, very few became rich overnight,
but they all came to San Francisco for entertainment. Everywhere that Johnson went he saw inflation and carefree men:

> The bar-rooms and hotels were crowded with revellers—
> money, wines, and liquor flowed like water. Gold dust, dou-
> bloons, and dollars were the only currency men would look at,
> old miners often scattering smaller coins in the streets by hand-
> fulls rather than to count or carry them. A French *café* was
> thronged with hungry customers at three dollars for a cup of
> coffee, bit of ham, and two eggs. Gambling prevailed to an ex-
> tent heretofore unheard of and unknown. The *monté* and
> *roulette* tables, encircled continually day and night by a dense
> mass were covered with bags of gold dust and heaps of dou-
> bloons and Mexican dollars, which were incessantly changing
> hands in enormous amounts. Pistols and revolvers, fired in
> recklessness or fun sometimes, made the air musical with loud
> reports or whistling messengers, while, at other hours, intoxi-
> cated men, mounted on fleet horses, were rushing to and fro . . .

It would be grossly unfair to leave the impression that all
Californians of the period sought either gold or entertainment
or both. There were many who came or stayed for other
reasons. They were the men who turned to farming and
lumbering. The great vintners and ranchers played less dramatic and colorful roles than the forty-niners but they, as well
as the fishermen and fruit-growers and merchants worked to
make California prosperous and great.

In the 'fifties, Montgomery Street, today the Wall Street of
San Francisco, was a brawling, rowdy thoroughfare lined by
the principal banking houses, shops, hotels and saloons of the
carefree city. In those days the broad Embarcadero was not
yet dreamed of. The bay was close to Sansome Street and
the bowsprits of the swift clipper ships extended over that
narrow street. Their tall masts fringed the town all along the
water's edge.

Night and day the streets of San Francisco were crowded. Local citizens, miners who had made their way to the assay office and the mint from the Mother Lode, policemen and screaming newsboys added to the din. There were frequent fires in the town and the mad clatter of the fire companies rushing through the streets was a common one.

At the far end of Montgomery Street rose the steep knob of Telegraph Hill, at the top of which was the famed semaphore that first signaled to the city the arrival of ships. Ships meant mail, newspapers and express packages from the East, and whenever one came in bells and whistles further announced its coming and all San Francisco raced through the streets to greet the new arrival. Hacks and buses and splendid private carriages added to the congestion. There was almost always a band to greet each ship and generally a fire company or two would be on hand. After the ship docked there was a customary rush to the post office and to the express offices where men clamored impatiently for their packages and mail.

By 1852 the gold-mining region covered about 20,000 square miles at the foot of the High Sierras. It embraced Yuba, El Dorado, Amador, Placer, Calaveras, Tuolumne, Merced and Mariposa Counties. The rich gold deposits were almost entirely in the valleys of the various rivers and gulches of smaller streams that led down from the Sierras: the American, the Sacramento, the Feather and the Yuba.

The principle of all placer mining is based on the breaking up of gravel or earthy material by the action of water which washes off the lighter particles, leaving the heavier gold.

Simple washing was done with a "pan"—a round, metal dish with sloping sides. A "cradle" was used for mining larger deposits. The cradle was a box, made with a perforated bottom, mounted on a rocker. The action of the rocker shook the heavier gold through the bottom onto a canvas screen. The "tom" was a cradle with an extended sluice placed on an incline. In 1852 "hydraulic" mining was invented. This dramatic type of mining was done by shooting a powerful stream of water against a gravel bank of considerable size. This was a

19

great advance over simple washing or panning for, by hydraulic mining, huge quantities of gravel could be processed. Placer mining could be done by the individual miner, although often groups of men worked together. On the other hand vein mining was an extremely expensive process requiring stamp mills and other expensive equipment which few individual miners could afford.

Four years after the discovery, steamboats poked through the streets of Carquinez and up the American, San Joaquin and Sacramento Rivers. It was possible for the miner, merchant or expressman to travel in comfort on a sizable boat to Stockton or Sacramento, both gateways to the Mother Lode. In each of these towns there were stagecoaches that went up to the mines—or near to them—to the creeks, streams and gulches where men prospected.

II

Panic

In all *Alta* California there was no other town so favorably located as Sacramento. Built on low land, at the junction of the American and Sacramento Rivers, almost at the point where they joined the San Joaquin, Sacramento had tide-water connection with the Pacific, through the Golden Gate a little more than one hundred miles away. By the 'fifties, Sacramento wharf was the destination for much of the steamboat traffic while the wharf also served as the starting point for the ever-increasing stagecoach traffic that fanned up into the Sierras.

The track of the Sacramento Valley Railroad ran right down the center of the broad levee. Twice a day the small yellow train left for Folsom, twenty-two miles away. After 1856, when it was completed, the railroad supplemented the work of the stages. Even in the 'fifties, far-seeing businessmen talked about building a railroad right up the Big Hill, as the High Sierras were called, and across Nevada. From the beginning, Sacramento was railroad-minded while San Francisco, hemmed in by salt water, looked to the Orient and considered itself primarily a seaport.

From the earliest days of the gold rush, Sacramento had grown with astounding speed. When California was admitted to the Union in 1850, the capital had first been established at Monterey. Then it was moved to Benicia and, finally, to Sacramento. The new capital boasted such enterprising men as Leland Stanford, Collis P. Huntington, Mark Hopkins, Darwin C. Mills and Charles Crocker who were shrewd enough to realize that mining, at best, was a hazardous enterprise. With the exception of Mills, who was a highly successful banker, they were merchants and shopkeepers who made their early fortunes selling food, clothing and supplies to the miners.

William Pridham has told me on numerous occasions of the busy days on Sacramento wharf in the early days. Pridham was a definite little man close to ninety when I knew him in 1912. He was white-haired, always immaculately dressed in a blue-serge suit, and carried himself with an air of independence. He had served as a Wells Fargo messenger on the steamboat *New World* in the 'sixties, plying between Sacramento and San Francisco, and although he did not know Sacramento before 1855, his description of the town and life on the wharf represents the spirit of the whole era.

There were steamboats, and good ones, in the Sacramento and San Francisco trade, but none seemed to catch the popular fancy quite so much as the *New World*. This craft, in her neat coat of immaculate white, with her yellow stacks, 'scape pipes and upper works, and her gayly striped paddle-boxes, was a pretty sight. Captain Ned Wakeman had brought her from the East Coast around the Horn in 1849, a tremendous feat of

22

navigation, considering that she was a flat-bottomed side-wheeler intended strictly for river traffic.

There were always plenty of people to see the departure or arrival of the *New World* and the other steamboats. They filled the levee, stood on the galleries and leaned out the windows of the small wooden hotels. Sometimes there would be a hundred stages to meet the night boat for San Francisco and there was much noise, dust and commotion when the stages came racing down the streets of Sacramento.

Almost all the stages were six-horse hitches. All the late afternoon they brought a motley lot of miners and travelers to the levee. Newsboys milled through the crowd, and, if you were wise, you watched your wallet. It was no easy task to load the boats with the vast numbers of trunks, bags and boxes. Of course there was always gold to transport. Upon occasion the bullion room would carry close to a million dollars' worth of the metal. The room, braced by timbers, would be filled by stevedores who carried the gold from the stages in slender bags, suspended from a pole, swung between the shoulders of two men.

In the morning the traffic would be reversed. In the early dawn the San Francisco boat would arrive at the wharf where the stages were waiting. Quiet came to K Street wharf only when the last of the morning coaches, loaded with passengers, supplies and mail, went dashing off to the diggings, to Placerville, Auburn, Marysville and the other inland towns reached by the ever-improving roads.

William Pridham was a real old-timer who knew his California. After a short time on the *New World* he was appointed Wells Fargo agent at Los Angeles. In the mid 'sixties the City of the Angels was nothing more than a dirty, muddy little Mexican village, situated on a broad plain well inland from the ocean. There was no railroad, not even a thought of one. Its nearest large neighbors, San Diego and Santa Barbara, long established and attractive seaports, looked on Los Angeles with contempt. They had good reason, too, for the town had a mission and a plaza, a few small brick buildings, a few hundred adobes and little else.

But Pridham considered Los Angeles his opportunity, and when it came he bought the mud lots that surrounded the settlement. The city expanded and Pridham made a fortune. That is why, in 1912, when I first met him, he was living, like other Wells Fargo oldsters, in the gorgeous Palace Hotel in San Francisco. He loved to be with his old pals, Homer King and Andrew Christeson. King had been with Wells Fargo from the beginning and in more recent years had been head of the highly important Bank of California. Christeson, at the time, was vice-president of Wells Fargo, a leonine old-timer who had become influential up and down the coast. The three old men were cronies. They loved to eat cracked crab in the great court of the Palace or up at the St. Francis, where Christeson lived, or in the Pacific Union Club atop Nob Hill, which Homer King liked best of all.

Sacramento was, in many ways, as colorful a town as San Francisco. Samuel McNeil, a shoemaker from Lancaster, Ohio, traveled to California in 1849 and wrote about his experiences in his book, *McNeil's Travels to the Gold Regions in California*:

> On landing at Sacramento city I entered a tent, kept by Mrs. Moore, the first American woman I had seen since leaving the States, who swore that her brandy was better than any *other man's* in that renowned city. Her price was fifty cents a drink. Sure enough, I soon found that she had a great deal of the masculine gender about her, and that she permitted other things (more expensive) in her tent than drinking brandy, considering one of her smiles worth an ounce of gold or $16.

McNeil, who was a pretty observing man about some things, found that California was "The only country in which I have seen true democracy prevailing."

McNeil didn't stay long in the gold region. He returned to Ohio and his wife after a few months. Before he had left for California his preacher had asserted, "That the straightest way to California was the nearest road to hell." Whether this preacher was right, or not, McNeil preferred shoemaking and Ohio. He had had enough of mines and miners and California.

24

Gold brought many problems. Among them were those of security and safekeeping as well as transportation of the metal. A man might stake his claim and squat on it. The claim might yield a fortune but once the miner had his gold what was he to do with it? The assay office and the United States Mint down at "the Bay" were a long way off. Indeed, even with the coming of the steamboat and stagecoach to California, transportation was still a major problem. If the miner left his claim, even for a day, there was always the possibility that he might return to find someone else on it.

The express companies and banks solved these problems. They not only brought the miner his mail, newspapers and packages, but they took his gold dust and cared for it. What's more, they shipped it—everywhere.

A steamer sailing from San Francisco to Panama, on November 17, 1854, reported the following shipment of gold:

Page, Bacon & Company $417,000.00
Adams and Company   350,000.00
Wells, Fargo and Company   177,000.00

A similar report from a ship sailing ten days later also showed Wells Fargo running a poor third in the gold race. However, the company could rely heavily on its powerful connections with the American Express in the East and the year 1854 saw the payment of the first dividends on the stock of Wells, Fargo and Company. Ten per cent was paid on the first of March and five per cent on the 12th of September. In the face of heavy competition, Wells Fargo was gaining business, friends and profits.

California was confidently prepared to back with gold the currencies of the whole world from its booming mines. But there were signs, even by 1854, that the golden glow might dim. There was little mining done in 1854 because of the scant rainfall. Without plenty of water in the streams, placer mining was impossible. Real estate in San Francisco slumped badly. There was a great deal of political and financial corruption, some of which was coming to light. San Francisco businessmen extended too much credit to the idle miners while produce from Eastern manufacturers, ordered months before, continued to pour into the city.

The East had also had a hard winter. Speculation had run wild and conditions in New York, Philadelphia and Boston were as bad, if not worse, than in San Francisco. California was gloomy. The *Daily Placer Times and Transcript* wrote:

> In a commercial point of view, the news which goes forward by the steamer of to-day is of the most discouraging character. Trade is utterly prostrate and the pecuniary embarrassments of the mercantile classes have never been equalled since the settlement of the country by the Anglo-Americans. The principal cause producing this state of things has frequently before been alluded to by us—the absence of sufficient rain to enable the miners to prosecute their labors.

The blow that temporarily dimmed the golden glow, that left Wells Fargo in command of the express business in California and that emptied John Parrott's stone building of its first tenants, came on February 23, 1855. On February 18th, the steamship *Oregon* arrived in San Francisco Harbor with news that Page, Bacon's parent bank in St. Louis had closed its doors. The parent bank had been speculating heavily in the Ohio and Mississippi Railroad being built between Cincinnati and St. Louis. When the railroad got into financial trouble, Page, Bacon in St. Louis failed. Prior to its failure, the parent company had received a million dollars from the San Francisco branch. When the *Oregon* arrived with the bad news, a run started on Page, Bacon. Since its funds were depleted, Page, Bacon couldn't weather the panic that ensued and, on February 22nd, closed its doors. Alvin Harlow in his colorful book, *Old Waybills,* describes the effects of the crash in San Francisco:

> On Friday, the 23rd, the following day, came the final crash. Adams and Company, Wells, Fargo and Company, A. S. Wright, a private banker, and Robinson and Company's Savings Bank all closed their doors. The whole city was in panic. The courts adjourned, and business, both wholesale and retail, was practically at a standstill. Montgomery Street from California to Jackson was filled with a surging crowd, which over-

flowed into the neighboring streets. The press was greatest around the Adams office. A large percentage of the crowd appeared to be workingmen and men of modest means. There were a few women among the rest, mostly Mexicans—all hit by the collapse of the great structure in which they had once had so much confidence. There were tears, threats, hysteria, but no great disorder. One man said he had $7,000 in the Adams bank, and had expected to take it and return to his family in the East, sailing on the *Uncle Sam* on Saturday, the day after the failure.

Adams and Company never reopened. The panic spread through California. Scenes such as Harlow describes were repeated again and again. At the time of the panic the Wells Fargo bank and express office in Marysville was prospering. It was the stronghold for thousands of merchants who sold their merchandise to the miners for gold dust and then sent the dust down to the mint at "the Bay" to be converted into gold coin. The Wells Fargo representative at Marysville was a man named Hodges. When Hodges got wind of the impending crisis he was anxious. Finally the telegram came from headquarters ordering him to close the bank. Noting that there were still twenty minutes before closing time he sat, watch in hand, until five past three. Then he told the porter to close the door, turned to the clerks and said:

"Go and get something to eat, please. Then return. I shall need your help tonight."

Hodges was deeply concerned over the thousand or more accounts in the bank, the balances of the men who had sent their dust down and who had credits there—the men who placed their trust in Wells Fargo. The dust was generally shipped into the office in buckskin bags, each of which when filled held from one thousand to five thousand dollars. When Hodges went to supper that evening, he stopped at a near-by store and bought all the buckskin bags that the merchant had in stock.

When the clerks returned, he explained that he had been ordered to close the bank. Then he added:

"Most of the money on general deposit was placed here by

27

my friends who believe I am an honest man. Wells, Fargo and Company have a parent bank in San Francisco and branch banks throughout the state. I know nothing of the others, but this bank is still sound. Still, if we get into general liquidation months will be exhausted before the final settlement. We will settle ours *tonight*. Every man who has money here on general account must have it on special deposit tomorrow morning. [Todd's early bank had also had two kinds of account.] The amount due each man must be paid in money and dust in one of these bags. The name of the man and the account due him must be written on the bag and marked 'special deposit' and the books must correspond with the marks."

Hodges and his men left the bank, all very tired, after two o'clock the next morning. In the morning a dispatch came up from San Francisco to open the bank as usual. Only a handful of men in the town knew of the night's work in the bank. Speaking of it in later years, Hodges used to say: "I never enjoyed a more pleasant evening than that."

The following previously unpublished letter, written by the Wells Fargo agent at Auburn to his father, gives many details of the effect of the panic in that town:

Auburn, California
Feby 24, 1855

My dear Father:

Yesterday & today have been days long to be remembered by me. On the night of the 22nd I was present at a ball given in the place where I remained till 4 a.m. at that hour I retired to bed to snatch a few hours sleep before beginning the days work. At 8 o'clock I was awoke by a messenger handing me a telegraphic dispatch from our firm below, to the effect that *Adams & Co.* had failed & to prepare for a run. Here was a pleasant message and I instantly got up & at the moment I reached the door crowds were running toward the office, I knew that our funds would not meet all our outstanding drafts certificates etc. and would not commence paying. Very soon Adams & Co. here had paid out all their funds and still were short some $20,000.00. The crowd were now furious and banking hours drawing nigh —What was worse still was my being alone in the office—My assistant a short time since being transferred to the Iowa Hill

Office. I saw no other plan but to open and let it go as far as it would—Paying out commercial and the work got pretty warm when two or three of my personal friends came forward and offered their assistance to the extent of their means. One of them being very popular and a *substantial* man his presence seemed to allay all excitement and to instill confidence, as to our means, to the crowd. As they dispersed and the matter became a little quieted I went outside and made arrangements for funds nearly to the amount of all the demands against us—the time ran smoothly till about 4 p.m. when it was telegraphed that *Wells Fargo & Co. had suspended in San Francisco.* This fell like a death knell to me but as far as this office was concerned I could weather it—When the news was spread around the crowd commenced assembling and pretty soon the paying out was lively—but there seemed to be no lack of funds & my giving personal assurance of their safety, all was quieted for the day—This morning I received a dispatch from San Francisco Office that their house would open on Monday next and through the day have received several of the same purport. We have had but little trouble so far today & I am in hopes we will go through the storm safely. This is certainly the proudest time of my life and I only wish that my *masters' other agents* together with themselves may be so successful in the end as I have been. The bankers have been put to a frightful test and many having abundant means forced to suspend. As I understand it W.F. & Co. in San Francisco had plenty of dust and assayed bars, but ran short of coin. Monday I feel assured will bring us a better day and one that will establish the credit of the firm to a greater degree than it has ever enjoyed heretofore. Of course their standing effects me in every way & their fall would be equal to the same thing with me. The steamer Uncle Sam on account of all the suspensions which have taken place is detained till Monday when she sails. I send you two daily papers which will give you some idea of the excitement throughout the country.

> In haste
> Your affectionate son
> Jno. Q. Jackson

At the height of the panic, Louis Remme made a ride from Sacramento to Portland which is a classic of the West.

Remme, a French-Canadian, had driven down the valley the day before the crash, sold his cattle for $12,500 in gold and had deposited the money with Adams and Company. As he breakfasted in Bremond's restaurant in Sacramento, the certificate of his deposit in his wallet, he opened the morning *Sacramento Union* and read that Adams and Company in San Francisco had failed. He ran out of the restaurant to the local Adams office. It was surrounded by a mob. Finally when he reached a clerk, his deposit certificate in hand, he was waved back to the end of the long line of men—all waiting to get their money from the bank.

First Remme considered going to the next town. As he considered the matter he realized that all towns in California would be affected and that he would have to go out of the state. Portland! He would go to San Francisco immediately and take the next ship, the *Columbia*, for Portland. There was no telegraph to the city and the news of the panic could reach Portland in no other way. But, Remme reflected, if he went by ship the bad news of the panic would ride with him, and it would be impossible to cash his certificates in Portland.

He must reach Portland before the ship. He must ride by horseback and beat the *Columbia*. It seemed like an impossible feat but Remme thought of his $12,500 which he had worked so hard for, and he set out. First he ran to the Sacramento wharf and there jumped aboard a stern-wheeler just as she was starting up the river for Knight's Landing, forty-two miles away. Old man Knight let Remme have the first horse. He rode it to Grand Island, bought a fresh one there and started straight north. He rode night and day, buying fresh horses where he could, snatching an hour's sleep at long intervals. Seventy hours out of Knight's Landing he rode into Yreka near the Oregon border. From there to Hungry Creek, Bear Creek and Jacksonville. On the morning of the fifth day he arrived in the small city of Eugene. At the dawn of the sixth day he was at French Prairie. By 10:30 in the morning he reached Oregon City and at noon of that day a boy ferried him across the Willamette River into Portland.

30

He immediately went to the Adams office where the agent, just back from lunch, looked over his certificate of deposit on the Sacramento office. It was valid and he paid Remme in gold. Forty pounds of pure gold worth $12,500. Almost immediately after the transaction had been completed a cannon boomed, announcing the coming of the *Columbia* into the river. Within an hour she would dock and when the news she carried reached the city there would be no more payments made at the Adams office. Remme had beaten the *Columbia* by little more than an hour. What's more, he had made one of the great rides of all time, 700 miles in six days.

Wells Fargo weathered the crisis without difficulties. All its branches were in good shape, as was the main office and bank in San Francisco. O. O. Winther in his fine book, *Express and Stagecoach Days in California*, carefully explains how Wells Fargo made out in the panic:

> The panic affected Wells, Fargo and Company very differently from Adams. Wells, Fargo banks, everywhere except in Sacramento, remained open on February 22, and the express business seems to have continued in full operation. But since they did not know how long the gold reserve could last, the San Francisco bank was closed on the 23 with this announcement on its doors:

> *To our Depositors*—We have deemed it prudent for the protection of your interests as well as ours, to close our doors today. We shall make such a statement of our affairs and abundant ability to pay as we trust will satisfy all.
>
>

WELLS FARGO AND CO.
San Francisco, Feb. 23, 1855

> Henry M. Naglee was immediately appointed temporary receiver for the firm and on the following day, February 24, made this statement regarding the status of the company:

> Wells, Fargo & Co. have completed a balance of their accounts this day, and find to the credit of their house above every liability $389,106.23, and only ask of their friends a few days to convert some of their assets to resume payment.
>
>

WELLS FARGO & CO.
Saturday, 10 P.M.

31

But the panic brought financial ruin for at least 197 business houses in San Francisco as well as for Adams. After Adams failed, the company was snarled in legal entanglements. Some of the California partners landed in jail. I. C. Woods, one of the partners, fled to Australia disguised as a woman. All in all, the panic was a great tragedy to the miners and merchants and others who had entrusted their money to banks that had seemed completely safe and solvent.

From the ashes of Adams Express emerged the Pacific Express Company. This new business, formed by a group of men previously connected with Adams, gave assurance that it would deal only in the express business and would have nothing to do with banking. The firm was incorporated on July 1, 1855, and remained in business until it was combined with the Alta Express in 1857.

With Page, Bacon and Adams gone, the stone building that John Parrott had built—in defiance of tradition—with stones imported from China was empty. However, in the summer of '55, Wells Fargo moved across Montgomery Street into the Parrott building. As the only major express company surviving the crash, Wells Fargo could look forward to prosperous days ahead.

The Chinese fervently wished to continue their friendship for Wells Fargo, but one couldn't be friends with the tenant of a building infested by evil spirits. Yet the obstacle was overcome. The Chinese friends of Wells Fargo spent much time and no little amount of money in liberal offerings to their God of Wealth to exorcise the evil spirits and to assure the welfare of the new tenants. Thereafter, for seventy-one years, Parrott's stone building was known to all San Francisco as the Wells Fargo building. Wells Fargo had moved in to stay.

The company was now supreme in the express field in all California. The board of directors, back in the East, assigned T. M. Ianes, the company's general treasurer, to go to California to replace William Pardee as general agent. Shortly after that Louis McLane was placed at the head of the California end of the business.

Once the shock of the panic was over, business recovered.

There was a new discovery of gold in the Kern River country that stimulated the entire state. In 1855 Wells Fargo again paid dividends as usual—twice, each of five per cent. In addition the company's capital had been increased to $600,000. Offices in Boston, New York and Philadelphia were in operation as the eastern terminals of its California to New York express service. Elsewhere back in the East, the company was represented by the American Express Company. And in California itself—well, in October of 1855, only eight months after the crash, the *San Francisco Bulletin* listed forty-five Wells Fargo express offices reaching from Portland, Oregon, down to San Diego.

III

The Little Green Box

President James Polk and the Congress were as much excited about the discovery of gold in California and the rush that followed it as the plain citizens of the country were. Administrative and military problems connected with the fantastic growth of population there took up a good deal of time in the debates of Congress in that year. Among other things President Polk recommended in December, 1848, that the Congress consider "extending the benefit of our post office laws to the people of California."

These words had a fine ring to them, but the difficulties in translating them into a fact were tremendous. Mail contracts on overland transcontinental routes were offered as subsidies for the encouragement of stage lines and railroads, just as in our own day they have subsidized the development of cross-country air lines. But the post office department in the 1850's was an inefficient, and often a corrupt, arm of the Federal government. And contracts did not automatically make a good postal service.

The inefficiency and the corruption both were demonstrated in the very beginning of the department's efforts to establish a mail service in California itself. The efforts of the post office were feeble, and the express companies of California for a long time were able to provide a regular, safe and reasonably inexpensive mail service that became a thorn in the side of the political appointees back in Washington. The express companies beat the department at its own game, and made a handsome profit to boot. The result was a war which lasted for a good forty years between the express companies, most definitely including Wells Fargo, and the post office.

The first government postal agent sent to California, William Van Voorhies, arrived in California in 1849. He carried instructions which probably looked fine on the charts back in Washington but which were out of date and inadequate by the time his ship arrived in San Francisco. He was instructed to install post offices in the towns which seemed to those in the East to be most important: San Diego, San Pedro, Santa Barbara, Monterey, and San Luis Obispo. None of these towns was in the Mother Lode country, and in fact, except that an agent had previously been appointed for San Francisco, one would almost think that the post office hadn't yet heard about the gold rush. But not quite. Van Voorhies was authorized and instructed to set up offices in the interior "conditioned upon the expense thereof being defrayed out of the net proceeds of such office."

This, of course, was a businesslike attitude, but ignored President Polk's advice that the "people of California" should be benefited by the post office. The people of California were not in towns which could "defray the expenses thereof." They were in tiny mining camps; they were living in Brandy Hat, Poverty Bar, You Bet, Jackass Gulch and Piety Hill. They were in Sublimity, Last Chance, Nip and Tuck, Two Cent Ranch, Mad Mule, Poker Flat, Dusty Bar, and Muggingville. And they wanted their mail. They wanted it whether or not the post office could "defray the expenses thereof."

Their letters back home were bitter on this subject. The newspapers criticized this narrow attitude of the post office department. Everyone, East and West, complained.

Three years after gold was discovered in California, when the state had a population of 300,000, there were still only sixty post offices in California; and few of those were located where they serviced any sizable section of the population. By 1855, criticism had become violent. One of the bitterest attacks on the postal system appeared in the editorial page of the *Alta California* in July of that year. It is a fascinating document and expresses in no uncertain terms the feelings of most Californians at the time:

> . . . the Post Office system, so far as California is concerned, is a humbug and a nuisance. It does not facilitate intercourse between different parts of the State, but it impedes it. It subjects correspondents to an onerous tax, if they select a more speedy and sure conveyance for their letters than the mail, and it benefits no one save office holders and contractors.
>
> Indeed, we have yet to hear the first argument in favor of it. . . . In no branch or department of business would the public be worse served than they are now, were the whole postal system for California discontinued. The Expresses willingly carry letters for a bit each, to the Atlantic States, and we believe they would for less, if they could have the entire business. Even now they charge but a bit, if they are enclosed in government envelopes, so that correspondents, after paying individuals for service, are obliged to pay nearly the same amount to the government as a tax. And yet our business men generally prefer to pay the double postage, and send their letters by the Express . . . The Express runs into nearly every town in the State where there is a Post Office, and in many towns where there is no

such nuisance deposited, the signs of the Pacific Express and Wells, Fargo & Co. may be seen. . . .

. . . The Government now pays about $1,000,000 for mail service to, from and in California, which service is a positive disadvantage to the State, and in order to justify it and compel us to pay for it, Congress at the last session, while everywhere else it materially reduced the rates of postage, increased it for us. . . . To sum all up, it is a tyrannical and worse than useless institution and ought to be abolished. Let this matter be borne in mind by the people, when they come to vote.

Not only did the *Alta California* reject the post office completely, it also praised the mail service of Wells Fargo.

The government, of course, had a tough job on its hands, even if its service had been organized in the most efficient possible way. Manpower, for one thing, was at a premium, except for the business of mining gold. Samuel McNeil, the shoemaker from Ohio, tells the story of a sailor offered $250 a month to ship on a voyage to Oregon. The sailor answered that he would pay the captain $300 a month *and board* for helping him in an expedition to the mines. It was in this atmosphere that the post office tried to find men to work in the offices and carry the mail. The government's pay did not hold much attraction for the average Argonaut. There were millions to be made in the mountains! And even for the meager pay the postmasters had to depend entirely on the earnings of their own offices.

The express companies whose business depended in establishing and maintaining regular connections with any camp where there was gold to be transported were not slow to see their opportunity. The Post Office was confused and inefficient, but they were on the spot, able to fill a real need of the miners.

We have already mentioned that Alexander Todd, one of the first "express companies," began a mail delivery service. He went to San Francisco and got himself sworn in as a postal clerk. To the postmaster's relief he took charge of all letters belonging to miners who subscribed to his service. In addition Todd bought all the New York newspapers he could lay his hands on in San Francisco. He besieged incoming travelers for

38

copies of the *Herald* and the *Tribune,* paying a dollar apiece for their papers already weeks old. These he carried back into the Mother Lode country and sold them for eight dollars each. It was a profitable business.

The postmaster at San Francisco began to think that Todd's business was altogether too profitable. He demanded a cut and assessed him twenty-five cents for each letter he took out of the mail for delivery to his customers. The graft spread and before long the postmasters at Sacramento and Stockton were demanding their own two bits a letter from the pioneer expressmen. Naturally the expressmen paid up. In the first years miners often paid two and three dollars for letters delivered to them. Of course, the official postal rate was much lower. The tariff for local letters was 12½ cents for each half ounce while letters from the East Coast cost forty cents per half ounce.

Most of the express companies did not bother to have their employees made postal agents. They set their own rates and carried the mail. The post office retorted quickly. Letters must bear U. S. stamps. Letters found in express company possession without them would be fined $50. On January 13, 1854, the Adams company and Wells, Fargo and Company announced in the *Alta California*:

> J. D. Frye, Esq. Special Agent of the Post Office Department, has given us official notice that all Letters sent by our Expresses hereafter, must bear the Post Office Stamp or Envelope.

Not that the ruling was always observed. The boys in Sublimity and Dusty Bar were not interested in licking postage stamps when they sent a letter over to Muggingville or Poker Flat!

Almost all Californians resented these petty restrictions on the express companies, as the editorial in the *Alta California* makes abundantly clear.

Wells Fargo acted in the miners' interests in the perplexing problem of the mails. Wells Fargo caught the boats leaving for the East; the post office rarely did. Wells Fargo reached the miner far inland and helped businessmen to transact their business by making mail deliveries frequently and reliably. As a result, when the government sought to hinder and even stop the work of the express companies, the public enthusiastically supported the private concerns.

Wells Fargo's mail service thus supplied a need not filled by the post office. It was not the first time that the company had helped out when California was in a tight spot. Once when the city of Sacramento was seriously embarrassed financially and did not know where to get the money to meet its ordinary running expenses, Wells Fargo dipped into its strong boxes and brought out $85,000 to stiffen the city's credit and to meet its immediate need for cash. Wells Fargo did the same for other California towns. It was not Lady Bountiful but both good neighbor and good businessman; and the people of California recognized the fact early.

In 1855, the Post Office Department in Washington ordered the postmaster in San Francisco to seize all mail carried by the express companies. The businessmen of the city, outraged by the ruling, dared the postmaster to put the order into effect. He balked and the order was not enforced. Public sentiment in those days was not easily defied.

In the latter part of September, 1856, a formal announcement appeared in the *Alta California* to the effect that after the first of October the express companies were prepared to accept letters for swift delivery when they were enclosed in their own prepaid envelopes, provided that they also had the correct amount of regular government postage on them. This was a major step forward and credit for the idea has been given to Louis McLane, who had become the general agent for Wells Fargo in California at the end of 1855. It was he who first conceived the idea of buying government-stamped envelopes in quantity and then having imprinted on one end: "Paid, Wells Fargo & Co. over our California and Coast Routes." These soon became known as franked envelopes. They were inexpensive and were sold in large quantities.

In the preceding year Henry Reed, a former employee of the Adams Company left to shift for himself after its failure, had organized a Penny Express, to carry letters from San Francisco to Sacramento, Marysville, Benicia, San Jose and Santa

40

Clara at the much reduced rate of five cents a letter. In an advertisement in the *Alta California* on June 25, 1855, Reed promised extensions to more distant parts of the state and north into Oregon. Five cents was his charge if the letter was prepaid; double if the postage was to be paid by the recipient.

At about the same time, Stimson's express was advertising for letter mail at 12½ cents an item. Then the Pacific Express, an offshoot of the defunct Adams Company, began to carry letters over routes in California and Oregon at ten cents each, including the three-cent stamped government envelopes. Wells Fargo met these rates and vigorously went forward to develop its new letter service.

The success of Wells Fargo's new franked envelopes was immediate. They sold at nine dollars a hundred (including the United States postage) and sold by the thousands and the tens of thousands. Thus the post office was relieved of a great burden in a region where its operating costs were at the very highest. By 1861, it was being said that the express companies were doing a larger business in California mail than the government itself; and their service was swifter and infinitely better. Figures given out by Wells, Fargo and Company in 1863 announced that it had, in the preceding year, purchased over two million three-cent envelopes, 15,000 six-cent envelopes, and 3,000 ten- and eighteen-cent envelopes, in addition to 70,000 extra three-cent stamps and 12,500 six-cent stamps. It had complied fully with the law, not alone in theory, but in spirit and in practice.

Wells Fargo won and kept friends for its letter service by the simple process of rendering a far better service than the United States Post Office Department proffered. Even before the post office put up its new red mailboxes around the streets of San Francisco, the bright-green mailboxes of Wells, Fargo and Company had been affixed to the lamp posts of the streets of the town. Sacramento and others of the larger California towns followed. Wells Fargo led; it rarely ever followed.

The handling of letter mail was no easy chore for Wells Fargo. Not only was it an expensive operation, of much minute detail and precision, but there were complications other than the sniping warfare of competitors and of the Post Office Department. It was difficult, for instance, for the company to deliver many of the letters from the East, when the express service charge was to be collected from the recipient. Frequently, the recipient was a highly elusive person. There were many times when he could not be found, and letters to him were, therefore, carried at a dead loss. At other times the consignee of the letters was reluctant to pay the charges, and the expressman had to use much tact and diplomacy in collecting from a person who could not see why he should receive any letters at all. There were other cases where the government stamps were missing, and things had come to a pass where express companies which delivered letters without them were subject to heavy fines, as we have seen.

Judge C. C. Goldwin, veteran editor of the *Salt Lake Telegram*, once told me that very early in its days Wells Fargo earned a good reputation as a postman. When a man had an important letter to go to some distant camp or town, he rarely hesitated as to which postbox to use. The bright-green mailboxes of Wells, Fargo and Company almost invariably won over the bright-red ones of the United States Post Office. The Judge used to recall the days when a letter arriving from the East with the familiar but baffling "John Smith in the Mines," left the postmaster on the coast in a good deal of doubt, particularly as "John Smith" was not a unique name. Moreover, the "mines" extended from Siskiyou in the north more than 600 miles south to Bakersfield. The postmaster would quietly hold such letters until the end of the month and then slip them over to Wells Fargo to find the rightful recipients. They usually did so because the local agents knew all the miners and where they were.

Remember, there were no roads except pack trails to many of the camps, and that the boys in the camps—there were no old men there—were hungry for news of the outer world and absolutely depended on the express for their letters and newspapers. Their dependence was not in vain. The messengers came, by muleback in summer and by dog sled and snowshoes in the dead of winter, but they came. That was the point. The

42

mails moved. To that end, every Wells Fargo man gave his very best efforts.

There is an anecdote illustrative of such efforts on the part of John J. Valentine, later to become a most capable and best beloved of all Wells Fargo presidents. In the early spring of 1864, when young Valentine, lately arrived from Kentucky, was Wells Fargo agent at Virginia City, he was summoned from that brisk community to the express headquarters in Montgomery Street, San Francisco.

He boarded one of the company's stages and started out. He progressed for only a little way, because the snow lay thick in the high passes of the Sierras and there came a place where the stage could no longer go forward. Nor could it turn back. It was caught, firmly and immovably, as in a vise. The driver and the shotgun messenger alighted, and, scraping away the snow, built a giant fire to keep horses and passengers warm until the messenger could go back and get more horses.

In spite of all these alarming and disturbing developments, Valentine remembered the company's mail bags. He knew they contained important letters, due to go through to Sacramento and San Francisco without delay. He knew it would be hours, if not days, before the coach would be able to move. Without further ado and consulting no one, he threw the heavy mail sacks over his shoulder and started down the snow-filled road through the forest. Frequently the drifts came to his knees, occasionally to his waist, and all the time the wind and the soft falling snow swept about him. Fortunately he knew the road (as a messenger he had traveled it before) and he kept on unfalteringly, until late that night he dropped into the little town of Placerville at the foot of the mountains, exhausted. The expressmen put him to bed and sent the mail forward. The businessmen of Sacramento and San Francisco who received their Nevada letters the next day little dreamed of the personal effort that had brought their mail over the mountains.

The Post Office Department back in Washington showed increasing jealousy of the express company. Wells Fargo was practically a monopoly in California and Oregon, and the government sought every means in its power to embarrass the express company. Continually it sought to end the letter-mail service of Wells Fargo, and in 1880 moved to put an end to it, through maneuvers in Washington. But public sentiment in favor of a private enterprise which was consistently well managed and had proved itself a good neighbor, made itself felt chiefly through the columns of the newspapers and the government was forced to let the matter drop.

Fifteen years later the government postal service had been brought to a degree of efficiency and the use of the express envelopes had fallen off greatly. The government was determined to end it entirely. A federal statute was passed against the practice of outsiders handling letter mail in any form whatsoever. Accordingly, in 1895, the bright-green Wells Fargo mailboxes in the streets of San Francisco, Sacramento and Portland were taken down and the privately run service was terminated. The long contest came to an end. Since then the franked envelopes bearing the inscription: "Paid, Wells, Fargo & Co. over our California and Coast Routes" have become of interest mainly to stamp collectors, keeping alive the memory of the days when Wells Fargo men saw to it that the mails went through.

IV

Stagecoach Empire

For fifteen or twenty years after the discovery of gold in California, Wells Fargo and the other express companies operating in the West relied almost exclusively on the stagecoach to transport their gold dust, bullion and express packages. The stage lines in California ran to the latest discovered diggings almost on the heels of the first miners. Mountains, narrow pack trails and rivers were obstacles quickly overcome by the companies in order to bring in from San Francisco mining equipment, food and supplies, and to carry back to the U. S. mint the gold dust

45

and nuggets. Quickly a network of roads and stage lines was constructed criss-crossing the mining country and leading to the coast.

In the days when California was a Spanish colony and later under the rule of Mexico there were a few roads along the coastal plain, notably El Camino Real, which connected the missions founded in 1769 by Father Junipero Serra. Over these roads traveled the great carriages of the grandees, visiting back and forth among the vast ranches or attending to business in San Diego and Monterey. As Americans came and began to crowd the lordly Spanish landholders, a few inferior roads were built to connect growing towns in the interior. For the rest there were narrow horse trails which sufficed for the *vaqueros* of the *rancheros* to round up the cattle, and for the business of settlers. It was a grazing and an agricultural civilization. The saddle horse and the pack mule furnished the transportation.

The find of James Marshall at Sutter's Mill changed all that. The miners had to have supplies and they had to get their gold out for safekeeping. Heavy transport was a necessity and roads were the answer. The era of the stagecoach, the most picturesque in all of California's colorful history, was being ushered in.

The early roads across the Sierras were blazed by the immigrants who crawled over the mountains down into the California valleys. The thousands of wagons that came from the East gradually made highways that were often little more than passable. In the high Sierras they were choked with snow in winter and in the rainy season they became seas of mud. In the long dry season the stages would raise clouds of dust to plague the passengers who must have cursed every boulder and rut in the path of the careening coach. Many of the mountain roads would have tried the courage and patience of the most stalwart goat. But somehow the stages came through, mostly on time, and with little loss of life, considering the hazards of wrecks and bandits. It took years to build good roadbeds, bridges and ferries, but it was done.

Wells Fargo at first was content to ride the stages; they

owned none. But wherever the stage lines went Wells Fargo rode along, with an armed messenger beside the driver to guard its shipments. The shotgun messengers were an intrepid breed, utterly fearless and quick on the trigger. But in the '60's the company began buying stage companies and for a short time was the proprietor of the greatest stage empire in the country. So let us go back a bit and see some of the details behind the coaches, the shotgun messengers, the Indians and the hold-ups, some of the excitement that went with linking the mountains of California with the clipper ships tied up along Sansome Street in San Francisco, and then the uniting of East and West by means of the Overland stage lines.

The first stage line in California was started by John Whistman in the fall of 1849. It ran between San Jose and San Francisco, a little irregularly, it is true, and it always was uncomfortable with its single old French omnibus pulled by scraggly mustangs or mules. A second company was founded by Ackley and Maurison operating between the same towns. They had, however, more modern equipment and forced Whistman out of business. Whistman sold out to Warren F. Hall and Jared B. Crandal, who were to become great stagemen. They were daring and enterprising, and they knew their business. In the *Alta California* of 1850 the following advertisement appeared:

San Jose.   San Jose.
BERFORD & CO's LINE
OF EXPRESS MAIL STAGES,
HALL & CRANDAL, Proprietors,
    Are now running every morning to San Jose, leaving Berford & Co's office in the plaza, at 8 o'clock, A.M., and the City Hotel in San Jose at 7 o'clock, A.M.
    The reduced rate of fare puts it in the power of every one to visit the beautiful and healthful valley of Santa Clara. There is no more charming drive in California than that from San Francisco to San Jose, and as one is whirled rapidly through the oak openings and across the level plains under the skillful driving of Professors Dillon or Crandal, who drive their own coaches, he finds that pleasure is united with business, and wonders he has never made the trip before.

The great advantage this line possesses over all others, is that the Stages were bought expressly for the road, and with a particular attention to *safety,* while the drivers, who have served a long apprenticeship from New England to Mexico, make the *quickest* time and *never meet with accidents,* which are so likely to occur with the old-fashioned stage coaches. We invite our friends to give the line a trial.

BERFORD & CO.

Crandal was an expert driver. He once drove Governor Peter Burnett just after California was admitted to the Union as a state in September of 1850 who told of the incident in his *Recollections*:

> Next morning I left for San Jose on one of Crandal's stages. He was one of the celebrated stage-men of California, like Foss and Monk. He was a most excellent man, and a cool, kind, but determined and skillful driver. On this occasion he drove himself, and I occupied the top front seat beside him. There were then two rival stage-lines to San Jose, and this was the time to test their speed. After passing over the sandy road to the Mission, there was some of the most rapid driving that I ever witnessed. The distance was some fifty miles, most of the route being over smooth, dry, hard prairie; and the drivers put their mustang teams to the utmost of their speed. As we flew past on our rapid course, the people flocked to the road to see what caused our fast driving and loud shouting. . . . I never can forget Crandal's race. He beat his competitor only a few moments.

Hall and Crandal sold out, in April, 1853, to Dillon, Hedge and Company. However, they weren't through as stage-men. They were just beginning.

James Birch and Frank Stevens were two of the most successful stage-men in the West. They had been stage drivers in New England and had come to California in 1849 by the arduous Overland route. Sacramento, in the 1850's, was the staging center of California. It was there that Birch started with an old rancho wagon which carried passengers to Mormon Island in Placer County. Stevens, in 1849, had built his first crude hostel on the wharf in Sacramento. A sign over its roof read: "Rest for the Weary and Storage for Trunks." Men bound for the diggings, who arrived from San Francisco by boat of every sort, smiled grimly at that sign. Rest was a thing long since denied any of them.

In this colorful scene Jim Birch drove his rancho wagon madly up and down the levee, shouting at the top of his lungs;

"All aboard for Mormon Island! Forks of the American River. All aboard!"

Then came the Argonauts with their bags and boxes and trunks, all striving to get aboard the clumsy vehicle.

Thus the new era of California transport was born.

There were, of course, many other lines. The Sacramento-Marysville route was first opened by John Sharp who sold out, in 1851, to Hall and Crandall. There was Charles Green's Sacramento to Sonora Line that linked the southern and northern mines. According to Green's announcement it passed through Ione Valley, Jackson, Mokelumne Hill, Chilean Gulch, Bay State Ranch, Jesus Maria, San Andreas, Yankee Camp, Kentucky House, Foreman's Ranch, South Calaveras Crossing, Angel's, Valliceti and Murphy's Camp, Campo Muerto, Carson Creek and Hill, Robinson's Ferry, Stanislaus River, Half-Oz Gulch, Soldier's Gulch, Tuttletown, Shaw's Flat, Springfield and Columbia to Sonora. You can't beat miners for choosing interesting town names!

Birch and Stevens as well as Crandall and Hall realized that there was great duplication and unnecessary competition among the lines. By late 1853 they began to consider steps to consolidate and merge the state's stage lines and on January 1, 1854, the California Stage Company came into existence. It is believed that the merger included five-sixths of all the lines in the state. Birch was the first president and Stevens vice-president. The firm, capitalized at one million dollars, became in a few years one of the outstanding stage companies in the country. It boasted that it had the largest and finest stud of horseflesh ever assembled. It bought horses from the East which were driven overland from Ohio, Pennsylvania, Kentucky and Virginia, costing from $2,000 to $4,000 per team, delivered. One year after it was established the new company had purchased several additional lines including the one owned

49

by Dillon, Hedge and Company which Hall and Crandall had obtained from Whistman. By 1860, their lines extended all the way to Oregon.

In addition to owning the finest horses the California Stage Company bought the finest Concord coaches. The first Concord coach had arrived in San Francisco in 1850. It came from Boston around the Horn. The coach took its name from the capital of New Hampshire where it was manufactured, and it made the name famous all over the Americas, in Europe and even in India.

It was the Concord coach which made staging possible over primitive roads and mountain trails. With only the European type of coach, staging in the West probably never would have succeeded. The Concord was built for trouble, close to the ground for sharp curves at high speed, with a light upper structure and heavy underparts, with a springing arrangement made of heavy leather straps called thoroughbraces to absorb the shocks of the rough roads. It was an American coach, designed to fill the specific needs of staging in the West.

The Concord was made by Abbott, Downing and Company. This firm had been building carriages and coaches since 1826 on South Street in Concord. Its work met with favor, and by the 'fifties its buildings covered four acres.

Leslie Downing was the founder of the company. He had come to Concord in 1813 and lived there until he died in 1873. Leon B. Abbott was his right-hand man who handled the construction problems of the various vehicles made by the company, including the Concord.

Abbott and Downing were precisionists. The 300 men who worked in their plant were carefully selected. Each man was a specialist, well trained in the job assigned to him. They all went to work after an early breakfast and continued working until after supper. At 9 P.M. the closing bell rang, ending the twelve-to-fourteen-hour work day.

The two founders took the English mail coach as their model and adapted it to the rough roads of North and South America. The precision and care in construction were matched in the selection of materials. The spokes, made from the finest

50

ash, were literally hand-picked and hand-fitted to the rim and hub. The wood was seasoned to withstand any climate. With the exception of the felloes which were cut with band saws, almost the entire construction was handwork. These band saws driven by horse power were the only machinery in the shop.

One of their coaches, sent around the Horn from Boston to San Francisco the winter of 1868-1869 went down with the ship which was wrecked just before it reached its destination. About thirty days later the coach was hauled out of the water and placed in service. It ran for fifty years.

The making of the curved panels of the coach was an intricate process. Basswood (American linden) was used, and the lamination of thin plywood was moistened and glued, then placed on a form until it dried. It was all a slow, painstaking job, a far cry from the modern mass-production methods.

It took four men to thread the end of an axle. The axle was placed in a vertical position and four men were attached to the die, with a man at each lever who walked around the axle until the thread was completed.

While the records of the company have been carefully preserved by the New Hampshire Historical Society at Concord, there seems to be no way of being sure how many coaches Abbott and Downing made and sold to Wells Fargo, or any of the other staging outfits. After they entered the staging business Wells Fargo bought many Concords. In 1867, for example, the company bought forty coaches, thereby becoming the largest single customer in Abbott and Downing's history.

Edgar Burgum, who, with his father, John, hand-decorated every stage coach that came out of the old shop in Concord, told me that the serial numbers ran high into the hundreds. At the New York World's Fair in 1939, Edgar Burgum scraped the grease from the axle of a coach that we were using in Railroads on Parade and found the serial number of the coach was 274. "That was just the beginning," he said, and then told me of the care that he and his father expended upon the decoration of those magnificent carriages. The elaborate striplings, the scroll work and the lettering were a work of art and the final touch were oil paintings on the panels of the doors. One was always a distant view of Mount Washington and the other —can you guess?—that sturdy New England crag, the Old Man of the Mountain.

The coach usually carried fifteen passengers, nine inside and six, including the driver and messenger on the outside. Thirty-five passengers have been known to ride on just one coach. The capacity was elastic!

Another type of coach, called inelegantly but aptly the "mud-wagon," weighed even less than the Concord and was built lower to the ground. Like the Concord, the mudwagon was slung on thoroughbraces. With its low center of gravity the mudwagon was especially useful on treacherous mountain roads and in wet, muddy weather.

There were many more, but the Concord was the finest, fastest and most useful of them all. It was, according to Captain William Banning, who drove one for many years, "as tidy and graceful as a lady, as inspiring to the stagefaring man as a ship to a sailor, and had, incidentally, like the lady and the ship, scarcely a straight line in its body."

These coaches were designed for various purposes, but the design of all of them had one thing in common. None of the carriage makers worried very much about the passengers. The coaches seemed to have been designed for everything except comfort. The passengers had some pretty definite ideas about the pleasures of coach riding in the Far West. The following anonymous poem quoted in William and George Banning's *Six Horses* is probably a pretty realistic appraisal of stagecoaching from the less romantic point of view:

Creeping through the valley, crawling o'er the hill,
Splashing through the branches, rumbling o'er the mill;
Putting nervous gentlemen in a towering rage.
What is so provoking as riding in a stage?

Spinsters fair and forty, maids in youthful charms,
Suddenly are cast into their neighbors' arms;
Children shoot like squirrels, darting through a cage—
Isn't it delightful, riding in a stage?

POEM RE CONCORD COACH

52

Feet are interlacing, heads severely bumped,
Friend and foe together get their noses thumped;
Dresses act as carpets—listen to the sage:
'Life is but a journey taken in a stage.'

Mrs. D. B. Bates, in her book, *Incidents on Land & Water or, Four Years on the Pacific Coast,* telling of the trying conditions encountered by women on the West Coast in the early 'fifties, calls staging in the mountains "perfectly awful," and adds:

> One night about eleven o'clock, a lady came into the hotel, (at Marysville) looking more dead than alive. She was leading a little girl, of about seven years of age, who was in the same plight as the mother. They were both covered with bruises, scratches, and blood, with their garments soiled and torn. They were coming from Bidwell's Bar, a place about forty miles from Marysville, in a stage-coach, in which were nine Chinamen. The coach was all closed, as it was rather cool in the mountains in the evening. All at once, they found themselves turning somersaults. The coach was overturned down a steep bank.
>
> All the Chinamen, with their long cues reaching to their heels, were rolling and tumbling about in the most ungraceful manner imaginable. They were vociferating at the top of their voices in a language which, if spoke calmly and with the greatest mellifluence, is harsh and disagreeable in the extreme. "And," said she (the woman in the hotel at Marysville), "such a horrid din of voices as rang in my ears, it was scarcely possible to conceive of; which, together with the fright, was almost sufficient to deprive me of my reason." The driver was seriously hurt, and so were some of the horses; but the inside passengers escaped without having any limbs broken, but their cues were awfully disarranged.

When the population of California swelled to several hundred thousand and the territory, ceded to the United States by Mexico after the Mexican War, became a state, a terrific impetus was given to the long-dreamed-of overland transport system. There was fierce competition among the stagecoach lines for routes, for business, for mail contracts, for the tremendous opportunities which went with the opening of a largely un-

53

touched empire. How great, even the most extravagant of the promoters could not dream.

All of this, of course, had tremendous political significance. The tension between the Northern abolitionist states and the Southern slave territory was boiling up to its climax. The fabulous treasure house of California was a prize coveted both politically and materially by both sides. The state held strong elements of the South, as well as of the North. Aside from the profit motive of the promoters, aside from the demand of the growing population of California for a link with the East, the government in Washington saw the necessity for holding the loyalty of California for the North.

Even so the first overland route which was surveyed by the War Department, then under Jefferson Davis, went south through New Mexico and Arizona, but with the outbreak of the war this line was closed and the more direct one through Colorado and Utah was opened.

It seems to be agreed that Birch and Stevens were the first to make concrete plans for a stagecoach route from the Mississippi to California. Aside from the political difficulties they encountered, they tangled with John Butterfield and many of the original American Express Company men who also had ideas about an overland route. And it was Butterfield, not Birch and Stevens, who got the one thing needed to make such a service financially possible—the government mail contract. John Birch went east in 1856 to try for the mail contract; he failed and returned to California. A year later he was returning to the East by ship and was lost at sea. Birch, however, had succeeded in developing a line almost 1,500 miles long from San Antonio to San Diego and blanketing California.

It remained for John Butterfield to complete the first so-called transcontinental stage line, the Overland Mail. In 1856, the government entered into negotiations with Butterfield, William Dinsmore, and William G. Fargo for a line to carry the mails from the Mississippi to California. On March 3, 1857, Congress authorized the Postmaster General to contract for the service. It was to cover a route from the Mississippi to San Francisco. The contract would run for six years; and the cost was not to go above $300,000 annually for a semi-monthly service, $450,000 for weekly service, or $600,000 for semi-weekly service.

On September 16, 1857, the government signed a contract with Butterfield and his associates who agreed to carry the mail twice a week and to cover the distance in twenty-five days. Under its terms the first mail had to be carried over the route within a year from the date of signing the contract.

The Butterfield crowd set to work at once. The line they had contracted to establish was the longest stagecoach run in the world, 2,700 miles, through Indian territories, across rivers, plains, deserts, over mountains, a large part of the run without roads, relay stations or settled towns of any kind.

The route, officially designated as No. 12578, began at two points: St. Louis and Memphis, converged at Little Rock, Arkansas, and then continued west via Preston, Texas, or (as the contract read):

> . . . as near as may be found most advisable to the best point of crossing the Rio Grande above El Paso, and not far from Fort Fillmore, thence along the new road being opened and constructed under the direction of the Secretary of the Interior to Fort Yuma, California, thence through the best passes and along the best valleys for safe and expeditious staging to San Francisco.

Butterfield, one of the founders of the American Express Company, knew the staging business from top to bottom, and he needed all the experience he had. The following passage, written by Waterman L. Ormsby, a correspondent for the New York *Herald*, the first through passenger to ride over the new route, indicates some of the problems Butterfield had to overcome:

> Considering that the contract was signed but just a year before the route went into operation; that an exploring party had to be sent over the road to lay out the details of the line, consuming nearly eight months' time; that during this time over 100 wagons had to be built, nearly 1,500 horses and mules bought and stationed, corrals and station houses built, men employed,

GOING WEST

Leave	Days	Hour	Distance place to place.... Miles	Time allowed Hrs.	Average miles per hour......
St. Louis, Mo., and Memphis, Tenn.....................	Mon. & Thur.	8:00 AM	—	—	—
P. R. R. terminus, Mo........	Mon. & Thur.	6:00 PM	160	10	16
Springfield, Mo..............	Wed. & Sat.	7:45 AM	143	37¾	3.79
Fayetteville, Ark............	Thur. & Sun.	10:15 AM	100	26½	3.79
Forth Smith, Ark............	Fri. & Mon.	3:30 AM	65	17¼	3.79
Sherman, Texas..............	Sun. & Wed.	12:30 AM	205	45	4½
Fort Belknap, Texas..........	Mon. & Thur.	9:00 AM	146½	32½	4½
Fort Chadbourne, Texas.......	Tues. & Fri.	3:15 PM	136	30¼	4½
Pecos river (Em. cross)........	Thur. & Sun.	3:45 AM	165	36½	4½
El Paso.....................	Sat. & Tues.	11:00 AM	248½	55¼	4½
Soldier's Farewell............	Sun. & Wed.	8:30 PM	150	33½	4½
Tucson, Arizona.............	Tues. & Fri.	1:30 PM	184½	41	4½
Gila river, Arizona...........	Wed. & Sat.	9:00 PM	141	31½	4½
Fort Yuma, Cal..............	Fri. & Mon.	3:00 AM	135	30	4½
San Bernardino, Cal..........	Sat. & Tues.	11:00 PM	200	44	4½
Fort Tejón (via Los Angeles) ..	Mon. & Thur.	7:30 AM	150	32½	4½
Visalia, do.................	Tues. & Fr.	11:30 AM	127	28	4½
Firebaugh's Ferry, do.........	Wed. & Sat.	5:30 AM	82	18	4½
Arrive					
San Francisco................	Thur. & Sun.	8:30 AM	163	27	6

GOING EAST

Leave	Days	Hour	Distance place to place.... Miles	Time allowed Hrs.	Average miles per hour......
San Francisco, Cal...........	Mon. & Thur.	8:00 AM	—	—	—
Firebaugh's Ferry, Cal........	Tues. & Fri.	11:00 AM	163	27	6
Visalia, Cal.................	Wed. & Sat.	5:00 AM	82	18	4½
Fort Tejón (via Los Angeles to)	Thur. & Sun.	9:00 AM	127	28	4½
San Bernardino, do..........	Fri. & Mon.	5:30 PM	150	32½	4½
Fort Yuma, do...............	Sun. & Wed.	1:30 PM	200	44	4½
Gila river, Arizona...........	Mon. & Thur.	7:30 PM	135	30	4½
Tucson, Arizona.............	Wed. & Sat.	3:00 AM	141	31½	4½
Soldier's Farewell............	Thur. & Sun.	8:00 PM	184½	41	4½
El Paso, Texas...............	Sat. & Tues.	5:30 AM	150	33½	4½
Pecos river (Em. cross)........	Mon. & Thur.	12:45 PM	248½	55¼	4½
Fort Chadbourne, Texas.......	Wed. & Sat.	1:15 AM	165	36½	4½
Fort Belknap, Texas..........	Thur. & Sun.	7:30 AM	136	30¼	4½
Sherman, Texas.............	Fri. & Mon.	4:00 PM	146½	32½	4½
Forth Smith, Ark............	Sun. & Wed.	1:00 PM	205	45	4½
Fayetteville, Ark............	Mon. & Thur.	6:15 AM	65	17¼	3.79
Springfield, Mo..............	Tues. & Fri.	8:45 AM	100	26½	3.79
P. R. R. terminus, Mo........	Wed. & Sat.	10:30 PM	143	37¾	3.79
Arrive					
St. Louis, Mo., and Memphis, Tenn.....................	Thur. & Sun.	——	160	10	10

Facsimile schedule of the Butterfield Overland Mail, 1858, illustrating the service in transcontinental travel by stagecoach.

and all these appurtenances disposed along the route—the work appears to me to be superhuman. Then it must be taken into consideration that food and clothing for all these men and horses have to be transported over the line, which is no mean item in itself.

Butterfield went forward swiftly with his plans. Coaches were ordered from Concord and elsewhere. Until Abbott, Downing and Company could make deliveries, Butterfield used cumbersome wagons made in Troy, New York. Everything needed was obtained; the necessary roads and relay stations were built and manned, and a year from the date of signing the contract the route was ready for service.

The matter of the relay stations alone appeals to the imagination. Strung out every eighteen to thirty miles over the breadth of what was then known as the Great American Desert, many of the stations were in hostile Indian territory, under constant threat of attack. The men in them had to maintain themselves and their horses, had to be ready to repair broken-down vehicles or doctor sick animals. Always they must be ready to fight Indians or white desperadoes.

In the annals of the West there are many stories which tell of a stage galloping up to a lonely relay station only to find it burned to the ground, the crew dead, frequently scalped, and the horses run off. That meant that with jaded teams the six-horse hitch would have to push on to the next station, never knowing whether the Indians would return from over the next hill or around the next curve.

William Tallack, a traveler from England, made the trip over the line shortly before it was discontinued, and described the way stations and other "arrangements" on the line:

> The stations of the Overland Company average about eighteen miles apart; but some are distant only twelve, and others more than thirty miles. They are mostly log houses or adobes (of sun-dried clay), and each tenanted by several men well armed, whose duty is to look after the mules and their provender, and have the relays punctually ready on the arrival of the stages.
>
> A conductor and driver accompany each stage, the former

changing every five hundred miles, and the latter at shorter intervals. Passengers and luggage are shifted into a fresh wagon about every three hundred miles. The average rate of travel is one hundred and twenty miles in every twenty-four hours; but of course the actual speed varies greatly according to circumstances. Over smooth and level prairie lands we sometimes dashed on at twelve miles an hour, whilst, on rugged or sandy ground, our advance was only two or three miles in the same time, and that often on foot. . . .

Meals (at extra charge) are provided for the passengers twice a day. The fare, though rough, is better than could be expected so far from civilized districts, and consists of bread, tea, and fried steaks of bacon, venison, antelope, or mule towards the two ends of the route—that is, in California and at the "stations" in the settled parts of the Mississippi Valley.

It can be seen from this description how well Butterfield and his associates settled the "superhuman" problems they faced a year earlier. Over this line stages ran with more regularity than could have been expected, and in less time, too. The attached schedule gives a detailed picture of the distances covered, and times allowed for them. Passenger tickets from either eastern terminal to San Francisco were $200. Local fares were usually about ten cents per mile.

On September 15, 1858, the last day of Butterfield's one year, the first of the Overland coaches left San Francisco for the East. John Butterfield rode with the westbound mail from St. Louis the following day, and continued as far as Fort Smith, Arkansas. The first western trip was made in twenty-three days and twenty-three hours, one day and one hour below contract time.

Waterman L. Ormsby, the New York *Herald* man previously quoted, rode west all the way to San Francisco on the first run. There seems to have been more interest in the Overland in New York City than there was in San Francisco. At least Ormsby describes the arrival of the first stage of the Overland in San Francisco in quiet enough terms. Of course, this may have been due to the fact that the coach reached the city after its long trip from St. Louis early on Sunday morning, October 10, 1858. Ormsby wrote:

58

... Soon we struck the pavements, and with a whip, crack, and bound, shot through the streets to our destination, to the great consternation of everything in the way and the no little surprise of everybody. Swiftly we whirled up one street and down another, and round the corners, until finally we drew up at the stage office in front of the Plaza, our driver giving a shrill blast of his horn and a flourish of triumph for the arrival of the first overland mail in San Francisco from St. Louis. But our work was not yet done. The mails must be delivered, and in a jiffy we were at the post office door, blowing the horn, howling and shouting for somebody to come and take the overland mail. ...

Ormsby is reputed to have said at a banquet given that night in his honor that he would do it all over again, but cynics noted that he returned to New York by steamer.

This first through coach brought not only Ormsby and the mail but also a small shipment of packages for Wells, Fargo and Company. Freight was limited on the Overland Mail; the greatest load that was carried, including the mail, was never more than about 750 pounds.

Although public reception of the Overland Mail in California was not especially enthusiastic, Butterfield's transcontinental service was of tremendous importance. It reduced the communication and transport problems of the eight-year-old state of California. No longer did mail and express have to go a long sea voyage to Panama, be unloaded, reloaded on mule trains, packed across the Isthmus of Panama, and finally loaded on ships for the trip to the West Coast ports.

Wells Fargo was quick to see the new line as a way of cutting down the time on their express and mail packages between the East and California. They shipped their express via the Overland for the next three years until the beginning of the Civil War brought about the abandonment of the Butterfield southern route of the Overland Mail.

V

The Fat Cat of Montgomery Street

While Birch and Stevens expanded the California Stage Company and John Butterfield developed his colossal Overland Mail, Wells Fargo was also growing richer and more powerful. By 1860 the company was already rich beyond the fondest dreams of the founders. Its surpluses were piling up in the bank (the largest of the six left after the crash of 1855); and the company paid dividend after dividend. Henry Wells already could contemplate endowing a college; two-fisted, hard-working, God-fearing William G. Fargo was setting

61

aside his shekels for the half-million-dollar mansion with the $10,000 chandelier of 3,000 bits of crystal that he was to build in Buffalo. Also he was putting aside money to buy the Buffalo *Courier* and enter journalism.

Wells Fargo was a powerful company in California in 1855, but five years later it was virtually a monopoly. In 1855 there were fifty-five offices; in 1860, 147. In the same period the capitalization was increased from $600,000 to $1,000,000. In the process it forced the Pacific Express Company, a major competitor, out of business.

The Pacific Express was founded in 1855 by men from the bankrupt Adams Express. At the time Wells Fargo did not consider it a particularly serious rival, but when Dexter Brigham, Jr. became president of the Pacific Express he proved to be a fighter. It was not long, however, before he was forced to send the following letter to the company's agents:

> P.E.C. (Pacific Express Company)
> Gents:—
>
> As Wells Fargo & Co. have instructed their agents throughout the country to reduce the rates of freight on treasure, etc. so as to obtain all the business, . . . you are hereby authorized to do the same, regardless of the former rates.
>
> D. Brigham, Jr.

Obviously the Pacific Express was making a desperate effort to retain its business and, equally obvious was the fact that Wells Fargo was cutting rates to embarrass it. The first rate war in the West couldn't last long, for Wells Fargo had too many resources. Neither the Pacific Express nor the old Adams crowd backing it had a sizable cash backlog and, after six months, they were begging for help. An armistice was reached, followed by a carefully concocted "compromise" on rates which set the pattern for similar doings on eastern railroads for the next twenty-five years. In 1857 the Pacific Express went under. It was succeeded by the Alta Express which, within a year, sold out to Wells Fargo.

Wells Fargo's specialty remained the transport of gold; although mining declined somewhat after 1855 Wells Fargo carried most of the gold available. In 1858 it handled over

62

$58,000,000 in gold bullion on its California lines. And it made large sums of money: through the 'fifties, dividends on its stock continued at ten per cent per annum. In 1860 an additional stock dividend of eight per cent was declared and paid on 6,000 shares. Two years later the company's capital was increased to 20,000 shares, and in that year four dividends of three per cent each were paid on the entire issue. Despite the obvious disadvantages of absentee ownership, the regular twelve per cent dividend was continued throughout 1863, but also cash dividends of twenty-two per cent and on December 22, 1863, a stock dividend of one hundred per cent on 10,000 shares was paid! And so was born the nickname for Wells Fargo which became current in San Francisco—the Fat Cat of Montgomery Street. A fat cat indeed!

The panic of 1855 marked the dramatic end to the gold craze. After that time men and business turned more and more to other ventures. Although Wells Fargo continued its business in gold and silver, especially whenever new discoveries of the precious metals were made in the West, it would never again depend entirely on such treasure for its life blood.

The tracks of the Central Pacific were building out of Sacramento in the late 'fifties; the disappointed miners were finding work in farming where wheat and other grains were cultivated; in growing grapes; in raising cattle and sheep. It looked as though the state might settle down to more prosaic occupations from then on.

But then, in 1859, California was off on another gold and silver hunt. In that year the Comstock Lode was discovered just over the California border in Nevada. Gold and silver poured from the earth, and Virginia City, on the slope of Sun Mountain on the eastern side of the Sierras, became the center of the newest bonanza. San Francisco and the Mother Lode were almost depopulated; California packed up and started for Nevada. It was 1849 all over again. Virginia City was the newest boom town. It was built 7,200 feet up on the side of a mountain so steep that there was as much as a fifty-foot drop from one street to the next. Within the first twelve months of its existence, Virginia City acquired a population of 20,000; a huge brick hotel, the *International*; innumerable eating and drinking places, saloons, bordellos and even a few churches. Alvin Harlow has a fine description of the city in his invaluable book, *Old Waybills:*

> Virginia City in the first three years of the '60's was in a fever of development—houses being thrown up with frantic haste, stamp mills thundering and belching smoke, stores jammed with buyers and making a hundred per cent profit on every sale, auctioneers yelling, newspapers dashing off extras, fire companies clanging to and fro, saloons open day and night, hurdy-gurdies, theaters and dance halls all alight and humming with activity, stage-coaches with cracking whips and "yip-yip-yipping" drivers clattering through the crowded streets amid flying dust and gravel, pulling up with a flourish at the door of the Wells, Fargo or other office to discharge passengers, bags of mail and bags of gold.

Virginia City occupied Wells Fargo's principal attentions for some years, as well as that of the other business houses of San Francisco. In 1861 Wells Fargo built its banking house at Virginia City with red brick brought by wagon over the Sierras and with the bright-green cast-iron shutters that Californians knew so well. It was the handsomest building in town. Louis McLane, general manager for Wells Fargo in California and Nevada, saw to that.

Louis McLane came to California from Baltimore, where his father had been president of America's earliest railroad, the Baltimore and Ohio. The McLanes were quite a clan. One of them, Robert, became United States Minister to France; another, Allan, was for some years president of the Pacific Mail Steamship Company; a sister married the noted Confederate General, Joe Johnston. Then there was young Louis, born in 1819, who attended Delaware College at Newark. He entered the Navy as a midshipman, later served with John C. Fremont's California Battalion when Fremont defied Mexican authority and proclaimed California an independent republic. One year later, McLane was with Commodore Stockton when he placed the American flag over the Monterey Custom House and proclaimed the entire sprawling *Alta* California a future state of the Union.

On the first day of January, 1850, Louis McLane resigned his commission and, as a civilian, made his way to San Francisco. He found San Francisco of the 'fifties very much to his liking. He entered the shipping business between San Francisco and Sacramento and named his first boat *Sophie,* after his wife. Later when the *Sophie* blew up, an unfortunate habit of steamboats in those days, McLane built a newer and better boat and called it the *Sophie McLane.* It also exploded.

Louis' younger brother Charlie, who had also come to California, was an ardent horseman and he plunged into the staging business. With Louis' help he organized the Pioneer Stage Line which operated between Placerville (Hangtown) and Virginia City. The line made money steadily and, by 1864, it was the most traveled road in the entire state.

The "main drag" as it was called was then, as now, one of the most beautiful drives in all North America. It climbed the Sierras, swept around the cerulean-blue Lake Tahoe at the summit, dipped down into the valley of the Truckee and almost straight up to Virginia City on Sun Mountain. It was carefully graded and generally well kept. In dry seasons it was watered down to lay the dust. It is a matter of record that the bright-red coaches of the McLanes once made the run of more than 100 miles in twelve hours and twenty-three minutes.

No wonder that Schuyler Colfax from Indiana, riding west in 1865 with the distinguished Samuel Bowles, editor of the Springfield, Massachusetts, *Republican,* declared that "It required more talent to drive a stage down the Sierras than to be a Member of Congress." He may have been right.

It was on this Placerville-Virginia City run that the reputation of the fabulous Hank Monk was made. Monk came to his greatest fame in 1862, when he drove over the High Sierras with Horace Greeley, editor of the New York *Tribune.* Mark Twain tells the story in *Roughing It,* and he adds that he couldn't recall whether he had heard it 481 or 482 times. Who are we not to repeat it?

Horace Greeley went over this road once. When he was leaving Carson City he told the driver, Hank Monk, that he had an engagement to lecture at Placerville and was very anxious to go through quick. Hank Monk cracked his whip and started off at an awful pace. The coach bounced up and down in such a terrific way that it jolted the buttons all off of Horace's coat, and finally shot his head clean through the roof of the stage, and then he yelled at Hank Monk and begged him to go easier—said he warn't in as much of a hurry as a while ago. But Hank Monk said, "Keep your seat, Horace, and I'll get you there on time"—and you bet he did, too, what was left of him!

Mark Twain concluded:

> Drivers always told it, conductors told it, landlords told it, chance passengers told it, the very Chinamen and vagrant Indians recounted it. I have had the same driver tell it to me two or three times in the same afternoon. It has come to me in all the multitude of tongues that Babel bequeathed to earth, and flavored with whiskey, brandy, beer, cologne, sozodont, tobacco, garlic, onions, grasshoppers—everything that has a fragrance to it . . . I have never smelt any anecdote as often as I have smelt that one; never smelt any anecdote that smelt so variegated as that one . . . I have seen it in print in nine different languages; and now I learn with regret that it is going to be set to music. I do not think that such things are right.

Whether this incident ever occurred, and Twain stoutly maintains that it didn't, Henry James Monk certainly had a way with him. It is recorded that a prominent San Francisco woman going up to Lake Tahoe had her trunk sent after her by Wells Fargo. When, after two days, it failed to arrive, she went to the door of her summer hotel, greeted Hank Monk and asked after the whereabouts of her trunk. He smiled at the lady quizzically and replied in a slow drawl:

"Jes' didn't have room for it, mum, on the stage, so I'm sawin' it in half. I'll bring the first half tomorrow . . ." The woman shrieked, "But my dresses!" Hank continued to smile. "Sawing them in half, too, mum. That's the way they look to me, anyway."

There was no gainsaying Hank Monk.

66

When he came to his final end, Mark Twain's old paper, the Virginia City *Enterprise* prepared this obituary (March 6, 1883):

HANK MONK—the famous stage driver is dead. He has been on the down grade for some time. On Wednesday his foot lost its final hold on the brake and his coach could not be stopped until, battered and broken on a sharp turn, it went over into the canyon, black and deep, which we call death. In his way, Hank Monk was a character. In the old days, before the leathers under his coach were soaked with alcohol, there was no better balanced head than his. There was an air about him which his closest friends could not understand. There was something which seemed to say that stage driving was not his intended walk; that if he pleased, there were other things, even more difficult than handling six wild horses, which he could do quite as well. In his prime he would turn a six horse coach in the street with the team at a full run, and with every line apparently loose. But the coach would always bring up in exactly the spot that the most careful driver would have tried to bring it. His eye never deceived him and his estimation of distance was absolute; the result which must be when leaders, swings and wheelers all were playing their roles, with him an exact science. His driving was such a perfection of art that it did not seem art at all, and many an envious whip, watching him, has turned away to say, "He is the luckiest man that ever climbed on top of a box."

It was not luck at all; it was simply an intuitive exact calculation from cause to effect, and his whole duty ended when he fixed the cause. The effect had to be. He has often driven from the summit of the Sierras down into the valley, ten miles in forty-five minutes. Other drivers have done as well, the only difference being that with others it was a strain upon the eye and hand and arm and foot; with Monk it was a matter of course. He was to stage driving what the German papers say Edwin Booth was to Hamlet, "It was not played, but lived."

In his gray shirt and tobacco-stained corduroy trousers, never too scrupulously clean, Hank Monk typified a breed of men of valor and nonchalance, never before known, and perhaps never again to grace the American scene, men who with equal ease could crack a whip or a shotgun and who could look down coolly into the barrel of a highwayman's gun without batting an eyelash.

Then there was John Blake, another stage driver—a sort of Beau Brummel in dress, who was a good fellow, and fairly talkative on the ground, but as silent as a clam when on duty.

On one occasion a traveling salesman had secured a seat on the driver's box beside him. After the start had been made and the stage was well under way, the passenger offered John a cigar, but the only response was a shake of the head. A little later, the passenger began to comment on the weather, upon the scenery, upon John's fine horses and the masterly way he handled them. Still no response. Later in the afternoon the passenger thought he would try again to break through the crust of the Sphinx, and asked: "Mr. Blake, what time do we arrive?" John looked at him for a moment and replied: "There is a clock in the office when we get there."

There were other drivers on the pioneer stages whose reputations ranked nearly, if not equally as high as Hank Monk's, such men as Charles Watson, Curly Dan (R.B.) Burch, Charlie Carroll, Coon Hollow Charlie (Charles Saddle) and Ned Blair. William Pridham remembered Charlie Crowell, Charlie Forbes, Dave Green, Jerry Crowder, the two Robbins twins, Dan and Jerry, and many others. In a later day there was James Stewart, known to all Wells Fargo in the West as the "Silent Terror," whose brace of old-fashioned muzzle-loading revolvers were never brought into action until actually needed, and then invariably with awful results. No one has recorded the number of outlaws who fell by the deadly aim of Jim Stewart in the wilds of Wyoming, Utah, Arizona and Nevada.

These were some of the famous "jehus" who drove the Pioneer coaches from Placerville up the Big Hill, down into Carson City and up the impossible slopes of Sun Mountain to Virginia City. They were in a class by themselves. George and William Banning in their well-known book, *Six Horses,* sum them up this way:

> Their life histories were not for the world. When they talked
> —and many of them would not talk except to their teams—

68

any sincere confidence from them could be taken as the highest compliment. Otherwise they were drolly insincere, spinning yarns to be taken with bushels of salt—salt which they frankly passed around for application. Their lives were strictly their own. . . .

Most of the jehus (despite what has been said of Hank Monk) were handsome and proud dandies, keenly interested in neat cravats, white shirts, fine gauntlets and highly polished boots. To top off their sartorial splendor they usually wore dashing hats of cream-colored felt. They had an eye for women whom they treated with respect and chivalry—at least while on duty. The whips on the Pioneer Line, or any other line for that matter, were not apt to be church-goers but they were a hardy, daring breed of men who invariably swore by Wells Fargo.

There were few opportunities for expansion in those days that Wells Fargo did not accept; not that they always worked out. For instance, there was the time at the beginning of the 'sixties when gold was discovered at the foot of the Blue Mountains up in Idaho. A rush, similar to that into the Mother Lode country more than a decade earlier, began. Wells Fargo saw this as a new opportunity and seized it. Superintendent Sam Knight at San Francisco sent one of his newest young men, Charles T. Blake, up into the Blue Mountain region as an advance agent for the express.

Blake outfitted himself for the trip at Portland. In the late spring of 1863 he traveled into the inland country by way of the Columbia, Snake and Boise Rivers. He wrote home in May from Placerville, Idaho, that he had arrived by a mule train which carried him all the way from Portland, except for a few miles by steamboat and the newly completed railroad around the Dalles.

At Placerville he was given a warm reception. A crowd gathered in the town square and a miner said to the guide in charge of the train, "Can you tell us anything about Wells, Fargo and Company? We understand that they are going to establish an agency here." "Yes," replied the guide, "they are, and that man in spectacles is the agent." The next moment there was much rejoicing in the town. People shouted gleefully, "Wells Fargo has come! Wells Fargo has come!"

Blake brought 400 letters with him for which he collected one dollar each. He also sold copies of the *Sacramento Weekly Union* at $1.50 apiece. Before leaving San Francisco, Knight had furnished him with a book of receipt forms, sealing wax, four quires of paper and forty envelopes. The envelopes were sold at fifty cents each for transmission to the West Coast, seventy-five cents if they were to go to the East.

The Idaho experiment wasn't continued for long. The route was too dangerous—even for Wells Fargo—and more important, the gold soon petered out. Blake returned to San Francisco. But wherever there were men and gold, Wells Fargo was sure to follow.

VI

The Pony Express

The words Pony Express are magic in America for they have excited and thrilled Americans for almost a century. There had been short-run pony expresses in the west before 1860 run by Wells Fargo and others but *the* Pony Express which rode the 2000 miles from St. Joseph, Missouri to Sacramento in nine days—on a regular schedule—is in a class by itself. No matter what the obstacles, blizzard, flood, hostile Indians, sandstorm or accident, the mail went through. And yet this short-lived express, the most famous and dramatic in history, was a financial failure. It lost money but it was magnificent. But that perhaps is a minor matter in the larger perspective, because it served a useful purpose in establishing rapid communication between the loyal North and California. It may be fairly said that the Pony Express played its part in keeping California in the Union. The firm of Russell, Majors and Waddell created it to dramatize to the nation the need of reliable and regular communication between California and the East by the central rather than the southern route. In achieving this purpose the founders as well as the hundreds of men who rode and maintained the long treacherous route, who did the impossible, created a legend in the land.

In all of this Wells Fargo played an active part because the Pony Express carried their mails under the Wells Fargo Pony Express stamp and many of the men active in the Pony Express were or had been Wells Fargo employees or officials. Later when Wells Fargo took over the Ben Holladay staging empire they became actual owners of whatever was left of the Pony Express.

For years before the Pony Express there had been a great clamor for a stage line running directly across the country from San Francisco to Salt Lake City and from there to St. Joseph or Independence. Indeed there had been lines. As early as 1851 Major George Chorpenning Jr. and his partner, Absalom Woodward, made a contract with the government to carry mail from Sacramento to Salt Lake and return. They were to cover the route once a month, each way, and were to be paid $14,000 per year for the job. The following account* of Woodward's fatal trip from California and the later trips made during the terrible winter of 1851-52 shows the courage and daring of these great pioneer expressmen:

> ... the following month, November 1st, [1851] Capt. A. Woodward, then a partner with Chorpenning, left California with the mails for Salt Lake. He had with him four good mountain men, as well mounted and armed as was possible for experienced men to be, and he had with him some $5,000 to $10,000 in gold coin,

* Taken from a printed pamphlet in the Coe Collection of Western Americana in the Yale University Library.

72

most of which was designed for the purchase of mules, horses, sheep, &c., in Salt Lake. This train was attacked at Clover Patch, below Stony Point, on the morning of the 20th, by some seventy Indians, who disputed the right of the white men to pass through *their* country as they termed it; but after some firing, in which several Indians were killed by the long range Government rifles in the hands of the men, they fell back and allowed the train to pass on, only, as it proved afterwards, to attack them at some more convenient or suitable point further on. The train traveled all day and nearly all night on a forced march, and next morning met the train on the way into California at Stockton Springs, which was the last heard of them till their remains were found. The history of the affair, as gathered from Indians afterwards met in the country, was that they had attacked Woodward's party in the "Big Cañon" on the Humboldt river, next day after they parted company with the California bound train, and killed the four men and wounded Woodward, who, being mounted on a good horse, got away, and traveled some 150 miles perhaps, where his remains were found by the roadside . . .

The train going into California for this month also had great difficulty. They were first driven back to the Salt Lake settlements by the Indians, and, gathering more strength, struck out again, but after parting with Woodward at Stockton Springs, were attacked several times; had one man wounded, and lost five horses and two wagons.

The trains for the month of December, 1851, and January, 1852, got stuck in the snows in the Sierra Nevada, and had to return to the settlement. The February mail was sent from Sacramento by what was known as the Northern or Feather River route. This train was some forty days reaching the station in Carson Valley, from whence fresh animals were taken, and they proceeded on toward Salt Lake. But while in the Goose Creek mountains all these thirteen mules and one horse were frozen to death in a single night. The men being short of provisions, dried choice portions of the flesh of their frozen mules, and with the mails, blankets, &c., on their backs, traveled on foot through deep snow nearly 200 miles to Salt Lake City . . .

The trail was so dangerous that Chorpenning had great trouble in getting men to carry the mail. So, with his partner dead and his contract to carry the mail in jeopardy if he didn't deliver the mail on the return trip, Chorpenning left Salt Lake City, probably on May 1st, alone, brought the mail into Sacramento and saved his contract.

In April, 1854, Chorpenning signed another contract with the government. This one allowed him to carry the mail between the two cities by way of the Southwest and San Pedro and from San Pedro to San Francisco by water.

Chorpenning's pack-mule express, known as the "jackass mail" was not equal to the job. Stages were needed. So in 1858 this daring expressman signed still another contract with the government. This time he would run stages over the mountains. But in spite of hard work and good intentions this line also proved to be inadequate. The roads were abominable and it was virtually impossible to maintain satisfactory schedules. Finally, in May, 1860, Chorpenning's contract was cancelled and it was taken over by Russell, Majors and Waddell, who had been developing staging lines east from Salt Lake City.

In the early days, before Russell, Majors and Waddell took over on the routes east of Salt Lake, things hadn't been much better. Colonel Samuel H. Woodson was the first to get a mail contract. In 1850 he signed an agreement to carry mail, once a month, from Independence to Salt Lake. But Woodson, like several men who later had contracts, found that he couldn't keep a regular schedule in the face of blizzards and Indian raids. And so for years the service was poor.

Then there was the firm of Hockaday and Liggett which, in 1858, got a government contract to run mail from St. Joseph, Missouri, to Salt Lake. But this firm wasn't successful either. Like the others, they faced incredible hardships and their service was irregular in every sense of the word.

Since 1848 Alexander Majors had been developing a freighting business from Independence and other towns to the military garrisons on the frontier. In 1855 he went into partnership with William H. Russell and William B. Waddell and, in 1858, the firm received a government contract to supply the army heading West to quell the Mormon "rebellion." When the gold rush to Pike's Peak started, Russell, always the gambler and plunger, planned to inaugurate a stagecoach line between

Leavenworth, Kansas, and the new settlement at the junction of the South Platte and Cherry Creek, known as Denver. Majors, the solid and conservative member of the firm, refused to go along with his plans and so Russell and John S. Jones started the Leavenworth and Pike's Peak Express. By May, 1859, service was started and, within a month, they bought Hockaday and Liggett's mail contract. Russell and Jones now had a mail route all the way from St. Joseph to Salt Lake.

Albert D. Richardson, the famed correspondent for the New York *Herald,* rode West from Leavenworth in 1859 on the stages of the Leavenworth and Pike's Peak Express. Eight years later he wrote about it in his book, *Beyond the Mississippi:*

> *May 25.*—I left Leavenworth by the overland mail carriage built in Concord, New Hampshire, known as the Concord wagon. In a dozen communities its manufacture is imitated with more or less success but never equaled. The little capital of the Granite State alone has the art of making a vehicle which, like the one-hoss shay, "don't break down, but only wears out." It is covered with duck or canvas [Richardson must have been riding in a mudwagon, from which the famous buckboard later evolved] the driver sitting in front, at a slight elevation above the passengers. Bearing no weight upon the roof, it is less topheavy than the old-fashioned stage-coach . . . Like human travelers on life's highway, it goes best under a heavy load. Empty, it jolts and pitches like a ship in a raging sea; filled with passengers and balanced by a proper distribution of baggage . . . its motion is easy and elastic . . .
>
> Two coaches, each drawn by four mules, leave Leavenworth daily and make the entire trip together, for protection in case of danger from Indians. A crowd gathered in front of the Planters' House to see our equipages start. Amid confused ejaculation of "Good-by, old boy," "Write as soon as you get there," "Better have your hair cut, so that the Arapahoes can't scalp you," "Tell John to send me an ounce of dust," "Be sure and give Smith that letter from his wife," "Do write the facts about the gold," the whips cracked and the two stages rolled merrily away.

When the gold rush in Colorado subsided (although there were untold millions yet to be made from Colorado mining) the Russell, Majors and Waddell freighting firm had to take over the Jones and Russell line which was in financial hot water. In 1860 the firm's name was changed to the Central Overland California and Pike's Peak Express Company. No Westerner would stand for that and so the firm became known throughout the region as the C.O.C. & P.P.

Horace Greeley who, in 1859, went west on the same line that Richardson traveled on—they went part of the way together—was much impressed with the work that Russell, Majors and Waddell were doing. He wrote in his *Overland Journey:*

> . . . Russell, Majors & Waddell's transportation establishment between the fort and the city, is the great feature of Leavenworth. Such acres of wagons! such pyramids of axletrees! such herds of oxen! such regiments of drivers and other employees! No one who does not see can realize how vast a business this is, nor how immense are its outlays as well as its income. I presume this great firm has at this hour two millions of dollars invested in stock, mainly oxen, mules and wagons. (They last year employed six thousand teamsters, and worked forty-five thousand oxen.)

A year later, in 1860, the entire nation was agog over the Pony Express. Not content with freighting and staging, Russell, Majors and Waddell who had years of experience along the central overland route, started and successfully developed the most daring and hazardous one-man express ever conceived. It was not a stunt but a bold venture that was operated for more than eighteen months. It was started on April 3, 1860, and officially discontinued on October 26, 1861, although it operated until November 20th.

The newspapers quickly recognized the founders' intentions. The San Francisco *Bulletin* on January 30, 1860, said that the firm's purpose was "not so much to make money at present as it is to prove by actual experiment the superiority of the Salt Lake route." The *Rocky Mountain News* in Denver hoped that the Pony Express would "shame" Congress into legislating a daily or tri-weekly mail run on the Central route.

On the other hand Collis P. Huntington, one of the shrewd and daring "Big Four" California promoters, all to loom large in the state's financial history, was pretty blunt in his criticism. He thought that the whole scheme was little else than "constructive murder" for, in his opinion, Indians would massacre the riders on the long and dangerous runs. But Huntington recognized an achievement when he saw it, for once the Pony Express was established the growing firm of Huntington & Hopkins used its services regularly.

The most interesting account of travel along the route of the Pony Express can be found in Mark Twain's delightful *Roughing It.* His book is filled with reminiscences, information and humor. It describes, at some length, the details of the trip and includes these interesting comments on the Pony Express:

> In a little while all interest was taken up in stretching our necks and watching for the "pony-rider"—the fleet messenger who sped across the continent from St. Joe to Sacramento, carrying letters nineteen hundred miles in eight days! Think of that for perishable horse and human flesh and blood to do! The pony-rider was usually a little bit of a man, brimful of spirit and endurance. No matter what time of the day or night his watch came on, and no matter whether it was winter or summer, raining, snowing, hailing or sleeting, or whether his "beat" was a level straight road or a crazy trail over mountain crags and precipices, or whether it led through peaceful regions or regions that swarmed with hostile Indians, he must be always ready to leap into the saddle and be off like the wind! There was no idling-time for the pony-rider on duty. He rode fifty miles without stopping, by daylight, moonlight, starlight, or through the blackness of darkness—just as it happened. He rode a splendid horse that was born for a racer and fed and lodged like a gentleman; kept him at his utmost speed for ten miles, and then, as he came crashing up to the station where stood two men holding fast a fresh, impatient steed, the transfer of rider and mail-bag was made in the twinkling of an eye, and away flew the eager pair and were out of sight before the spectator could get hardly the ghost of a look. Both rider and horse went "flying light." The rider's dress was thin, and fitted close; he wore a "roundabout," and a skull-cap, and tucked his pantaloons into his boot-tops, like a race-rider. He carried no arms [many of them did]—he carried nothing that was not

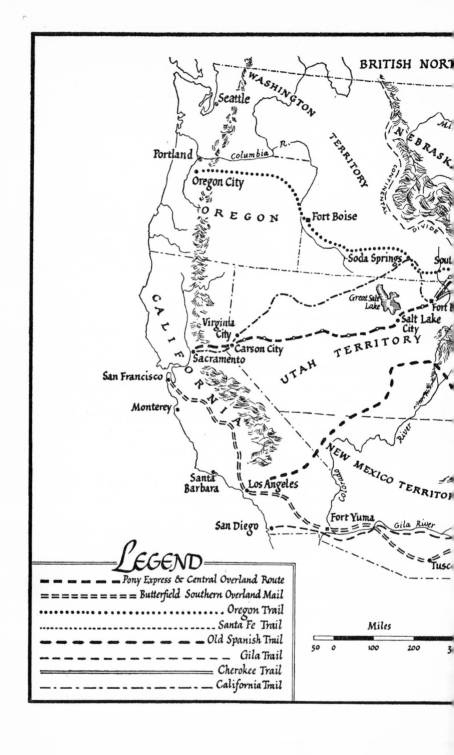

BRITISH NOR[T]

WASHINGTON
Seattle
TERRITORY
Portland
Columbia R.
Oregon City
O R E G O N
Fort Boise
Soda Springs
Sout
NEBRASK
Mt
CONTINENTAL
DIVIDE
Great Salt Lake
Fort [
Virginia City
Salt Lake City
Carson City
Sacramento
UTAH TERRITORY
San Francisco
Monterey
C A L I F O R N I A
River
NEW MEXICO TERRITOR[Y]
Santa Barbara
Los Angeles
Colorado
San Diego
Fort Yuma
Gila River
Tusc

LEGEND

— — — — — Pony Express & Central Overland Route
========= Butterfield Southern Overland Mail
•••••••••••••••••••••••••• Oregon Trail
·························· Santa Fe Trail
— — — — — — Old Spanish Trail
— — — — — Gila Trail
══════════ Cherokee Trail
—·—·—·—·— California Trail

Miles

50 0   100   200   3[00]

Sketch Map of the Route of the Pony Express, the Butterfield Southern
Overland Mail Trail, the Oregon Trail and Other Trails by Which the
Westward Course of Empire Made its Way. Redrawn from several old maps.

absolutely necessary, for even the postage on his literary freight was worth *five dollars a letter*. He got but little frivolous correspondence to carry—his bag had business letters in it mostly. His horse was stripped of all unnecessary weight, too. He wore a little wafer of a racing-saddle, and no visible blanket. . . . There were about eighty pony riders in the saddle all the time, night and day, stretching in a long, scattering procession from Missouri to California, forty flying eastward, and forty toward the west. . . .

The Pony Express which started in St. Joseph went from there to Seneca, then to Marysville, up the Little Blue River, across the Platte to Fort Kearney. It then proceeded along the famed Oregon Trail, through the Platte River Valley to Lodge Pole Creek, through Old Julesburg, Chimney Rock, Fort Laramie, South Pass, Fort Bridger (long since established by the renowned Jim Bridger) and into Salt Lake City.

From the Mormon capital the Pony Express used the old Chorpenning route through Camp Floyd, Deep Creek, Ruby Valley, Fort Churchill, Carson City, Genoa, Placerville, and on into Sacramento.

To save time at the relay stations the saddles remained on each horse; it was the *mochilla* or saddle-bag that was changed in a trice. The *mochilla* which fitted snugly over the saddle horn had four *cantinas* or pockets. Three were locked and only opened at military posts or Salt Lake City. The fourth contained mail picked up en route and the time slip recording the arrivals and departures of each rider. There was a key for this *cantina* at each way station.

The *mochilla* had to be light and so the load was limited to twenty pounds. As a result, letters sent by Pony Express were written on tissue paper. For a time a few Eastern newspapers printed limited editions on thin paper for transport to California by Pony Express.

The relay points, where horses were speedily changed were, at first, twenty to twenty-five miles apart, later ten to twenty miles apart. The station buildings were often built of logs, but stone and adobe were used to rebuild the stations destroyed by

80

Indians, for these materials offered greater protection from the hostile red men.

There is some question whether Ben Ficklin, superintendent of Russell, Majors and Waddell's stage lines at Salt Lake or California's Senator William Gwin, originated the idea for the Pony Express. There are also those who claim that John Butterfield or the Overland Mail (on the southern route) contemplated a "horse express" first. Whatever the truth in the matter, the Pony Express brought to a climax the fight between the advocates of the central and the advocates of the southern route. It brought the two great firms of Russell, Majors and Waddell and Butterfield running on these two routes into direct competition. It was the Civil War that settled the struggle.

The start of the Pony Express from St. Joseph, Missouri, the eastern end of the line, was a major event in the town. About a year before, a small and crudely built railway had poked its way from Hannibal on the Mississippi to St. Joe. It was called, quite logically, the Hannibal and St. Joseph Railroad, but for a good many years now it has been part of the Burlington system. The little road was ambitious and decided to share in some of the glory surrounding the inauguration of the Pony Express service. Mail from the East came over the railroad via the present Wabash from Toledo; east of Toledo it was hauled on the main lines of the Lake Shore and New York Central Railroads.

Superintendent J.T.K. Haywood of the St. Joe road planned the whole thing carefully. He picked the *Missouri,* the road's fastest engine, for the run. In back of the locomotive there was a specially constructed mail car, with seats for just a few passengers. All the operating officers of the road were in the car on the big day. They would not order their engineer to gamble with death without sharing the risks. The danger was not imaginary for the roadbed was new and green and the rails were light. There was no rock ballast and when the short train swung around the frequent curves, the passengers hung on for dear life. But the train went through on record time.

For several days in advance people along the line knew that the St. Joe road was planning a life-or-death run for the government mail contract. For those few days the impending Civil War was almost forgotten. On the day of the run, people lined the track to watch the train flash by.

Orders had gone out to all fuel agents to be on the alert for telegraphic directions. They were to be ready to load the tender with wood, and to lose no time about it. St. Joseph was reached on schedule, the precious mail pouches were quickly transferred to the waiting pony and the Pony Express was off on its first westward run.

It is not known, definitely, who that first rider was. His name appears to have been drawn by lot. In later years it was said that Johnny Frey, a twenty-year-old boy who was later killed in the Civil War, rode the first pony west. Other candidates have been advanced for the honor, but a few years ago a St. Joseph newspaper suggested the name of Billy Richardson (John William Richardson). This claim has been confirmed in the pages of the *Missouri Historical Review.*

There has also been a good deal of discussion as to who carried the first mail east out of San Francisco. For years Harry Roff was given the honor, but it is believed today that Bill Hamilton rode the first horse east. Because the mail started from San Francisco and went up to Sacramento by boat, Hamilton began his stretch of the eastward run at Sacramento. He left at 2:45 in the morning and reached Placerville in just four hours. From there he went on to Sportsman's Hall, twelve miles farther, where Warren Upson took over. Upson made Carson City on schedule in spite of the heavy snow on the mountain trails. The rider out of Carson City was Bob Haslam, one of the greatest of them all.

It took just a few hours less than seven days for the other mail, coming west, to reach Carson City from St. Joseph. Warren Upson was waiting for it and he retraced his trip to Sportsman's Hall where Bill Hamilton picked up the mail and raced back into Sacramento. His welcome made history. He was met before he reached the crossing of the American Fork. Men, old and young, rode with him and ahead of him, escorting him into town. It is said that Charlie Crocker, who at the time was building the Central Pacific Railroad, behaved like a madman. With others he raced ahead of Hamilton just to be

82

able to say that he had beaten the Pony Express to the dock. Hamilton must have been dazzled and startled by the racket of shotguns, cannon, shooting anvils and the band on the levee. He certainly couldn't have been blind to the beautiful women who stood on the galleries of the houses on J Street and threw him flowers and kisses. It was a royal greeting. Even the skeptics, who said, "It can't be done," cheered Hamilton as he rode into town. Hamilton, with his pony, boarded the *Antelope* for San Francisco, and when he arrived there the tumultuous welcome of Sacramento was repeated. There was a band, firemen and a mad populace. There were bonfires and dancing as well as a parade (there was a parade in San Francisco on every occasion)—for the mail, all of twenty-five letters, had come through in ten and a half days and California was celebrating as only she could celebrate.

People all over the country had many occasions to marvel at the feats of the Pony Express. Lincoln's inaugural address was carried to California in seven days and seventeen hours.

One of the great feats can be indirectly credited to the Piute Indians. In the spring of 1860 the Piutes went on the warpath against the Pony Express relay stations Ben Ficklin had built across the lonely stretches of Nevada. Stations were burned, horses stolen and relay crews killed. The Pony Express appealed to the Army and whole companies of the Army policed the route east of Carson City and finally were able to drive the Piutes off the trail and north into the mountains.

During this siege of "Indian trouble" Pony Bob Haslam made one of the greatest rides in the history of the West. His route lay between Friday's Station and Bucklands (Fort Churchill). When he pulled into Reed's Station on his eastward run there were no horses, since they had been taken by the troops fighting the Indians. So, after feeding his mount, he rode fifteen miles farther to Bucklands, the end of his seventy-five-mile run. However, Johnny Richardson, the next rider, refused to set out for Carson Sink since the danger from Indians was so great. Marley, the superintendent of the station, offered Haslam $50 to ride Richardson's route and ten minutes later Pony Bob headed out across the alkali-covered trail. At the

Sink, he changed horses and continued on to Cold Springs. From there he completed Richardson's run, finally reaching Smith's Creek, where a rider took his *mochilla* and continued eastward. Pony Bob had traveled 185 miles, stopping only to change horses.

He spent the night at Smith Creek and, in the morning, when the exhausted rider from the east arrived, Haslam picked up the westbound bags and rode back over the trail he had come in on the night before. At Cold Springs the station was a shambles and the keeper dead. The horses had disappeared with the Indians. There was nothing to do but ride on through the night to Sand Springs. From there he galloped on to Carson, where the men tried to prevent him from going on since they feared that the region was surrounded by Indians. Haslam, however, insisted on riding through with the mail and so he rode on to Bucklands. Marley, who was still there, doubled the bonus he had offered him and Bob, after resting for a little more than an hour, galloped on across the Sierras and back into Fridays. He had covered 380 miles through hostile Indian country with about eleven hours rest.

Operation of the Pony Express, once it had been thoroughly organized, approached perfection. Precision, as well as the utmost speed, became its watchword. Despite the superhuman obstacles against which it worked, it achieved an astonishing regularity. In the entire eighteen months of its history, over 150 round trips were made between the Missouri and the Sacramento, 650,000 miles had been ridden, and but one trip ever was lost. Only one rider lost his life in the service.

The men who rode the Pony Express were handpicked, but no more so than the horses they rode, which were the best that could be bought. The riders were closer to jockeys in size, and few of them weighed more than a hundred pounds. What's more, they were young, for it took stamina to cover routes twice each week that covered at least fifty-five miles in mountainous country and sometimes 120 miles on level terrain. The job of riding the Pony Express was the most glamorous and prized in all the country. Millions of boys dreamed of being express riders some day. Most of them didn't realize that the pay

84

ranged from $50 to $150 per month. It wasn't bad pay for the times, but you never could get rich riding a horse—not even in the old days.

But the great feats of riding and endurance could not hide the handwriting on the wall. The Central Overland California and Pike's Peak Express Company, the backer of the Pony Express, was being called the "Clean Out of Cash and Poor Pay" outfit. William H. Russell was in serious trouble with the government and Butterfield's southern route stages were discontinued in the spring of 1861 and transferred to the central route. Then, too, there was Ben Holladay who had advanced the C.O.C. and P.P. Exp. Co. a good bit of money. He held a first mortgage on the line. Finally there was great pressure in Washington to establish a *daily* stage across the continent on the Central Overland route. And finally the magnetic telegraph was nearing completion. It would soon span the continent and make the "fast" service of the Pony Express obsolete.

William H. Russell, who had always been the most enterprising member of the firm, was arrested in New York in December, 1860. He and Godard Bailey, a clerk in the Department of the Interior, were charged with the theft of Indian Trust funds. The whole affair has been interpreted as a plot against Russell by the eminent historian, H. H. Bancroft in his *Chronicles of the Builders:*

> In January, 1861 . . . Russell, president of the company, fell into difficulty—if, indeed it were not a trap set for him by friends of the southern route [John Butterfield's]. The company was largely in debt, owing about $1,800,000; and, although a large company, and with considerable assets, was embarrassed to a degree which made borrowing necessary to a greater amount than was convenient. The Government was also in debt to the company on its contracts, Congress having failed to pass an appropriation bill. While Russell was in Washington, endeavoring to secure some relief, he was induced to take $870,000 in bonds of the Interior Department, as a loan, and giving as security acceptances on the War Department furnished him by Secretary Floyd, a part of which was not yet due. The bonds, as it turned out, were stolen by Godard Bailey, a family connec-

tion of Floyd's and law clerk in the Interior Department . . . In the temporary confusion which followed the discovery of the fraud, Russell lost his opportunity, as perhaps it was meant that he should and Congress in February authorized the Postmaster General to advertise for bids for a daily mail over the central route.

As Russell battled in the courts, both he and his firm lost their golden opportunity. On March 2, 1861, Congress passed a law which authorized a six-day-a-week mail service from the Missouri to California. The contract was worth $1,000,000 per year. Butterfield's southern route was abandoned because of the war and the contract was let to his firm—the Overland Mail—which had always been closely connected with the men who controlled Wells Fargo. The Overland Mail had a new president, William B. Dinsmore, who had replaced John Butterfield when the latter had disagreed with other members of the firm over the establishment of a Pony Express on the southern route.

The Overland Mail, by its contract with the Government, had the privilege of making arrangements for carrying the mail across the entire central route. The Pioneer Line, operated and owned by Louis McLane, was to operate the run from Placerville to Carson, the Overland Mail moved in to carry the mail from Carson to Salt Lake, while the C.O.C. and P.P. Express covered the Salt Lake to St. Joseph run. Service under the new contract started on July 1, 1861. It was decided that the Pony Express should continue until the transcontinental telegraph line was completed.

Beginning in April, 1861, Wells Fargo sold Pony Express stamps of its own design in $2-red and $4-green denominations, for use on letters. In accordance with the Overland Mail Act of March, 1861, the express postage was reduced to one dollar per half-ounce, or less, and new Wells Fargo stamps were issued to comply.

By August, 1861, the magnetic telegraph was 100 miles east of Fort Churchill, Nevada, and a week later fifty miles farther east. At the same time, Hiram Sibley was pushing the telegraph line west from Fort Kearney. The ex-sheriff from

New York State was both go-getter and diplomat. When the Indians west of the Missouri River looked on the telegraph lines with considerable suspicion, Sibley summoned the chief of the Sioux. The old chief noted the upstanding figure of the white man and grunted his approval. Then Sibley affixed a telegraph sounder to the end of the copper wire that was being spun across the continent. Before his eyes, Sibley completed an electric circuit. The telegraph sounder began to click, faintly at first and then more distinctly.

"The voice of the Great Spirit is speaking to you," Sibley said to the Chief.

The Indian bowed low. It is a matter of record that from then on, no Indian ever again interfered with the wonderful machine that spoke from the heavens.

By August 9th, the telegraph reached fifty miles west of Fort Kearney, by September, 115 more miles had been added, and by October 8th, when the race between the crews working east and west had reached fever pitch, 368 more miles had been added. On the 20th of October the transcontinental telegraph was joined at a point just west of Salt Lake. The click of the telegraph key in Wall Street was instantly repeated in Montgomery Street, San Francisco.

The days of the Pony Express were numbered and few. The express which operated more than eighteen months was officially discontinued on October 26th, although, as we have seen, it continued to run, unofficially, for a few more weeks. It had lost its owners, the C.O.C. and P.P., some $200,000 and that company never really recovered from the loss.

From that time on California relied more and more on the great Overland Mail. The Pony Express had been a gallant gesture and it deserves a prominent place in the dramatic picture of the development of transport in the United States. It played an important role as well. Just what the Far West would have done in the early days of the Civil War without the swift and reliable communication that it offered, is hard to say. It was the Pony Express that kept Utah and California informed of the progress of the war. It is not too much to say that the Pony Express played an important part in the preservation of the Union. It helped greatly in placing California on the side of the North.

The stage was now set for the battle of the titans. Wells Fargo was soon to play a major role in the staging activities on the central route. Toward the close of 1864 president Danforth N. Barney in the company's main office in New York City announced to the stockholders that Louis McLane's Pioneer Stage Line had been bought. The name "Pioneer" on the letterboards of its stages was replaced by "Wells Fargo and Co." It would, in the future, not only ship its cargoes by stage, it would own the stage lines. The tremendous system of staging firms that had been developed throughout the central route was to become a part of the expanding Wells Fargo empire. In entering the stage business in the 'sixties, Wells Fargo bucked the oncoming Central Pacific and Union Pacific railroads. But, before it controlled the great stages of the West and before the railroads brought a new problem, Wells Fargo ran into Ben Holladay—head on.

Ben Holladay, to put it mildly, was a controversial figure. Henry Villard, the financier and journalist, thought him "illiterate, coarse, pretentious, boastful, false and cunning." John Hailey, the Idaho historian, thought differently. To him, Holladay was "sociable, generous, energetic, open and frank." There can be no doubt, however, that Holladay was a mighty shrewd, cunning, bold business man.

He was born in the hills of Kentucky in 1819 and schooled in a rough country store. In 1836 he came to St. Louis and three years later he was clerking in Weston, Missouri, a town just across the river from Leavenworth. In short order he owned a hotel, became postmaster. At different times he was a druggist, proprietor of a general store and, with his brother David, he owned a factory.

In 1846, with the advent of the Mexican War, Holladay became interested in transportation, moving freight to General Kearney's army. In 1849 he brought a wagon train of goods to Salt Lake where, with Brigham Young's blessing, he sold his freight at a large profit. He did business, successfully, as far west as California and, in the course of the next few years,

88

he made a great deal of money. He made enough so that when Russell, Majors and Waddell began expanding their stage business, Holladay was able to supply them with equipment. The firm borrowed from Holladay and was soon deep in his debt.

The financial failure of the Pony Express which lost at least $200,000 for Russell, Majors and Waddell, brought them to the brink of financial disaster. In March 1862, the Central Overland California and Pike's Peak Express company failed to meet its obligations and Holladay, who held a first mortgage on the company, took it over.

He changed the name of the company to the Overland Stage Line, added new equipment, bought finer horses, changed the route in places, built new way stations and managed to get additional government contracts. In four years he built a staging empire that spread into Idaho, Montana, Washington and Oregon. However, before he could reign supreme in the region east of Salt Lake City, he had to contend with a competing line which ran between Atchison and Denver. This line, popularly known as the "B.O.D.," was operated by David Butterfield, who was not related to John Butterfield in any way. The Butterfield Overland Dispatch or "B.O.D." used the Smokey Hill route to Denver which was approximately seventy miles shorter than Holladay's. The "B.O.D." was financed by Eastern money; the President of the Park Bank in New York was also President of the staging company. The following prospectus* of the new outfit was prepared by David Butterfield. It is a very interesting document for it shows much about the business methods of the day:

> Pres. of the Park Bank—
> . . . The cost of stocking an Express line to Colorado alone will not exceed $365,000 at present high prices.
> The running expenses per month will not exceed, including interest on stock, $13,500. On this basis the Express Company will have a capacity of moving two thousand pounds per day, a less weight of light merchandise than is now going forward by the existing organization. All freight, outside of the ordinary

* From the Coe Collection of Western Americana at the Yale University Library.

mule teams, goes West by stage at the rate of one dollar per pound, and no package taken of more than five pounds.

Two thousand (2000) pounds per day, at fifty cents per pound, *less than one-half of the present rates,* produces a monthly earning of $30,000 from freight alone.

These Express wagons are adapted to bring passengers to the Missouri river on their return trip. The charges overland from Denver now are one hundred and fifty dollars per passenger. Reducing this rate to fifty dollars each, *one hundred dollars less than now charged,* and carrying ten passengers daily, will produce a revenue of $15,000 per month.

It is estimated that Colorado . . . will send to the East this year *sixty million dollars* bullion. . . . The present rates of taking out currency and bringing in bullion, is *three per cent.* each way, and with sixty million gold coming East, it is safe to conclude that forty million currency will go West, making one hundred million dollars annually to be transported by some company. At *three per cent.* charges (the present rates), the receipts for handling this gold and currency would amount monthly to two hundred and fifty thousand dollars.

Reducing this to *one per cent.* (a living rate), the Company would realize $83,000 per month.

Receipts per month for Express freight	$30,000
Receipts per month for Passengers	15,000
Receipts per month for Bullion and Currency	83,000
	$128,000
Running Expenses per month	13,500
Monthly Profits from Express	$114,500

The above prospectus was signed by D. A. Butterfield. It appeared that the "B.O.D." would give Holladay a good fight. Furthermore, the company planned to extend its lines beyond Denver to Salt Lake City.

In February, 1866, Holladay in his magnificent downtown New York office read reports of this new threat to his growing empire. He had also learned that three sister express companies —Wells Fargo, American and United States—were proposing to stock and open a stage line of their own between Salt Lake City and Denver and to operate east of Denver on David Butterfield's Overland.

To meet these new threats, Holladay sent two men to look over the "B.O.D." and report their findings to him. When their report was completed and he had looked it over, Holladay knew that the line was operating at a deficit. His next step was to meet with the then president of the "B.O.D.," Edward Bray. Bray, of course, was also president of the Park Bank.

Some historians say that they met in the evening at Delmonico's while others say that Holladay invited Bray to his office where lunch, delivered from Delmonico's, was served. Wherever they met, they apparently did eat the fine food prepared by Delmonico's and Holladay convinced Bray that he knew more about the "B.O.D." than Bray did and that unless the "B.O.D." sold out while the selling was good, the company would be forced to the wall. The result of their meeting was that Holladay bought out the line and thus blocked Wells Fargo's plan for expansion to the East.

But Holladay wasn't through yet. Wells Fargo wanted to buy stage lines and Holladay unloaded. The transcontinental railroad was just around the bend and "Old" Ben saw it coming.

Regardless of what Ben Holladay saw, or thought he saw, on the horizon, the Wells Fargo record of earnings for that period is interesting. In 1863 they amounted to $255,000, in 1864 $254,000, in 1865 $269,000. The earnings for the first ten months of 1866, up to the time Wells Fargo bought the Holladay stage lines, amounted to $231,000. The last two months of the year they amounted to $24,000. In '67, '68 and '69 the earnings were respectively $199,000, $176,000 and $170,000.

By the middle of July, 1866, Holladay moved the terminal of his stage lines 100 miles west, from Omaha to Columbus, Nebraska, then the temporary railhead of the Union Pacific Railroad. Two months later the railhead was at Fort Kearney and the Holladay terminal retreated to that point. Surely, and not too slowly, the stage was giving way to the oncoming Iron Horse. Wells Fargo had arranged for a coupon-ticket for passengers on which change points from rail to stage, and then from stage to rail, had been left blank, subject to constant readjustment. Holladay knew that this was just a makeshift arrangement and that in three or four years the stage would no longer be the connecting link between East and West. He prepared, with infinite care, to sell his entire stagecoach holdings to the wealthy and expanding Wells Fargo and, on November 1, 1866, Wells Fargo, represented by Louis McLane, purchased Holladay's entire stagecoach empire which from early 1866 had been named the Holladay Overland Mail and Express Company. For his empire he received $1,500,000 in cash and $300,000 in Wells Fargo stock. Less than two weeks later all the interests, Wells, Fargo and Company, the Pioneer Stage Company, the Overland Mail Company, and Holladay's organization adopted the name of Wells, Fargo and Company. Wells Fargo took over Holladay's Colorado charter and has operated under it to this day. To do all this Wells Fargo increased its capitalization to $10,000,000. Louis McLane was elected president of the new Wells Fargo, Ashbel H. Barney became vice-president and Calvin Goddard, treasurer. In 1867 the directors were: Louis McLane, James C. Fargo, D. N. Barney, Johnston Livingston, Ashbel H. Barney, Ben Holladay, Benjamin P. Cheney, William A. Fogg, Eugene Kelly. In June of 1867, William Fargo and John Butterfield were also made directors. Henry Wells, now sick and tired, was not made a member of the board.

The express company that had been organized in 1852 and started in a very modest way in San Francisco, was by 1867 a growing colossus. It was rich and powerful. It had come a long way. Wells Fargo now controlled and owned virtually all the stage lines from the Missouri River to California. The only cloud on the horizon was the transcontinental railroad that was fast nearing completion.

VII *Bullion and Bandits*

The record of few other commercial organizations in all America glows with as many stories of genuine heroism, always accompanied with a risk of life, as the record of Wells Fargo stage drivers, messengers, and guards in the first forty years of the company's career.

The saga of the hold-up and robbery of stagecoaches and of trains bearing treasure and goods given into the care of Wells Fargo for safe transport would fill a dozen volumes such as this. For years there was unending battle between the express company and thieves who sought to relieve it of the treasure entrusted to its care. These bandits worked in a wide variety of ways. There were small thieves whose takings were relatively unimportant and then there were the big and dramatic fellows like the renowned Black Bart (more about him later) whose operations were skillfully conceived and carried out on a large scale.

Yet one part of this saga is unchanging in the entire history of the company. From its beginnings nearly 100 years ago down to the present, not one person ever lost a dollar, in property or in money entrusted to the care of Wells Fargo.

To set the record that makes such a statement possible often was an expensive business, both in human life and in money.

The earliest express companies found that hold-up worries began almost as soon as their business. From the beginnings in 1848 there were tales of easy wealth and easy money in El Dorado; of gold nuggets lying around, of Alexander Todd bringing $200,000 in gold dust in an unmarked box from Stockton to "the Bay"—and completely unprotected. The tales were fantastic but true: of the movement of gold dust into San Francisco—think of it, a million dollars on the Sacramento boat in a single night—tales that lost nothing in the telling as they filtered their way back East, tales that excited the interest and the envy and greed of men. Some thought they might strike it rich far more easily than by swinging a pick and shovel. The good claims were all taken anyway. Far easier to get the gold in another way. Help yourself to it! By fair means or by foul.

The soft spot in the entire mining picture was the transporting of gold from the lonely and remote diggings in the Sierras to the strongboxes of the San Franciso mint, many miles away. This soft spot was the opportunity for those easygoing gents who were loath to lift a pick. Wells Fargo and the other expresses took the responsibility off the miners' shoulders by establishing branch offices throughout the Mother Lode and elsewhere as required.

But this step did not solve the problem of the easygoing gents. It merely transferred it. When the miner deposited his dust in the Wells Fargo office in the nearest town, almost in-

94

variably a dignified two-storied red-brick building standing like a fortress above the little one-story shacks along the main street, and was given his receipt by the express agent, responsibility had not been discharged. The problem was to move safely thousands, and perhaps hundreds of thousands, of dollars in gold from the mining towns to San Francisco. And it was Wells Fargo's baby.

There was a tradition in Wells Fargo which had its beginnings the first time one of its treasure boxes was rifled. The company paid the shipper the money lost, no matter how large the amount. Then it found the box, and the bandit. Not the least loss went unnoticed by Wells Fargo. There is a record in the company's annals of a lost treasure box stolen by highwaymen from a stage and a search for it which lasted four months, when it finally was found in an obscure corner of the great Oregon forest, torn open with only a thin Canadian dime remaining in the chest. That search cost Wells Fargo upwards of ten thousand dollars, but the company carried it through to the finish. It always did. Wells Fargo never forgot!

Wells Fargo's hold-up troubles began early in its history, and on a big scale, too. It was near Shasta. A mule train with $80,000 in gold dust was held up successfully in 1855 by the gang led by a young desperado called "Rattlesnake Dick."

Dick had been born twenty-odd years before in Quebec, as Richard Barter, the son of an officer in the British Army. He arrived in California in 1850 and at once started a promising career as a horse-thief down around Rattlesnake Bar: hence his nickname.

Horse-thieves were not popular one hundred years ago. Stealing a horse was regarded as one of the orneriest and dirtiest of crimes in the whole book. You might under certain conditions murder a man and get away with it, but you were a gone goose if anyone ever caught you stealing horses, because, it was argued, to set a man afoot in the wild desert or mountain country was to seal his doom. But this did not disturb the erstwhile Dick Barter.

Dick went on to better things. He became a member of the Reelfoot Williams gang and after Williams' sudden departure for healthier counties Dick took over the gang.

95

In 1855 came the robbery noted above which brought the gang to Wells Fargo's attention. A year later the gang took $26,000 from Rhodes & Lusk's Express in the same part of the country. Neither haul, by the way, was ever recovered. People say the swag is still buried somewhere in the wilderness at the foot of Mount Shasta.

Wells Fargo finally caught up with Rattlesnake Dick. By 1855 the company had already begun to organize its own defense and to recover stolen treasure. Its police were sent into the hills and after a thorough scouring, assisted by sheriffs all the way, they finally rounded up the Rattlesnake Dick gang in a hide-out near Folsom, captured four of them and killed the fifth. Dick was taken to the jail at near-by Auburn, from which he presently escaped and went to hide in San Francisco.

Rattlesnake Dick was arrested again and again, but he always seemed to make his escape. The jails in the Mother Lode, where he was a frequent guest, became a joke to him. He seemed to lead a charmed life. But the law finally caught up with Dick in 1859. He was shot during an attempt to avoid arrest, and his body was found the next morning with two bullet holes in his chest and another in his head.

Dick was the first hold-up man (except for Reelfoot Williams' short attempt) to organize a gang that used their collective information and weapons in planning and carrying out stagecoach robberies. But such gangs became common. Alvin F. Harlow in *Old Waybills* describes the hangout of such gangs:

> The Mountaineer House, kept by one Phillips, on the Folsom Road about three miles from Auburn, was a hangout for many of the bandits, including Tom Bell's outfit and some of Rattlesnake Dick's henchmen, who operated first under one banner and then under the other. So numerous were the men who collaborated with Bell in his heyday—about fifty, some chroniclers assert—that an elaborate system of signs and passwords was necessary for their identification at the Mountaineer House. If, for example, a man came into the bar and as his drink was set before him, covertly exhibited a bullet with a string through it, Phillips had reason to believe that he was one of the field staff, and further signals were exchanged.

Tom Bell, another famous hold-up man, worked on more extensive lines than Rattlesnake Dick and became more feared in the Mother Lode country. He was an educated man. He came from Rome, Tennessee, born Thomas J. Hodges, and he had graduated in medicine just at the outbreak of the Mexican War, in which he served as a non-commissioned officer.

After the war was over he went to California, prospected for gold with no luck, and drifted into bad ways. In 1855 he was convicted of theft and sent to the old state prison on Angel Island, in San Francisco Bay. It wasn't too difficult to escape from there, and Hodges with four others (later to form the inner circle of the Tom Bell gang) turned the trick. Hodges now changed his name to Bell and definitely decided upon a career of high crime. Let Alvin Harlow tell the story:

> Hodges or Bell was now a little past thirty, tall, muscular, agile, restless and possessing great physical courage. He had light blue eyes and a mop of sandy hair and wore a yellowish moustache and goatee. But his nose! His nose was the curse of his existence. Once straight and handsome in outline, it had been smashed flat at the bridge in some violent episode of his past and reduced to a mere button. That nose made description easy, disguise impossible and shortened his career.

Bell often used his medical knowledge when his men were wounded. It was said that as a doctor he was as gentle as a kitten. But at all other times he was a bullying, swaggering, bragging bandit who all through 1856 went his evil way with his gang through Yuba, Nevada and Placer counties, preying on everyone as he went.

But fear never dwelt in the heart of Wells Fargo. Gradually it prepared to close in on this medico-bandit who was terrorizing the entire mining district of central California.

Bell and his gang had two hide-outs in addition to the Mountaineer; one of these was the Western Exchange known to many as Hog Ranch on the Nevada City road; the other was the California House on the Camptonville road, two-hours by stage from Marysville.

On August 12, 1856, the Tom Bell gang set out from the latter place to waylay Sam Langton's Marysville and Camptonville stage. One of Bell's scouts, dressed in the familiar gray

97

shirt and slouch hat of a miner, and posing as a passenger, got off a stage at the California House, waved the stage on, and then rushed inside to pass the word to the gang that the now-familiar green wooden box under the driver's seat of the stage from which he had just alighted, was marked with the old familiar W.F. & Co. and was loaded with not less than $100,000 in dust. The "passenger" settled down for a drink in the bar and the coach rolled on. After it rode Tom Bell's men, armed to the teeth.

At Dry Creek Gulch, a few miles below, the stage was overtaken and held up. John Gear, the driver, reined up his horses and confronted the five or six bandits who had made a short cut through a little-known trail and faced the coach. Bill Dobson, the Langton messenger, rode beside Gear. He showed fight. With five armed men facing him, he fired his shotgun point-blank, and calmly proceeded to draw his Colts. More than forty shots were exchanged. One of the most heroic fights in the entire history of California staging was on. Dobson, with a deadly aim, had succeeded in unhorsing Tom Bell; other armed passengers in the coach came to his aid and the entire bandit gang was driven off. The embattled coach drove on. One of its passengers had been killed, two wounded, and driver John Gear had a flesh wound in his forearm. But he succeeded in driving the coach with its dead and wounded into Marysville.

Bill Dobson had escaped unscathed. Word of the hold-up already had reached Marysville, and Dobson was greeted by the town band and a madly cheering crowd. He became the hero of the hour.

The law swung into swift action. Sheriff's posses gathered in one after another of Bell's gang, but the desperado himself succeeded in avoiding them for nearly ten months. Then, one day in early October, the law in the form of a posse of nine men headed by the sheriff of Calaveras County, picked him up. With that button nose of his he could not hide his identity.

There was no trial. The sheriff of Calaveras decided that. Hodges, alias Tom Bell, was given just four hours in which to write farewell letters to his folks back in Tennessee. At the end of that time he was left hanging by a rope from the branch of a convenient tree, while the posse slowly descended through the ravine where he had been trapped, bearing the precious letters the men had promised to mail home.

Tom Bell was gone, but there were plenty of other hold-up artists and hold-ups.

There was the time that same year that two stages running closely together (for mutual protection) from Nevada City to Sacramento Wharf were held up. In the first of these was a banker's agent from San Francisco—Dawley, his name was—who had $20,000 in gold dust in his carpet bag. The Wells Fargo green box rode the second coach, and it held $21,000 in gold. It also had a small safe belonging to the Alta Express Company.

Not far from Nevada City, in the lonely forest, the two coaches were held up by a gang of highway robbers and, following the usual custom, the passengers were compelled to alight. Dawley played fox. In order to save his own treasure he told the road agents that the stage carried no express safe, but hinted that the companion coach, a few minutes behind, had the treasure shipment. The bandits searched the first coach anyway—saw for themselves—and disgustedly told the driver to go on.

They waited for the second coach. Once halted, its driver handed the small Alta Express safe to them, and then they demanded the Wells Fargo box. When they got it they quickly smashed it in and were removing the gold when there was a clatter of hoofs up the road. The bandits hastily escaped into the woods with their loot.

A moment later three horsemen dashed up to the stalled coach. Two of them were gold-dust buyers who had missed the coach at Nevada City and were riding furiously to overtake it; the third was the owner of the horses, who was to lead them back to town. The dust buyers had another $16,000 in their carpetbags. But they escaped the bandits.

The *Calaveras Chronicle* reported a robbery near San Andreas in January, 1871:

BOLD AND SUCCESSFUL STAGE ROBBERY!

The down stage from Murphys to San Andreas, connecting at the latter place with the through line to Stockton, was stopped on Tuesday morning last, by two highwaymen and robbed of Wells, Fargo and Co.'s treasure box. For the following particulars of the affair we are indebted to the politeness of C. M. Whitlock, Esq., Wells, Fargo and Co.'s Agent at San Andreas.

About 2 o'clock on the morning of the 17th, when the Stockton stage arrived at a point about three miles west of Angels Camp, on the road to San Andreas, the driver—Dick Flanders—was hailed from the roadside and a voice said, "Throw out that express box!" Flanders stopped and seeing the shadows of two men by the side of the road, he answered: "My horses won't stand; come and get it." The voice answered, "Throw out that box, you son of a b—— or I will blow your head off." The driver then threw out the box, when he was told to "get," an order he was not slow in obeying. The highwaymen kept in the shadows, away from the light of the lamps. The driver can give no description of them; thinks one of them was armed with a shotgun. The only passenger in the stage—a Mr. Clayes—heard the conversation, but did not see the robbers, "as he could not see well from the bottom of the stage." On the arrival of the stage at San Andreas, Sheriff Thorn was notified and started out immediately. The express box was found within a few feet of the place where the driver threw it off, broken open and rifled of its contents, letters, waybills, and about $2,000 in treasure having been taken by the robbers. The highwaymen having had four or five hours start, had ample time to make their escape, and the ground being hard and dry they left but little trace of their movements. Sheriff Thorn is now out with his deputies working up the case with some hopes of finally arresting the robbers. Wells, Fargo and Co. have offered a liberal reward for the arrest of the robbers and a further reward for the recovery of the treasure.

Seven days later the same paper gave the account of a second stage robbery on the grade from San Andreas down to Stockton. *"Another 'Sight' Draft on Wells, Fargo & Co."* it headed the item, and added that the robbers first took the green treasure box, then demanded the driver's watch ". . . but he told them to take his coat, the watch was a present from his mother and he regretted very much to part with it. They permitted him to retain it, saying, 'Well, you are a pretty good fellow and out of respect to your mother you may keep the watch.'"

Another robbery was perpetrated that spring two miles south of Mineral Hill, Nevada, when the Woodruff and Ennor stage, with eleven passengers including one woman, and the veteran Hank Knight on the box, was held up by two armed men. One obviously was a professional and the other, equally obviously an amateur. Hank was ordered to pull up and throw out the treasure box which he promptly did. Muzzles of two rifles were pointed at him and the man beside him who said that the mouth of the gun that he was facing was as big "as a flour barrel." Even Hank admitted that he could put his fist into the muzzle of the one that confronted him.

The passengers were ordered out of the coach and to strip off boots and coats. They obeyed orders. Then Knight was asked to "fork over" and he replied that it all was unethical. Said he to the leading bandit:

"You are the meanest man I ever saw in the business. There never was a driver before who was asked to give up a cent."

The bandit smiled in acquiescence, thus respecting the rules of the game. He ordered Knight back on the box and to drive to the next station, eight miles distant, without stopping, which he did. The green box that morning contained very little treasure, but there was $11,000 in coin in the boot of the stage which the robbers missed entirely. Stage robbery was such an uncertain business.

These stories might be multiplied a hundred times. You can find them for yourselves in the fading files of the Sacramento and San Francisco newspapers. Also in such of the records of Wells, Fargo and Company as escaped the devastating San Francisco holocaust of April 19, 1906.

The company's old books showed the constant sums that were paid out: "Stage robbery at Sonoma, $750." "Robbery at Rattlesnake Bar, $2,250." "To hold-up of company stage near Dutch Flat, $5,000." So it all went with dismal regularity.

Wells Fargo lost, and lost aplenty. But its patrons never lost a dollar. It was laying the foundations of its reputation for responsibility in such matters.

To prevent hold-ups Wells Fargo very early in its history evolved the stage-coach guard, the "Wells Fargo shotgun messenger." He rode the box beside the driver, the unobtrusive green wooden treasure box beneath his feet, maintaining unceasing vigil. The crack of a twig, the movement of a tree branch might spell instant danger. The messenger had to be always on the alert. His vigilance had to be unceasing, and he needed courage to match. He had it. The Wells Fargo shotgun messenger early took an honorable place in the history of California transportation. More than once the messenger's reward was to be death. Here was to be the Legion of Honor of the express, the picked battalion of the men who carried the freight and defended it faithfully.

Among these couriers of the early Wells Fargo appears the name of James B. Hume, whose whole long life was to be identified with the protection of the express, along with his assistants, T. B. Thatcher, Eugene Blair and George Hackett. Then there was Shotgun Jimmy Brown, Mike Tovey and John Brent. And there was Francis Bret Harte, in all probability the best known of all of them to the world at large. He was only employed for a short time by Wells Fargo. His fame, of course, came later for his books.

Bret Harte was a young man who had come west from Albany, New York, in 1857, to seek his fortune in California. He found work with Wells Fargo and served as messenger for the company on stage lines in Humboldt, Trinity and Siskiyou counties. After a few months he became dissatisfied with the job and turned from it to teaching school. Ten years later he was on a San Francisco newspaper and laying the foundation of his career as a writer.

The stagecoach, its drivers and its messengers, lingered unforgettably in his memory and they crop out over and over again in his writing—his greatest character, the famed Yuba Bill, is full enough proof of this. In *A Night at Wingdam,* Harte drew a picture of a Wells Fargo messenger:

... The gallant expressman, who knew everybody's Christian name along the route, who rained letters, bundles and newspapers from the top of the stage, whose legs frequently appeared in frightful proximity to the wheels, who got on and off while we were going at full speed, whose gallantry, energy and superior knowledge of travel crushed all us other passengers to envious silence. . . . I stood gloomily, clutching my shawl and carpet-bag, and watched the stage roll away, taking a parting look at the gallant expressman as he hung on the top rail with one leg, and lit his cigar from the pipe of a running footman. . . .

These were the shotgun messengers, the men who defended the treasure boxes of Wells Fargo. If a messenger put up a brave fight during a hold-up and was not killed, Wells Fargo usually gave him a gold watch with his name and the occasion engraved inside the case. That was long before the days of employees' pensions, and watches were cheaper anyway, even gold watches. There must be a lot of those Wells Fargo testimonial watches scattered around the West.

It was not always the messenger who paid the full price of his devotion to Wells Fargo. For instance, there was the case of the much-loved Samuel Knight, in 1866 superintendent of the company in John Parrott's stone castle in Montgomery Street, San Francisco.

It was in April of that year that the Panama Mail Steamer, *Sacramento,* up from Panama, brought, among many other things, a wooden box consigned from Europe via New York to Wells, Fargo and Company, to be forwarded to a destination in Los Angeles.

There was nothing on the outside of the box, nor in the waybill, to indicate the nature of the contents, but it was noticed that it was leaking a liquid that looked like maple syrup and smelled like banana oil. It arrived at the Wells Fargo depot on Friday, April 13th, and for three days stood in a corner of the courtyard, apparently unnoticed. Superintendent Sam Knight decided to get rid of the thing and sent for the porter, William Jester, also freight clerk F. E. Webster, and for William H. Haven of the Pacific Mail Steamship Company which had brought in the mysterious box.

The porter Jester had gone out to lunch, so the three others did too. They went up the iron stairs that led from the court-yard to the Union Club atop G. W. Bell's Assay office next door. At one o'clock they returned and Jester met them with a hammer and chisel.

The Wells Fargo building was crowded with patrons. At the noon hour many San Franciscans made a practice of call-ing for their mail, of which Wells Fargo was now handling upwards of a thousand letters a day. Jester started work. But not for long.

People in John Parrott's stone castle never knew exactly what happened. There was a dull roar, a terrific flash of light, and a column of yellow-green smoke ascended to the sky. Two blocks up Montgomery Street men were knocked flat by the impact of the explosion. A human head went into the window of an auction room across the way, a man's arm into another office. Bell's Assay office was a shambles, and so was the Union Club upstairs. A three-story brick building next door was moved two inches from its foundation. Only John Parrott's stone castle stood steadfast. It was scarred and burned and gutted—but it stood, smoking and forelorn.

Nitroglycerine is a pretty thorough destructive agent. And nitroglycerine was the contents of the damaged carton with the noncommittal waybill. Ten men were killed in the explo-sion and eleven were injured. Three of the waiters in the Union Club disappeared without a trace. No faint vestige of Webster or Haven or Jester was ever found.

For days the courtyard was filled with the wreckage. Yet when the debris was cleared away, it was seen that Parrott's building had hardly been touched; its thick stone walls were not even cracked. And forty years later when it was rocked in the greatest earthquake that North America had known, those same walls stood unscathed. The fire that followed upon the heels of the earthquake swept through it and gutted it. But the walls stood intact.

Besides its shotgun messengers, besides its trusted agents and superintendents, Wells Fargo began and built up an elaborate police service for the protection of its passengers and property.

For more than thirty years the head of this organization was

Captain James B. Hume. Hume, one of the great detectives of all time, was a large man with a soft black felt hat and the mustache common in his day. He passed among the crowded San Francisco streets unnoticed. He never was interviewed. He had no newspaper cronies. He wrote no magazine stories of his prowess. He never revealed his methods, which were various and canny.

When he died on May 18, 1904, there was genuine sorrow not only in Wells Fargo's ranks, but almost everywhere else in San Francisco. Of him, the San Francisco *Chronicle,* in its death notice, said:

> James Bunyan Hume, chief of Wells Fargo & Co's detective force and one of the best and most favorably known figures in Pacific Coast criminal work, if not in the whole police world of the country, died yesterday afternoon at his home after a lingering illness, during which, although his body was enfeebled, his mind never lost its keenness until the very last hours . . .
> Detective Hume was seventy-seven years of age and had been on the Pacific Coast since 1850, when he arrived here with the early pioneers from his childhood's home in New York. From the very start of his western career he became identified with criminal work, engaging his wits, talent and courage against the lawlessness of the early mining communities.

Almost to the very minute of his death Hume was on the job for Wells Fargo, following the reports of the Copley train robbery in the autumn of 1903. At the age of seventy-six, he had gone east to Michigan, captured an absconder, and had him placed behind prison bars.

Long before he joined Wells Fargo, Hume had made a reputation for himself both in California and Nevada as a law-enforcement officer. When he came to California as a young man he was a raw-boned product of the Catskill mountain country of New York State. Soon after his arrival he was made Marshal of Placerville. His shrewdness and his perception, his unfailing courage and coolness, soon led him to the sheriff's office in El Dorado county. Hume took to all of it easily. His reputation for getting after evil-doers of every sort spread rapidly, and soon he was in every corner of California, ferreting out criminals, especially highwaymen, who roamed far too easily in the Golden State in those stirring days. He quickly grew to a figure of dominating importance in the police world.

In 1872, local police called him to Nevada where lawlessness was reaching new heights. The foul old prison at Carson City was filled with desperadoes of all sorts. Murderers were thicker than thieves without its stout stone walls; while the whole institution was presided over by a drunken and imbecile warden. The conservative folks of the state shuddered every time they thought of that black blot on the desert, just outside Carson City. There was one jailbreak after another; the worst of them all came in September, 1872, when four of the most desperate criminals in the place succeeded in making their escape. It was almost as easy for them as walking out of a children's home.

Then it was that the Governor and the State Prison Board of Nevada reached across the state line and asked for Jim Hume. The young California sheriff came at once. The former warden was released, and Hume slipped behind his desk. But he was never at a desk very long; within a few days he was off and away and after the escapees. By train, stage and horseback he traveled alone, with resolution and vengeance in his heart. Two of the escaped convicts he found in California, another in Oregon, the fourth in Utah. They all were manacled and one by one brought back to Carson City. Hume again sat at his desk in the lonely prison and smoked his inevitable cigar.

With the express robbery problem growing more acute, Lloyd Tevis and John J. Valentine, the active heads of Wells Fargo, sent for Hume to come join their company in 1873. As the business of the treasure express increased, so its responsibilities had increased. Law enforcement in certain parts of California still was a good deal of a joke. Highwaymen and the crimes they committed against lives and property were all the while on the increase.

James B. Hume turned the tide in the other direction. With firmness and decision, he took hold of the problem and for thirty-two years he remained at the head of the Wells Fargo police service. He was known as the man who, once he had started upon the chase, *never* gave up. Defeat was a word unknown to him. His quick wit and steady thinking were tremendous assets. The frontier sheriff gradually became a shrewd detective.

The criminals that faced him were not often fools. Moreover, they had the courage of desperation; but the courage of Jim Hume was the courage of the man who knows that he is eternally right.

Both the extent of stage and express car hold-ups and the record of James Hume in tracking down bandits who molested Wells Fargo can be seen in the interesting table quoted by Neill C. Wilson in his book, *Treasure Express.* It was drawn up by the company in 1884 to see how the unending battle between bandits and Wells Fargo was coming:

Number of stage robberies	313
Attempted stage robberies	34
Burglaries	23
Train robberies	4
Attempted train robberies	4
Number of Wells Fargo guards killed	2
Number of Wells Fargo guards wounded	6
Number of stage drivers killed	4
Number of stage drivers wounded	4
Number of stage robbers killed	16
Number of stage robbers hanged by citizens	7
Number of horses killed	7
Number of horses stolen from teams	14
Convictions	240

Treasure stolen (promptly made good to customers)	$415,312.55
Rewards paid	73,451.00
Prosecutions and incidental expenses	90,079.00
Salaries of guards and special officers	326,417.00

Total cost to Wells Fargo due to highwaymen operating against 8 trains and 347 stages, during 14 years	$905,259.55

It had been an exciting (and expensive) fourteen years; the company had set an enviable record. It was a record of unending vigilance that few companies in the United States could equal.

VIII

The
Treaty of Omaha

In 1858 the West was first linked, feebly to be sure because of Indians and a thousand other hazards, to the Mississippi by the stages of John Butterfield's Overland Mail. Only eleven years later, however, East and West were bridged firmly and irrevocably by a railway line. This was an engineering and business accomplishment that amazed the entire world. In a few brief years of building, a railway system was completed 1,700 miles across plains populated only by enormous herds of bison and the Indian tribes who lived by them, across the

Great American Desert, through bad lands and over two of the most formidable mountain ranges in the world. It was a system flung across 1,700 miles with no revenues in sight except from the terminals at either end.

It was a feat demanding the energies of the whole American nation, a government as well as the individual businessmen who owned a railway empire when the job was done. No comparable railway construction job had been done before.

The completion of that first line—the Central Pacific and Union Pacific railroads—ended the transcontinental staging empire that Wells Fargo had built up. In 1866, Wells Fargo bought out Holladay; they became, almost at one stroke, the proprietors of the greatest staging business ever to be run in the West. Louis McLane headed the company; and his brother Charlie managed the network of lines in California, throughout the Sierras, and along the whole length of the cross-Rockies line. Only three years later this empire collapsed; Wells Fargo lost its hold on transcontinental express and mail, and the company was confronted with ruin. The transcontinental railroad did it.

Is it so unbelievable that the McLanes, Wells and Fargo, shrewd businessmen all, could have been so blind as not to see what the completion of that railroad would do? Eighty years afterwards it seems so, but it is perhaps understandable that even the shrewd proprietors of Wells Fargo shared the amazement of the rest of the world that greeted the completion in less than ten years of a transcontinental railroad.

To tell the whole story of how that railroad was built would take a book longer than this one. But there are a few things that we can sketch in here about the conception of the road, the physical job of building it, and the principal men whose brains and confidence not only completed a railroad but changed the whole future of Wells, Fargo and Company, Express.

"Visionaries" began talking about a transcontinental railroad at about the same time that gold was discovered in California. The pioneer efforts of two such men, Asa Whitney and Hartwell Carver, to stimulate the building of a line all the way from the Atlantic to the Pacific did not fall on deaf ears, even though neither man was ever to reap any benefit from his vision.

Jefferson Davis was Secretary of War in Washington in 1851 and to him Congress entrusted the task of having the Army engineers locate and survey in a general way not less than four rail routes from the Mississippi to the Pacific coast. It took four routes to appease the conflicting interests in the country at the time. In those days the South was very strong in Washington. Its fear and jealousy of the rich North was growing, and it intended to use all its political power and influence to see that the first railroad to the Pacific began in Southern territory. The cotton planters and shippers of New Orleans were particularly determined about this.

Four major routes were surveyed under the direction of then Secretary of War Jefferson Davis. The most southern of these ran from the west bank to the Mississippi at New Orleans straight across Louisiana and Texas, then along the Mexican border through New Mexico, and Arizona to a point on the Pacific somewhere between San Diego and Santa Barbara. The Southern Pacific operates over this route today.

Two routes were surveyed for the central section. One ran from Kansas City across Kansas to La Junta, Colorado, to Albuquerque, New Mexico, across the Colorado River Plateau near Flagstaff and Gallup and into California by way of Needles. This is now the route of the Santa Fe. The northern of the two central routes—now the Union Pacific—extended from Council Bluffs in Iowa across Nebraska to Cheyenne, Wyoming, across the Great Divide to Salt Lake City, up over the Sierras by way of the Donner Pass, and down into California at Sacramento. This was the first line to be completed.

The most northerly route, from Duluth across North Dakota, Montana, and Washington to Puget Sound (the present Northern Pacific) was surveyed by General Isaac L. Stevens in 1854, but it was not until 1883 that it was finished and open from Duluth to Portland.

The Civil War determined the selection of a central route as the first over which a railroad would be completed. Shortly after that conflict ended, two companies were hard at work on

111

plans for its completion. From California east the Central Pacific was chartered. At its head were Charles Crocker, Darius O. Mills, Lloyd Tevis and, doing the yeoman's work on subsidies from California counties and from the Congress, Leland Stanford and Collis P. Huntington. It was a powerful combination, but in the first year of laying track the line was able to reach only four miles east from Sacramento. Early in this chronicle these men were mentioned as playing a big part in California's commercial life. Some of them were merchants and enterprisers in the early days of Sacramento, fattening on the traffic to the gold fields. Charles Crocker, Leland Stanford, Collis P. Huntington and Mark Hopkins were later to be known as the Big Four who ruled the roost in West Coast big business which included the building of the Central Pacific and the Southern Pacific. Tevis, later president of Wells Fargo, also became a great and powerful landholder.

The Union Pacific was building from Council Bluffs westward, but in its first two years it constructed only forty miles of railroad.

In 1864, when Wells Fargo bought the Pioneer Stage Line, the situation of the transcontinental railroad was not, as can be seen, so impressive as to bother Louis McLane and his brother Charlie.

The Pacific railroad, the McLanes persuaded themselves, was, even if it could be completed, only a part of the development of the West. There was much territory that the Iron Horse could not reach for years. And in that region the stagecoach would remain the only major means of transport. There were frequent new discoveries of gold and silver. These new strikes clamored for stage routes and to Louis and Charles McLane the prospects for further development of the staging and express business looked rosy indeed.

All of this was true, and to an extent stage lines *would* be important in the company's business until the 1890's, but what the McLanes did not foresee was the effect on the main part of Wells Fargo's business of losing the transcontinental mail contract, nor did they estimate highly enough the business shrewdness of Tevis, Crocker and Mills.

In the spring of 1868 Wells, Fargo and Company began extensive buying of stagecoaches for its lines. It bought more than thirty in that year. Certainly the McLanes were not much concerned with the Pacific railroad. But by spring of 1868 the tracks and trains of the Central Pacific were up over the Big Hill, through the Donner Pass, and at Reno. The Union Pacific had crossed Nebraska and was well into Wyoming. Only one and a half incredible years of building were needed to finish the last lap.

Now the directors of Wells Fargo were ready to take the Pacific railroad seriously, even if the McLanes were not. On May 16, 1868, the board of directors authorized and directed the president to sell all of the company's stage lines. The authorization also provided that the privilege of transporting express over each line was to be retained. The great transformation of Wells Fargo had begun. Louis McLane was brokenhearted and resigned the presidency late in 1869. Neither he, nor his brother Charlie, could quite understand why the magnificent stagecoach organization they had built up should be so ruthlessly abandoned. They were horsemen, and would remain so until the ends of their lives. But Wells Fargo was beginning to become "railroad minded."

On October 30, 1868, Wells Fargo received its final contract for carrying the transcontinental mail. It was a fat contract, paying $1,750,000 a year. Of course, there were deductions for the shortening distance between the railheads of the Central Pacific, now well over the Sierras, and only 100 miles east of Sacramento. The Union Pacific still had many a mountain to cross before it reached Salt Lake City.

Wells Fargo, however, underestimated the railroads. In their final year of building, the railroads performed miracles. Charlie Crocker on the Central and Granville Dodge and Jack Casement of the Union were drivers. The final year saw tunnels built in the mountains, fleets of ships delivering supplies to the terminal of the Central, gangs of thousands of men on the Union. The Central burst onto the great desert west of Salt Lake City. The Union laid seven and a half miles of track in a day and bragged about it. The Central Pacific, with a bit of extra planning, to be sure, answered with a world record: its gangs of Chinese laborers in one day on the great salt flats of Utah laid ten miles of track, moving up and unloading by hand 1,000 tons of rails. And on May 10, 1869, the golden spike was driven at Promontory Point north of the Great Salt Lake, and the transcontinental railroad was a fact.

But the exclusive transcontinental mail and express arrangements of Wells, Fargo and Company were unhappily for the company only a memory. There was now, they saw only too plainly, *no* distance between the railheads. Wells Fargo, if they wanted to move express to California, would have to move it on the trains of the Central and the Union Pacific. Otherwise, they faced ruinous competition. To use the trains, Wells Fargo needed contracts with railroads. And these they had made no arrangements to get.

The railroads had their own ideas about express contracts over their lines. The Union Pacific organized the United States Express Company and gave it the exclusive contract to carry the express between Ogden, Utah, and Omaha.

Tevis and Crocker controlled the Central Pacific, and they intended Wells Fargo to carry their express, but they also intended to control Wells Fargo. And to the astonishment of William G. Fargo and his partners, the Central Pacific was able to do just that.

While they were still struggling to build track across the Sierras, Charles Crocker and Lloyd Tevis organized the Pacific Union Express. It was no secret to Wells Fargo or to anyone else. When the Central Pacific reached Reno, the Pacific Union Express opened a stage line from that point to Virginia City in competition with the Pioneer Stage Line of Wells Fargo.

The McLanes seemed to welcome competition. They brought in some of the best riders from the defunct Pony Express to race Pacific Union messengers the twenty miles from Reno to Virginia City. There were exciting contests between the two companies. The *Sacramento Union* reported one such race in July 4, 1868:

> The rider for Wells, Fargo & Co. was Bob Haslam. Frank Henderson rode for the Pacific Express. Both riders were wait-

ing for the mail at Reno. Each rider had four changes of horses about four miles apart and both received their packages before the cars had stopped. The Pacific Express rider got about ten yards start (Bob delayed until his bag was firmly fastened on his back) but Bob soon overhauled and passed him (in one mile) and kept ahead of him the rest of the distance. . . . Bennett, the driver of the Wells Fargo lightning express wagon, a light buckboard, came near beating both ponies, but having worn-out horses could not keep up.

The McLanes saw to it that Wells Fargo beat the Pacific Union Express pretty regularly on this run. Charlie Crocker and Lloyd Tevis, however, were seeing to other things, and were not much bothered by these twenty-mile races. They saw to it that the Pacific Union Express Company (which they owned) got a ten-year exclusive contract for carrying express on the Central Pacific (which they also owned). They waited. for the price of Wells Fargo stock to go down as the railheads approached Promontory Point. And as the stock went down, they bought. Thus when Wells Fargo looked into a contract for carrying express on the Central Pacific, they found that the company they had beaten on the Virginia City–Reno run already had it. They also found that Tevis and Crocker and their associates owned enough stock in Wells Fargo to control the company. William Fargo and his partners had no contract, and their company itself was in danger.

William Fargo, his brother Charles and A. H. Barney in October of 1869 left their comfortable quarters in New York and went into conference in Omaha with Lloyd Tevis. It was a business conference issuing no communiques and not inviting reporters. When the New Yorkers emerged, Wells Fargo was not quite the same company that had complacently controlled all the express-lines business west of the Mississippi.

Wells Fargo bought the Pacific Union Express at that conference and obtained the vital contract to carry express on the Central Pacific. The price, however, was high. Wells Fargo paid $5,000,000 for the Pacific Union Express. It did it by increasing its capitalization from $10,000,000 to $15,000,000. Lloyd Tevis, of the Pacific Union and the Central Pacific, called before Congress to explain the transaction, claimed that actually Wells Fargo had decreased its capitalization from $10,-000,000 to $5,000,000 before the deal was made. If so, then they paid only $1,666,666 for the Pacific Union. Either way, Wells Fargo paid out one-third of its stock for this company which had few assets except the express contract with the Central Pacific Railroad. And without that Wells Fargo would have been finished.

There were other changes in Wells Fargo as a result of the "Treaty of Omaha." The headquarters of the company were moved from New York to San Francisco (Lloyd Tevis lived in San Francisco). Early in the spring of 1870 an order went out to pay all remittances from offices west of the Missouri to the San Francisco office. The control of Wells Fargo by Lloyd Tevis and the Central Pacific was a fact; and early in 1872 Lloyd Tevis became president of the company, a position he held for twenty years; William G. Fargo was vice-president; Calvin Goddard, treasurer; James Heron, secretary; and Theodore F. Wood, assistant secretary. On February 8, 1872, John J. Valentine (whose devotion to the company's mail is described in Chapter III) was appointed general superintendent at San Francisco.

Wells Fargo was again on even keel. It was fimly established on the railroads, it had 463 branch offices, almost all of them on the West Coast. Things had changed: the day of the stagecoach was passing and from this time on Wells Fargo's destiny would ride the rails.

Lloyd Tevis, who represented the interests behind the Central Pacific Railroad, brought to Wells Fargo shrewd business acumen plus keen financial ability. He was no visionary. There was not a detail of the business that was to escape him.

Born at Shelbyville, Kentucky, March 20, 1824, he was the first of a dynasty of Kentuckians that were to succeed the group of upstate New Yorkers who founded Wells, Fargo and Company. His father, Samuel Tevis, had moved out to Kentucky from Maryland as far back as 1800. Once located in Kentucky, the elder Tevis had quickly found his place as a lawyer and a citizen of distinction. He sent his son Lloyd to Shelby College, after which the youth read law with his father, traveled exten-

THE
FOUNDERS

Left:
HENRY WELLS

Right:
WILLIAM G. FARGO

*Courtesy of Wells Fargo Bank
and Union Trust Company*

WHERE IT ALL STARTED
Sutter's Mill, Scene of the First Great California Gold Discovery

From *Sketches and Notes of Personal Adventures in California and Mexico*
by William McIlvaine, Jr., 1850

SAN FRANCISCO IN 1850

From *Personal Adventures in Upper and Lower California*
by William R. Ryan, 1850

SACRAMENTO IN 1848
Jumping-Off Place for the Gold Fields

From *Personal Adventures in Upper and Lower California*
by William R. Ryan, 1850
Courtesy of the New-York Historical Society, New York City

SAN FRANCISCO IN 1848

From a sketch by J. C. Ward in *El Dorado* by Bayard Taylor

THE SAN FRANCISCO POST OFFICE IN 1850

From a lithograph by William Endicott

*Courtesy of the **New-York** Historical Society, New York City*

SAN FRANCISCO AS THE '49ERS SAW IT

THE ADVANCE OF CIVILIZATION

San Francisco "Gambling Saloon" Just a Few Years Later

From *Mountains and Molehills* by Frank Marryat, London, 1855
Courtesy of the New-York Historical Society, New York City

THE STANISLAUS MINE IN 1850

From *Personal Adventures in Upper and Lower California* by William R. Ryan, 1850

PANNING GOLD IN THE EARLY DAYS

Wells Fargo Served the Miners in these Early Days Bringing Them Mail and Supplies and Taking Out Their Gold.

From *The Pioneers of '49*—A History of the Society of California Pioneers of New England
Courtesy of the New-York Historical Society, New York City

THE STAGE FROM CARSON
Arriving at Strawberry Valley

Courtesy of Behrman's Collection

THIRD HOME OF WELLS FARGO IN SAN FRANCISCO
The famous Parrott Building at California and Montgomery Streets
occupied by Wells Fargo from 1856 to 1876

Courtesy of Wells Fargo Bank History Room

THE GREAT MEN OF WELLS FARGO IN THE '70s AND '80s

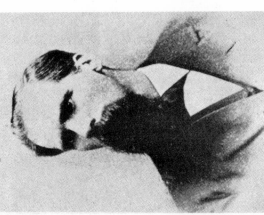

JAMES B. HUME

Head of Wells Fargo detectives who fought and conquered stage and train robbers

JOHN J. VALENTINE

President of Wells Fargo from 1892 to 1901

LLOYD TEVIS

President of Wells Fargo from 1872 to 1892

Courtesy of Wells Fargo Bank History Room

On Such Stagecoaches as this Wells Fargo Carried the Treasure of the Miners and the Mails. This Line Ran Along the Famous Smoky Hill River.

Lithograph by Vincent Brooks, Day and Son, London. Courtesy of the New-York Historical Society, New York City

A RELAY STATION ON THE OVERLAND TRAIL: This is a modern reconstruction taken from the Paramount motion picture *Wells Fargo*, showing exactly what one of these lonely posts in the wilderness looked like.

CHANGING TEAMS: Ready with a fresh six-horse hitch to take the place of the jaded animals who have just brought the Wells Fargo stage over a tough stretch of road. This is a modern reconstruction of a typical scene, from the Paramount motion picture *Wells Fargo*.

Copyright Paramount Pictures, Inc.

STARTING FROM RAILHEAD: Three Wells Fargo coaches departing from the Wells Fargo office at Central Pacific Station, Colfax, California, for the gold fields in the High Sierras, in 1865.

Courtesy of Wells Fargo Bank History Room

WELLS FARGO, THEN AND NOW

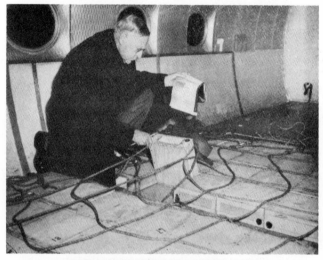

THE PONY EXPRESS RIDER

From a painting by Maynard Dixon

TODAY'S EXPRESS MESSENGER

Elmer R. Jones, President of Wells, Fargo and Company, inspecting a shipment of $3,500,000 gold which he accompanied by plane from Ottawa, Canada to Mexico City.

Photo by George Van—Newark Airport

THE TREASURE CARRIERS

THE CONCORD COACH

Upon this staunch vehicle was built the stagecoach empire of Wells Fargo.

Courtesy of Wells Fargo Bank History Room

WELLS FARGO ARMORED CAR

In such cars millions of dollars of gold and silver are transferred from
bank to bank. Beside the car stands James O. Ellis, Vice-President of
Wells Fargo and affiliated companies (left) and William F. Whitbeck,
Vice-President of Wells Fargo Armored Car Service Corporation.

$800.00 Reward!
ARREST STAGE ROBBER!

On the 3d of August, 1877, the stage from Fort Ross to Russian River was stopped by one man, who took from the Express box about $300, coin, and a check for $305.52, on Grangers' Bank of San Francisco, in favor of Fisk Bros. The Mail was also robbed. On one of the Way Bills left with the box the Robber wrote as follows:—
"I've labored long and hard for bread—
For honor and for riches—
But on my corns too long you've trod,
You fine haired sons of bitches.
BLACK BART, the P o 8.
Driver, give my respects to our friend, the other driver; but I really had a notion to hang my old disguise hat on his weather eye." (fac simile.)

It is believed that he went to the Town of Guerneville about daylight next morning.
2.
About one year after above robbery, July 25th, 1878, the Stage from Quincy to Oroville was stopped by one man, and W., F. & Co's box robbed of $379, coin, one Diamond Ring, (said to be worth $200) one Silver Watch, valued at $25. The Mail was also robbed. In the box, when found next day, was the following, (fac simile):—

Courtesy of Wells Fargo Bank and Union
Trust Company

BLACK BART,
THE PO 8
Outstanding stage robber
of all time

FREDERICK L. LIPMAN

PRESIDENT AND CHAIRMAN OF THE BOARD

OF THE WELLS FARGO BANK AND UNION TRUST COMPANY

Mr. Lipman has served Wells Fargo for 66 years. In 1949 he resigned as Chairman of the Bank's Board but remained as a director.

ELMER RAY JONES

President of Wells, Fargo and Company

sively and finally located with his wealthy uncle, Ben Tevis of Philadelphia, whose drygoods house he entered. When, a little later, the business was involved in serious financial difficulties, it was young Lloyd Tevis who, as assignee, succeeded in rearranging the business and in discharging its liabilities. He made so fine a job of it that he was immediately offered a post in the Bank of Kentucky at Louisville, which he declined; he went to St. Louis instead, where he found a position with a marine and fire insurance company, which unfortunately was wiped out of existence in the great St. Louis fire of May, 1849.

And all of this happened before Lloyd Tevis was twenty-five years old!

As the ashes died in the St. Louis fire, the gold rush to California was sweeping the country. Lloyd Tevis joined it. And so, apparently, did an evil jinx. For on the trip across the country one mishap after another happened to him. The covered-wagon party in which he had joined endured an unusual number of upsets. There were many privations, and the party was all but exhausted before it hailed in sight of El Dorado. But at no time did Tevis give up. He had a capacity for hard work, and he was an influence that kept up the determination and the morale of the entire party. When he arrived in El Dorado (the county) misfortune still was with him. He made his way into the diggings, living alone in a tiny miner's shack, but he found no gold. He was smart enough, however, to get out and to seek his fortune in other ways. He decided to go where business, not mere luck, was the highway to wealth.

And so he went to what was then the chief city of California, Sacramento. With his legal training he quickly secured a position in the recorder's office where it is said that he worked twelve hours a day and did the work of three men whom he had succeeded. He was frugal, and he saved his money, and within a few months after he arrived in Sacramento he made his first investment there—buying a lot for $250, which presently tripled in value. His fortune had begun. It increased by leaps and bounds. Ten years later he was able to build his great house at Taylor and Jackson Streets, San Francisco. It cost $12,000 which for those days was a tidy sum.

It all sounds like a Horatio Alger story. And in a way it was. So, too, was the story of James Ben Ali Haggin, another Kentuckian, with whom Lloyd Tevis joined forces. The two young men with much in common formed a friendship that was to last through the years—in outward form it was a legal partnership, that, starting in October, 1850, continued for almost fifty years, developing into a financial association. Haggin and Tevis gradually became one of the outstanding business concerns of the entire Pacific coast. It bought land, land at wholesale until it was not only the largest partnership landowner in California, but perhaps in all the country. Of course the railroad corporations were getting vast land grants in these days too.

Following the trend of the time, Haggin and Tevis moved from Sacramento to San Francisco, which was swiftly becoming the dominant city of California, and there the partners began their shrewd investments in one business after another; the California Steam Navigation Company; the State Telegraph Company, which was sold (a few days after its incorporation) to Ezra Cornell and Hiram Sibley's Western Union outfit for $200,000 without a real dollar of investment on the part of Haggin and Tevis; the California Dry Dock Company; the California Market; the Pacific Ice Company. All these were jewels that Tevis added to his crown.

The Southern Pacific Railroad, a little line struggling its way out of San Francisco down the peninsula, in a seemingly hopeless effort to reach Los Angeles, was another Lloyd Tevis enterprise. He became its first president in 1869. And then there was the Pacific Union Express Company, by means of which he and his fellows wormed their way into the strongboxes of Wells, Fargo and Company—and Tevis himself into a twenty-year job as the head of the conquered company. In after years he was to find other avenues for expansion: the Risdon Iron Works, the Spring Valley Water Company, the California Street Cable Railroad and, with Adolph Sutro, the great Sutro Tunnel under the Comstock Lode in Nevada.

He was a heavy owner of gold and silver mines in California, Nevada, Utah, Idaho, Montana and South Dakota. These included the Homestake Mine in the Black Hills and the Ontario in Utah, in both of which he had George Hearst for a partner. Tevis, Haggin, Hearst and Marcus Daly owned the Anaconda copper properties in Montana; the Hearst share was sold to an English syndicate in 1897 and two years later the others sold their share to a syndicate headed by John D. Rockefeller. Tevis is said to have received $8,000,000 for his share in this transaction alone.

By the time of his death at the end of the century Lloyd Tevis was one of the richest men in California, a land of rich men. But the thing that he liked best in all his long career was his post as president of Wells, Fargo and Company.

Opinions may differ as to the quality of his administration of Wells Fargo. It is sometimes said that he used too generously the funds of the fat cat of Montgomery Street for his own enterprises, but it has never been said that he failed to return to the cat his cream. In those days lines were not drawn too finely when it came to using funds entrusted to one's care for one's own enterprises. Wells Fargo's records are filled with stories of branch managers using the company's money from their strongboxes for their own speculations. It was all right if the money finally got back to the place from which it was taken and if you were not found out. Those were the business ethics of the day.

Wells Fargo, aside from Tevis' own investments, financed more than one great California project desperately in need of ready money and ready to pay Wells Fargo's price for it: the Southern Pacific railroad, the vast wheat and wine developments of Southern California, and in a later day, and under a different administration, the regeneration of the Union Pacific railroad—of which more in good time.

Through the 'seventies the company grew. Men spoke admiringly of Lloyd Tevis, of his shrewdness and of his daring. Aided by his most competent general superintendent, John J. Valentine, who a little later was to be made vice-president, Wells, Fargo and Company made real progress under Tevis.

Eight and ten and twelve per cent annual dividends were paid with the surplus in the banking department of the company. Into its banking department Wells Fargo poured the tremendous earnings from its steadily growing express monopoly on the West Coast. In those days there were no inquiring and dominating state commissions to inquire into just what a man (or corporation) was earning; no Interstate Commerce Commission back east, or Treasury Department in Washington to demand just what you were receiving for your labors. It was all free enterprise, and easy.

There was infinite hush-hush in those days about the earnings of Wells Fargo. There were no public reports, no public relations men, no income tax returns. However, reference to the old records of Wells Fargo today indicates that in the '70s and '80s annual income fluctuated from $375,000 to $1,000,000, most of which was paid out in dividends. In 1881 the books showed a surplus of $250,000 which remianed unchanged until 1892.

The completion of the Pacific railroad marked the real beginnings of railroading on the West Coast. The Central Pacific was completed from Sacramento to San Francisco—or at least to Oakland—in 1871. In that year the construction of the present large passenger and ferry station and trainshed was finished and the terminal placed in operation. The same buildings serve as the terminal today. Wells Fargo moved into the terminal with Central Pacific.

The company never was able to get express contracts on the eastern half of the Pacific railroad except in through-cars sealed in transit between Council Bluffs and Ogden while they rode the rails of the Union Pacific.

But the now rich and prosperous Central Pacific, whose construction it once had so violently opposed, was its meat. In 1878, the original ten-year express contract with the Central Pacific expired, and Wells Fargo entered into a new deal with that railroad, as well as with the Southern Pacific which finally had found entrance into Los Angeles and was pushing its way toward the East. The two roads by this time were virtually one, and at a slightly later date were to become one in fact.

The new contract, finally signed October 4, 1878, was a curious document, and yet rather typical of the express-railroad contracts of that time.

Briefly, it had these chief features:

120

Wells, Fargo and Company, in consideration of the contract itself, was to pay $825,000 of its capital stock to the Central Pacific Railroad Company, and $425,000 to the Southern Pacific railroad. This sum of $1,250,000 in shares Wells Fargo met very easily in November, 1878, by increasing its capital stock from $5,000,000 to $6,250,000. All done with a few scratches of the pen—merely bookkeeping.

For this the company received the exclusive express privileges for fifteen years on the passenger trains of the two railroads. It was to pay quadruple first-class freight rates for every ton of its express carried, provided that the aggregate did not exceed 100 tons. At that figure charges were lowered to triple freight rates, and, in excess of 150 tons, dropped to double rates. The difference between these charges and its express rates, Wells Fargo pocketed.

Considering the fact that Wells Fargo was the only company that could transport express in California on this railroad it fixed its rates high. And the profits, as we have seen earlier, were good.

IX *Train
Number One*

Tevis and Valentine had many problems in the 'seventies and
'eighties, and not the least of them was the highwayman.
The increase of Wells Fargo territory toward the southeast
as the company shipped express over the eastward-advancing
rails of the Southern Pacific served to widen the operating
territory of the desperado. Sometimes it must have seemed to
Hume, who was the head of the Wells Fargo police service,
that operating on the railroads only exposed the company's
strongboxes to more bandits in more places.

123

Tevis had extended Wells Fargo's activities to the train, but he did not abandon the stagecoach express. And neither did the highwayman. The county jails and the state prisons did a thriving business. Bandits plagued Wells Fargo long before Tevis became president, and they were still busy twenty years later after he had left the company.

Hardly had the chief carrier of Wells Fargo express changed from the old-time six-horse stage to the picturesque early railroad before brigands in the fastnesses of the High Sierras turned their attention to the Iron Horse. The transcontinental route had been open only a year and a half before there occurred on the Central Pacific, not far from the California-Nevada state line, a train robbery of proportions great enough to rock not merely the West but the entire land.

On the morning of the 4th of November, 1870, the Central Pacific's Train Number One, bound east for Ogden, Utah—a forty-eight-hour trip—pulled slowly out of the long train shed at Oakland Wharf. In addition to a combination baggage-express car and day coach, it carried a brand-new car with rounded ends similar to those George M. Pullman was building back in Chicago. Only this was not a Pullman sleeper, but one of the glittering Silver Palace cars that the Central Pacific was operating on its own account. It had its own kitchen and eating facilities, specializing chiefly in tinned dishes. No luxury was too great for the new Silver Palace cars. Indeed the advertisements stated that they possessed all the comforts in creation. That very year *Appleton's Railway Guide to the United States and Canada* said of them:

> In no part of the world is travel made so easy and comfortable as on the Pacific Railroad. To travelers from the East it is a constant delight and to ladies and families it is accompanied with absolutely no fatigue or discomfort. One lives at home in the Palace Car with as much true enjoyment as in the home drawing room. . . . The slow rate of speed, which averages but twenty to thirty miles per hour day and night, produces a peculiarly smooth, gentle, and easy motion, most soothing and agreeable. The days of boisterous times, rough railroad men and bullies in the Far West, are gone.

Spoken like a gentleman, Mr. Appleton. The days of the Diesel-electric and the silvery streamlined train making its way from Chicago to San Francisco in thirty-nine hours still were far ahead. But the days of roughness upon the railroad were *not* gone, as events upon the Central Pacific railroad demonstrated that very day.

Train Number One was an important train indeed. Not only did its small, brisk locomotive with red trim and balloon stack haul the splendid Silver Palace Car and the little yellow day coach of the Central Pacific, but in its express car rode the United States mail and the valuable packages entrusted to the care of Wells, Fargo and Company. On this particular morning of November 4th, the express included a heavy shipment of gold and silver bullion and greenbacks, much of it for the payroll of the prosperous Yellow Jacket Mine at Virginia City. It was consigned from the banking room of Wells Fargo in Montgomery Street, San Francisco, to the Wells Fargo branch at Virginia City. Only those in charge of the express were supposed to know the nature and magnitude of the shipment.

The little engine was to haul Number One only as far as Sacramento, 150 miles from Oakland Wharf. In those days the Central Pacific trains took a round-about route to Sacramento through Niles Canyon and Stockton. The far shorter route by way of Benicia and the Contra Costa train-ferry was yet to come.

At Sacramento Number One would change locomotives. An even stouter iron horse would carry it up the Big Hill to Truckee at the summit of the Sierras, 7,000 feet above sea level. It was a long haul up and over the Big Hill, and that stretch was the most ambitious feat of railroad engineering that America had yet accomplished. A long pull and a beautiful one, with the constant vista of the magnificent canyon of the American River far below, and a halt at Sandy Hook so that passengers could stretch their legs and gaze upon one of the finest views in the land.

On this day in 1870 there was a two-hour halt at Truckee due to a freight wreck up the line. The passengers did not much care. Freight wrecks were not uncommon on the Central Pacific in those early days. The main street along the railroad track at Truckee was lined with gambling houses, brothels and saloons and for two hours the Silver Palace Car was neglected. When Number One finally managed to pull out of Truckee, it was after midnight. Conductor Mitchell noted the hour and spoke of it to the Wells Fargo messenger, Marshall, who had come through with the train all the way from Oakland Wharf. It was down grade and easy sailing now all the way to Reno and the Humboldt Plain, and Conductor Mitchell thought that Number One should make up some of her lost time.

But then there was an unexpected halt at Verdi, seven miles to the east.

Mitchell did not recall that anyone had pulled the bell-cord. Just another of those unexpected stops, he thought, perhaps caused by a group of carousing men and drunken miners with a lantern, or a silly brakeman playing tricks.

But the men who stopped C.P.R.R. Number One at Verdi in the very early morning of November 5th were neither drunk nor carousing. They were cold sober, and they meant business. A code telegram from San Francisco had advised them that the money for the payroll of the Yellow Jacket Mine was in the express car. "Am sending you sixty dollars," the message had read laconically, which meant $60,000 to them. Without hesitation they had gone into action.

The train once flagged and halted, the bandits climbed aboard. Two of them clambered into the engine-cab. They covered Engineer Small with their sawed-off shotguns. "Keep quiet and obey orders," they told him. The fireman dropped off the other side of the cab and began running through the woods. Five more masked men climbed into the combination express and baggage car. Quickly they covered Marshall, the Wells Fargo messenger.

Back in the day coach Conductor Mitchell fumed and fussed. What was holding up Number One, already two hours late? Through the end door he went into the baggage-express car. A sorry sight greeted him. The place was a shambles,

126

and he was at once subdued and held quiet at the muzzle of a shotgun. The bandits were taking the gold bullion and coins, nearly $42,000 of it, and were preparing to throw it out through the side door of the car at their own good pleasure. By quick thought and no little strategy, Marshall had managed to hide a few bars of gold bullion in among the firewood that had been cut and neatly stacked for his little stove. The robbers never saw them.

The bandits decided that it would altogether too dangerous to make their getaway from the train, considering the Palace Car full of passengers back of the express car. Two of the brigands shoved Mitchell back into the day coach. With a knowledge born of experience one of them reached down between the car platforms and pulled out the link-pin of the old-fashioned coupling. After that Engineer Small, under command of the men in the cab, started the engine and the baggage-express car down the grade. For five miles more they went. Then they halted beside an old quarry. The bandits took off their boots, tossed the gold and specie into them, opened the side door of the car and disappeared into the night with their loot. With the locomotive and tender once more hitched to the cars, Train Number One proceeded to Reno.

"Boisterous times" in the Far West with a vengeance!

It would seem as if that November day in 1870 was to be an exceedingly unfortunate one for Train Number One of the Central Pacific. It was not twenty hours after the first hold-up when it was in trouble again. This time it was in eastern Nevada, not far from the Utah line, 385 miles from Verdi. The tactics were much the same as in the first hold-up. As Number One pulled out of the small hamlet of Independence, four men jumped aboard; two on the locomotive and two on the rear platform of the baggage-express car. These last two pulled the link-pin of the coupling. (It might be noted that right after this the Central Pacific adopted a car-coupling device so constructed that the link-pin could not be easily removed, at least from the car platform. Necessity invents a good deal!) Engine and express car continued up the grade

127

ahead of the rest of the train which slowly came to a stop at Pequop siding. At this safe distance the engine was halted and while one of the bandits stood guard over the crew, the other three robbed the Wells Fargo car.

After the previous experience that day, anticipating what was happening, the messenger had hidden some $10,000 in treasure which had been taken aboard after the first robbery in a crevice of the car. It came through safely. The bandits took out $4,000 in bullion and gold coin, twenty-three packages of mail and a bar of silver, a mere pittance compared with the affair at Verdi. They got away safely across the desert. The locomotive and the baggage-express car backed down the hill to the rest of the train, and Number One went forward again, while warning was given to the authorities and another country-wide search began for the robbers.

Both jobs had been planned with care and precision. Even telegraph wires had been cut. James B. Hume, that exceedingly wise chief detective of Wells Fargo, saw it all as an extremely well-planned operation. This he told to John J. Valentine; Valentine might have cursed, but instead, being a pious man, he contented himself with putting up a reward of $10,000 for the apprehension of the bandits: $5,000 for identity of the bandits and another $5,000 for bringing them into custody. The United States Post Office, apparently not so exercised, offered $500 as a reward; and then the State of Nevada added $20,000 of its own.

From San Francisco up to Reno and to Virginia City, and far beyond, the sheriffs and the Wells Fargo police went to work. Not for one moment was the double hold-up taken lightly. The *San Francisco Chronicle* wrote hysterically:

> We Americans get terribly indignant when we read of the doings of brigands in Spain, or Greece, or Italy. We wonder how such things can take place in a civilized country. We make no scruples of accusing the government of supineness, or the population of complicity, in the acts of the robbers. We have our own brigandage and it promises to eclipse the European institution in audacity and magnitude. The evil has been developing for a long time and it now has reached a stage where it threatens

the welfare of the entire Pacific Coast. From horse-stealing it ascended to stagecoach-plundering and from that it has advanced to seizing and robbing railroad trains. If it continues to progress, the next step will be the sacking and burning of towns.

We trust that energetic steps which are being taken to secure the arrest of the brigands will succeed . . . so that the criminals will either stretch hemp or receive their quietus from the bullets of their pursuers' rifles. If they should escape it will become the duty of the railroad company to send an armed guard with each train, in order to protect the lives and property of the passengers. Unless this is done there can be no guarantee that the Verdi affair will not be repeated as often as the Knights of the Road think it necessary to replenish their purses at the expense of the public.

We have seen the two train robberies. Now let us see what Wells Fargo and the law enforcement agencies did about them.

The first hold-up at Verdi had happened just a little after midnight on a Saturday morning. It was dawn before Train Number One pulled into Reno and the first alarms had been spread; before Jim Kinkead, the veteran sheriff of Washoe County, was on the job. By night the countryside was aroused. Posses had been sent in every direction. All roads were closed to traffic. Every man who tried to pass over them was stopped and closely questioned before being allowed to go on.

In Sardine Valley, just northwest of Verdi, Nicholas Pearson and his wife kept a modest tavern hardly larger than a small farmhouse. Yet the Pearsons were popular, and many patrons came to their tiny hostel in the forest. The stranger who arrived that Saturday evening of the hold-up was a shy, quiet fellow, plainly dressed, and fairly typical of many casual travelers who had come to them for nearly twenty years past. He gave his name as John Squires and asked for a room for the night. He got it, and a rousing good supper as well. He went up to his room immediately afterwards. A little later two other men, who gave their names as Parsons and Gilchrist, also came to the tavern, had supper and were given a room just across the hall from the one assigned to Squires. Parsons

129

returned downstairs and sat in the common room of the inn with the innkeeper and his wife.

Mrs. Pearson was an exceedingly shrewd and alert woman. Twenty years of tavernkeeping had made her a good judge of people. Sitting in her rocking chair with her knitting, she heard Squires cross the hall upstairs and go into the room occupied by Parsons and Gilchrist. Somehow that aroused her suspicions. But she kept her counsel and her patience.

The next morning a little after the late November dawn, Parsons and Squires rode off to the north. Hardly had they disappeared over the thin snow and through the pines in one direction before Nels Hammond, Wells Fargo agent at Reno, accompanied by Deputy Sheriff Lamb of Washoe, rode in from the other on the track of the bandits who had held up Train Number One at Verdi. Gilchrist was in the common room of the inn, apparently unconcerned by the new arrivals.

Hammond and Lamb asked Mrs. Pearson if any other guests had spent the night. When she said that there had been two who had ridden off for Sierra Valley, the two agents of the law, in search of their quarries, pushed on. Gilchrist watched them disappear, then went out himself. Mrs. Pearson watched him making his way to an outhouse just below the tavern. Something was wrong. Just what she could not tell. Nels Hammond and Lamb had told her that there were not fewer than seven men involved in the Verdi robbery.

She put a scarf over her head and went to the outhouse herself, but by a different path than Gilchrist had taken. A thin wooden wall separated the men's section from the women's. There was a knot in the wood and, unabashed, Mrs. Pearson pried it out. This was no time for false modesty.

Gilchrist was in the other part of the shack, fully dressed. He was seated with an old boot in his hand and out of it he was pouring coin, bright, shiny, twenty-dollar gold pieces, into the other hand. Mrs. Pearson was transfixed. Never before had she seen anything like that amount of money. Although she did not know it, she was looking at nearly $12,000 in gold, part of the loot from Verdi.

Slowly Gilchrist replaced the money he had taken out of the

130

boot. Then he lowered the boot into the vault of the privy, went whistling back to the tavern. He looked for Pearson, but Pearson was gone. He too had had misgivings and had slipped out of the place and up the road, expecting at almost any moment to be felled with a bullet in his back. He had gone to find a sheriff.

Generally when you most want the police, they are extremely difficult to find. With the entire countryside at that moment filled with officers, Pearson went a full dozen miles afoot before he ran into Sheriff Jim Kinkead of Reno.

Kinkead had been inspecting the abandoned stone quarry where the robbers had first taken their loot from the train. Aside from a broken green treasure box, the pick-ax that had broken it apart, and a shotgun left behind in the flight of the robbers, there was nothing. With innkeeper Pearson he returned to Sardine Valley. They hunted for Gilchrist and found him hidden in the loft of the barn back of the tavern. He offered no resistance to arrest. More than that, he talked quite freely of his accomplices.

The master mind of the entire plan—there almost always is a master mind—had been A. J. Davis, a likable fellow who had once been superintendent of the San Francisco Mine at Virginia City and who was known and liked from one end of the Comstock Lode country to the other as Big Jack. Sheriff Kinkead immediately telegraphed Captain Downey of the Virginia City police, old friendships were forgotten and Big Jack Davis immediately was put under arrest. He confessed his part in the crime at Verdi and led Downey and Kinkead to a culvert under the railroad near Verdi and from it drew forth $19,760 in gold coin.

From then on the law moved swiftly indeed. Tilton Cockerill, a former army officer, who was one of the gang, was found in a public house located over the state line, but there were no complications because of that. In those simple days extradition generally was accomplished at the muzzle of a gun. Sol Jones was arrested with him. Together they led the police to a place where $7,345 had been buried. The $41,600 gradually was being brought together.

131

J. E. Chapman was the man who had sent the "sixty dollars" warning telegram from San Francisco. Detectives searched that town for him, then they searched Oakland. Next they took the first Central Pacific train to Reno. Chapman rode the same train, although at the time they did not know it. Upon arrival all hands adjourned to the grog-shop near the depot. Two more detectives (local men) came into the place. They had with them the crestfallen Sol Jones. Jones espied his fellow bandit and gaily said, "Hello, Chapman! What brings you here?"

That remark cost Chapman a sentence of eighteen years.

Having turned state's evidence, Gilchrist and a man named Roberts went free. Squires, Jones, Cockerill and Parsons were given sentences of twenty-one years each; but Big Jack Davis who had engineered the entire project and had confessed it all, escaped with only a ten-year sentence which a kindly governor of Nevada cut to three. "He died by an error of judgment in '77," says Neill Wilson. "His error of judgment was in trying to stop a stage defended by Wells Fargo messengers, Eugene Blair, who never lost a battle, and Jimmy Brown."

So much for the first robbery and its prompt solution.

Out in the easterly edge of the Nevada desert, the second hold-up of Train Number One also was being avenged. Nevada law seemed to work with equal efficiency on both sides of the state. The second band to descend upon Number One in twenty hours was composed of deserters from Fort Halleck, two of whom had carelessly worn their uniforms. That brought the Army into the chase and a round-up party was duck soup for the Army. Four posses went into the field together with a troop of cavalry. The entire gang was rounded up within the area eighty-five miles south of the Great Salt Lake. All the loot was recovered and the Army administered justice in its own efficient way.

Train Number One was robbed again in 1882, involving this time the only figure on either side of the train robbery business that I ever knew personally, Aaron Y. Ross. Ross stood six-foot-four in his stocking feet, and he must have weighed all of 250 pounds. When I first saw him he was seventy-five years old. A State of Maine man, he first came to Wells Fargo at the end of the 'sixties. In 1857 he had journeyed from Maine to New York, had stopped there just long enough to climb to the top of the spire of Trinity Church at the head of Wall Street to get the view of the city. From New York he had taken ship by way of the Isthmus of Panama to San Francisco. Once in California he tried his luck in the Mother Lode for a time, but the digging was thin there in 1857. He worked his way, prospecting, up into eastern Oregon and into Idaho, finally into Montana. Next he was driving stage up around Helena, then known as Christmas Gulch.

It was an easy enough matter for Aaron Ross to move from one side of the box seat of the coach to the other, to become a shotgun messenger for the express. For a long time he operated as Wells Fargo messenger between Helena and Corinne, Utah. After that he rode between Bodie and Carson guarding raw silver by the ton. There was a stage run for a time, between Pioche and Salt Lake, but finally Aaron Ross found himself in clover, in charge of the Wells Fargo car on trains One and Two of the famed Central Pacific.

So stood his record one January morning in 1882 when he was alone in the express car of Number One, slowly moving across Nevada toward the Utah line. It was the dull hour just before dawn and Ross rested his giant frame upon a cot in the car, while Number One plugged forward through the sagebrush.

At the little signal stop of Montello stood a single wooden shack, bunk-house for the Chinese who worked as a local track gang. A dozen of them lived in the stuffy, unventilated, over-heated place. Three hours before the arrival of Number One, there had been callers at Montello, uninvited and unwanted. Five of them had ridden up from the dark of the desert on a moonless night, had pelted the shack with rocks —putting in a few pot-shots for luck—and the Chinese, not accustomed to such raids, piled out of their shack into the night and up the track toward Toano, twenty-five miles away, just as fast as their legs could carry them. Their visitors replaced them in the bunkhouse and awaited the coming of the eastbound express train.

A baggage car followed the tender of the big-stacked locomotive, then came the Wells Fargo express car, finally three or four coaches and a Pullman sleeper or two. With the exception of the men in the engine cab, passengers and crew were mostly asleep.

Ross was awakened by the sudden stopping of the train. For a moment he thought that they were at Toano, a divisional operating point where he was accustomed to receiving silver from the mines to the south, and a must stop for every train. He looked at his watch. For once they were well ahead of time, a most unusual happening on the Central Pacific of those days.

As Ross rubbed his eyes there came a tap on the end door of the express car. A man's voice shouted to him to "Hop out!"

Ross looked more closely and saw the muzzle of a rifle pointed through a crack in the door.

Now Aaron Y. Ross had been brought up carefully in the Wells Fargo doctrine that express cargo was to be delivered at destination. He decided then and there that he would not "hop out" or get out in any other fashion, or even open the heavily barred doors of the express car.

Aaron Ross did not get out. He held the fort alone. For three hours and twenty minutes he held it against unceasing and terrific attack. It must have seemed an eternity to him. Afterwards they found the stout wooden sides of the express car riddled with bullets. Forty had entered the car. Ross was wounded, several times, but not seriously; his hands, his face, and his body were covered with blood. But he managed to bandage his wounded left arm and still keep on loading and reloading his faithful Winchester. Fortunately he had plenty of ammunition—and even more grit.

The bandits, tired of shooting at the seemingly impenetrable fortress, tried other tactics. At the point of a revolver they induced the engineer to uncouple the mail car, which was between the locomotive and the express car, take it down the track and then catapult it against Ross's fort, full steam on. This didn't work, either. The engineer saw to that. Once, twice, three times they tried the trick, then abandoned it. The fuel in the engine tender was getting low.

Next they crept along under the edge of the express car and talked to one another in loud voices:

"We've got to build a fire. We'll burn him out."

Ross listened to them in silence, but not in fear. Seemingly he never knew the meaning of the word fear. He reloaded his rifle. There was no fire; there was no firewood and not enough left in the engine tender for a worthwhile blaze. The ruse failed.

Ross waited, waited, and waited. A train, the westbound Number Two, came past. It took the siding at Montello, stopped for a moment, and then moved on. The engineer of Number One, still at revolver point, had motioned it on. Number Two's engineer had been tempted to get out and investigate. But he pulled his throttle and Number Two headed down the long straight track into the west. Aaron Ross's heart must have sunk a bit as he heard it disappear in the distance. But he merely held his gun and waited.

Finally the bandits were quiet.

Suddenly horses' hooves were heard. Ross put his keen eye to a bullet hole in the side wall and saw the five bandits rapidly ride away. At last they were under pursuit. The conductor of Number Two had given an alarm at the next station, some ten or twelve miles to the west, and a posse had come to the rescue. Ross unbolted the door of the express car and let them in. The danger was over. And in the saga of Wells, Fargo and Company he was to be forever known as "Hold-the-Fort" Ross.

Wells Fargo agent W. P. Bannon at Ogden telegraphed Superintendent Valentine at San Francisco, saying: "Ross's hand badly torn by bullet and groin discolored by spent ball. Feels jubilant and will probably want day off one trip."

Which was surely a modest reward for a great deal of effort.

The treasure box in the express car had been saved. There was, after all, only $600 in gold in it. But in the mail car

135

just ahead, which the bandits had used as a battering ram, there was nearly half a million dollars in unminted silver which entirely escaped their attention. The best of bandits sometimes are that way.

When Aaron Ross came into my office in the old Wells Fargo building on lower Broadway in New York, he was still on the job at the age of seventy-five, one of the most trusted messengers of the company. In fact, he had just brought in a heavy shipment of silver, bound all the way from San Francisco to England. There were 342 bars of it, valued roughly at a little over half a million dollars and Ross had been given the shipment at Oakland, to bring it through to Ogden. At Ogden his relief messenger had turned up ill, and Hold-the-Fort continued with it to Chicago, and then on to New York where he turned it over to the Wells Fargo bank.

It was Ross's first visit to New York in fifty-five years, and it was all too short a one. He got in on Erie Nine in the morning and went west on the Erie that evening at eight. But we made the best of it for him. We took him uptown in an automobile along Riverside Drive to Grant's Tomb, through Central Park and down Fifth Avenue to lunch at the old Waldorf-Astoria. Then we returned to lower Broadway on the subway and went to the top of the Woolworth Building, then the highest in New York. I stood with him as he gazed at downtown Manhattan, at the busy harbor with all its waterborne traffic, at the great bridges over the East River.

"How do you like it, chief?" said I.

"I liked that view from the top of Trinity Church spire that I got the other time I was here," he answered.

That was all. Aaron Ross was not much given to casual conversation. A few months later I rode with him on a Wells Fargo car over the Rio Grande through the Colorado mountains, one of his final runs with the express. I plied him again and again for the details of his earlier days with the company. He was courteous, but he would tell me nothing.

"I'm not used to talking about myself," he finally said to me.

I understood. Aaron Y. Ross was not that sort of a hero.

Throughout those early days and even into the recent past

136

the business of train robbery continued. The number of hold-ups, and the gun battles between express messengers and bandits is legion. It would take many books to chronicle them all. However, I do like the story of the contribution of one iron-nerved express messenger whose name never got into the records. He evidently was a man who valued his life and who had an inventive turn of mind. To him, whoever he was, goes the credit for the "train robber eradicator." This simple device consisted of a short "L"-shaped gas-pipe extending through the floor of the car and down under it. When the messenger was suspicious of trouble all he had to do was to extinguish the lamps in this car and drop a lighted signal fuse into the pipe. It flared with a brilliant white flame, like a searchlight, which illuminated the entire space under the car and around it, while the messenger in the open door was left in complete darkness —so complete that he could almost feel the tip of a bandit's rifle without being seen himself. Before the invention of the "eradicator" it had been the other way around. Standing in the door of a well-lighted car he was a shining target for bandits in the outer darkness. The "eradicator" reversed conditions. It was one factor that helped wipe out the train robber's profession.

There were other causes, of course. Not the least of them, the long-distance telephone and the automobile. But these things, after all, are only mechanical. The great factors in the elimination of the train-robber west of the Mississippi have been the unending courage, strength and ready wit of the men who have been chosen to guard the treasure-cars of the mail and the express.

X   *Black Bart,*
the Po 8

Six years had passed since the last railroad spike was driven at Promontory Point by the Great Salt Lake. In these six years the completion of the Pacific railroad had worked a change in the life and habits of the people of the Far West. The old carefree days were passing. The Gold Rush was history; most of the mining camps of California were abandoned or were changing to little villages and towns that began to bear something of the stamp of the East. Gone, too, were the long caravans of covered wagons from the East, the surprise attacks by angry Indians. People traveled across the continent now in the gaudy cars of the Silver Palace Car Company or the sleeping cars of Mr. Pullman. Refinement was spreading its silky gloves over the West, even if you still could take an occasional pot-shot at a prairie dog or a buffalo from the train.

Soon San Francisco would be as civilized as Boston, but much more entertaining—or at least, San Franciscans thought so.

"Farewell to romance," the Forty-niners were chanting over their drinks. "The old days are gone, we shall not see their like again." But they were wrong.

One fine day there appeared in Calaveras County—the same Calaveras of the Jumping Frog—a man as daring and picturesque and, if you like, as romantic as the West had ever seen. Once again the harassed old Wells Fargo was in for a time of it. He was a thin, wiry, stern-featured man who looked a little like a country parson or a schoolteacher; "the Sleepy Schoolmaster" was a name not infrequently given him in after days.

When he first entered the life of Wells Fargo in 1875, rather violently, he was getting along past middle age, and his dark hair, which was beginning to recede from a high forehead, was sprinkled with gray. Tipped back on his head, for he was usually hot and covered with dust, was an ancient black derby hat. All the rest of his attire, with the exception of heavy well-worn boots, generally was covered by a long linen duster.

Though he was most of the time many a tedious mountain mile from any railroad, he carried a large valise.

Harry Morse, a detective whom James B. Hume called in to help the company make this gentleman's acquaintance, described him as "elegantly dressed, carrying a little cane. He wore a natty little derby hat, a diamond pin, a large diamond ring on his little finger and a heavy gold watch and chain. He was about five feet eight inches in height, straight as an arrow, broad-shouldered with deep-sunken bright, blue eyes, high cheek bones, and a large handsome gray moustache and imperial: the rest shaven clean . . ." This was how Morse described Charles E. Bolton (or Boles) when he finally met him

140

in Bush Street in San Francisco. Obviously this was not his garb when professionally engaged.

In the mountains, however, his head was usually covered with a flour sack with roughly cut eye holes—and the linen duster. This, you might say, was his business dress. It was in this dress and firmly entrenched behind a double-barrel shotgun, which he was never known to use, that Black Bart (his business name) introduced himself to many an unfortunate stagecoach driver and Wells Fargo messenger.

This was the Black Bart who, in Wells Fargo annals, was to become for a long time more prominent than president Lloyd Tevis himself. At least there was vastly greater newspaper comment on his comings and goings.

On a bright July day in 1875, several persons afterward remembered, he was striding along one of the well-traveled roads of Calaveras County. He stopped at a ranch house and, following the hospitable custom of the country, broke bread with the family. The ranchman and his family found him a genial waggish soul, fond of cracking jokes. They enjoyed having him at the table. But later they recalled that he had been most reticent about himself. Indeed, that was the way everyone found him, and if there had been anything of particular interest in his past career he never divulged it. Yet, from the fact that there was an old bullet-hole just below his ribs—something that nobody in Calaveras knew in those days—he must have had something in his past well worth talking about.

To anyone who might have chanced to meet him in the wilds of Calaveras County seventy years ago, after first sight he would not have seemed to be a country parson or schoolmaster. Although he was a quiet, unpretentious fellow, extremely polite with almost everyone he met, especially when ladies were present, there was something about the look of the grim mouth under the heavy, drooping mustache, and of the very sharp, cold, steady blue eyes that would suggest an early Californian or a professional gambler. There was nothing sleepy about those eyes.

Later that July day the stage from Sonora to Milton, bearing the express and the treasure boxes of Wells, Fargo and Company came rumbling down the dusty road through the soft, green forest. Holding the reins over the six horses was Billy Hodges, an outstanding overland stage driver with a record nearly as colorful as that of any man in the service. Behind him on the top of the smart Concord coach, as well as inside, was a handful of passengers.

Then, suddenly, Billy Hodges pulled up his horses sharply, put on the long brake rod with all the strength of his seasoned hands and the creaking wheels locked. The stage squealed to a stop. In the middle of the road directly in front of the lead horses stood a man in a linen duster. He was tall and those cold, blue eyes shining through the holes in the enshrouding flour sack, looked over the top of a sawed-off double-barreled shotgun, straight at Billy Hodges.

"If they dare to shoot, give them a solid volley, boys," spoke the man in the linen duster. Billy Hodges glanced at the rocks alongside the highroad and thought he saw at least half a dozen gun barrels pointing at him. That was enough for him.

"No use trying to do anything," he said. "He's got a gang with him. Look at those guns. If you want to live, don't monkey with your guns."

The man in the linen duster ordered Hodges to throw the green wooden treasure-box of Wells Fargo onto the ground at once. He lost no time in complying. The highwayman produced a hatchet from under his linen duster and in a moment he had chopped the box open and was stuffing the money and the valuables it contained into his pockets.

"That will be about all, boys," he called out. Then jovially he added: "Hurry along now and good luck to you."

That evening the stage rolled into Milton bringing the first tale of the man in the linen duster, who, for the next eight long years, was to be the scourge and terror of the California roads.

The men who sat around the taverns of Milton that night got the story dramatically, but entirely wrong. Everybody in town was talking of how a whole band of robbers had held up Billy Hodges' overland stage and the Wells Fargo express. But the next day came the sequel. It seemed upon investigation that

142

the man in the linen duster had worked alone. The "guns" pointing over the rocks were only sticks.

Five months went by before the lone robber of Calaveras was again heard from. Perhaps he had found the holiday expensive, for it was just three days after Christmas when he jumped out in front of another Wells Fargo stage, this one bound north from San Juan to Marysville. He still wore his linen duster and still carried his sawed-off shotgun and his hatchet. Stooping low as he got the drop on the driver and messenger, he tried to shield himself in front of the lead horses, a trick that he occasionally practiced later. This time, as before, there was no hesitation in obeying his command to throw out the express box. Again, he ripped it open and disappeared in the woods with its valuable contents stuffed in his clothes.

Five months more and another hold-up was added to his record. This time it was the stage from Yreka to Roseburg, up near the Oregon state line. Again it was a successful job. The reputation of the man in the linen duster was spreading. Weird tales, some fanciful and some true, ran through the countryside. Women kept their children locked in their homes for fear of a visitation. But they had nothing to fear, for the brigand was a gentle soul indeed who was not interested in robbing women and children. On one of his hold-ups a woman passenger in the stage became hysterical and tossed her purse at Black Bart's feet. He returned it to her and said courteously: "Madam, I do not wish your money. In that respect I honor only the good offices of Wells Fargo." A gentle man, devoted only to the small, green boxes from Montgomery Street.

Wells Fargo was outraged. President Lloyd Tevis and General Superintendent John J. Valentine called in James B. Hume, chief of the Wells Fargo police, and the latter went to work on the case. He did more. He engaged a helper, one Harry Morse, a private detective in San Francisco, and put Johnny Thacker, a veteran member of the Wells Fargo police, to work. But the mysterious man in the linen duster was to prove the toughest problem that they ever tackled in all their long experience. No one knew his name or where he came from. Stage drivers and express messengers seldom could give much of a description of him because of the usual flour-sack mask. Some of the mountain people, however, had met him face to face and had talked with him. They reported that he was a polite and agreeable man, who came from the East and who said that he had been a miner and that he suffered from a disease of the throat; he had to rest a good deal. But for a man who was not in the best of health and who was fond of sleep he was astonishingly active. Once in three days he lugged that old valise of his for all of eighty miles over the mountains. As the valise held his unbreeched gun and his blankets, under which he spent many a night in the open, it must have been a fairly heavy affair. And it takes a pretty good walker to cover twenty-six mountain miles between sun-up and sun-down, even without a heavy valise. The Wells Fargo detectives on his trail found that following a robbery he never stopped to make camp and cook a meal until he was twelve or fifteen miles away from the scene of the hold-up. Quite a wonderful walker was the man in the linen duster.

Eventually Black Bart found his valise, stuffed with gun and blankets, too heavy, for he discarded it and carried his gun in his blanket-roll. The abandoned valise was found beside a mountain creek. Hume and his fellows searched it carefully for some clue of its owner. No luck.

Black Bart rid himself finally of his reticence and took to leaving facetious notes at the scene of his hold-ups, tormenting his pursuers.

On a day in August, 1877, he held up the stage from Fort Ross to Russian River. From the express box he took $300 in coin and a negotiable deposit check for another 300. Then he cut open the mail sacks and helped himself. He left behind in the rifled express box this exquisite bit of verse:

> I've labored long and hard for bread
> For honor and for riches,
> But on my corns too long you've tred,
> You fine-haired sons of bitches.
> *Black Bart, the Po 8*

So at last the man in the linen duster was named and it was

a good one. How pious John Valentine must have groaned when Jim Hume handed him that bit of poetry!

Black Bart it was, and Black Bart it was to remain throughout the years to come. For a full year thereafter the people of Northern California seemingly spoke of no one else. In the entire history of the Western frontier there never had been so mysterious and so elusive a highwayman as he, nor one so original in his methods. Superstitious folk began to think that there must be something uncanny about him, something unearthly like the great legendary figure of Paul Bunyan. Consider a bandit who never once was known to ride a horse, but who, within a single twenty-four hours, had robbed two stagecoaches thirty miles apart, hold-ups separated by the roughest of mountain country! It was all but inconceivable. What seven league boots did this Black Bart have that enabled him to dart here and there through the thicknesses of the great forests of the high Sierras?

Thousands of miles of rough mountain country the indefatigable Po 8 must have covered afoot, for eight years, carrying his valise or his blanket roll with him. During those eight years his name carried more dread to the drivers of the stages than to the people of the countryside. The country folk were safe. It is not known that ever once was any of them disturbed. Wells Fargo was his quarry. Against Wells Fargo he continued his course, unrelentingly: from Calaveras county to Sonora and to Yuba, to Sierra and Butte and Plumas and Shasta and Trinity. And all the while he wrote his little verses, eventually to find their way to Montgomery Street, San Francisco, and to give no comfort there. But James B. Hume waited his turn. Wells Fargo never forgot.

Black Bart was a gay wag who grew to enjoy notoriety. On a summer day in 1878 he held up the Wells Fargo stage bound from Quincy to Oroville. After he had helped himself to the contents of express box and mail pouches he left behind these verses, written in a meticulously even handwriting:

> Here I lay me down to sleep,
> To wait the coming morrow;
> Perhaps success, perhaps defeat,
> And everlasting sorrow.

I've labored long and hard for bread,
For honor and for riches,
But on my corns too long you've tread,
You fine-haired sons of bitches.

Let come what will, I'll try it on,
My condition can't be worse,
And if there's money in that box,
'Tis money in my purse.

Black Bart, the Po 8

Two stanzas added to the original version.

Verses like these were the only clues he ever left for the perplexed police service of Wells Fargo. Year after year, robbery followed robbery. Black Bart was here; Black Bart was there; seemingly Black Bart was everywhere, but still there was no clue to his identity. And the cost to Wells Fargo was coming to a pretty penny. The company, however, was used to that sort of thing. Its ledgers contained one item after another of expenses paid in the pursuit of thieves, as well as in the repayment of sums lost or stolen in transit.

But there came one occasion when the man in the linen duster escaped only by the barest chance.

It was in 1882, when he held up the stage from LaPorte to Oroville. Black Bart, stooping low as was his custom, was screening himself in front of the lead horses and at the same time trying to keep his shotgun pointed at his victim, when Wells Fargo man George Hackett took a desperate chance, brought his gun to his shoulder and fired. The horses reared and plunged and the highwayman was thrown aside, unhurt. Then the whip of the driver cracked over the backs of his six-horse team and the stage jerked forward, while Hackett fired again at the man lying helplessly in the road. The shot went wild and, as the stage rolled on, Bart got up and darted into the deep woods which came down close to the roadside.

Then came the day!

It was the third day of November, 1883, and Black Bart had returned to the scene of his debut, the rough and winding old road from Milton to Sonora in Calaveras County. The stage was coming from Sonora and its treasure-box was well filled. It contained $4,100 in amalgam and $500 in cash. Black Bart in some way, occult or otherwise, must have known of the contents of that little green box. At any rate there he was back on the road where eight years before he had made his first appearance as a highwayman.

The coach came rattling on. Suddenly from behind a rock stepped Black Bart just as he had done that July day in 1875. His technique was unchanged.

The driver, Reason McConnell, was alone on the stage. His only passenger, young Jimmy Rolleri, had got off a short way back to see if he could scare up some game. This bothered Black Bart. He didn't know where the passenger might be, but he proceeded as usual. "Throw down the express box," he ordered McConnell. But the box was fastened to the floor of the stage. Bart forced McConnell to unhitch his team and walk the horses over the crest of the hill, while he went to work on the treasure-box with his hatchet.

This was getting to be the most complicated hold-up Bart had ever rigged. By the time Bart had got the loot and was backing out of the coach, McConnell and Jimmy had joined forces. Jimmy's rifle blazed away at the retreating Bart, but he managed to slip into the brush. Either Jimmy or McConnell had scored a hit, for Bart was seen to falter as he faded out of sight.

Black Bart had been more than a little shaken by the unexpected angles of this hold-up. He left behind, not his latest verses, but a handkerchief, his hat, a magnifying glass, and a case for field glasses. On the handkerchief (to the joy of Montgomery Street and James B. Hume) was a laundry mark— F.X.O.7

This hold-up near Sonora was Black Bart's twenty-eighth, and it was his last. The Wells Fargo detectives lost no time in tracing the laundry mark. It was a long search. The laundries of a dozen towns were visited, and a little laundry agency on Bush Street, San Francisco (the 91st visited in San Francisco), identified the mark. It belonged, the manager said, to a thin, sharp-eyed man with a drooping mustache, who always brought his wash and called for it himself. His name? C. E. Bolton, living at 37 Second Street.

The Wells Fargo detective, Johnny Thacker, got a warrant, searched this room, investigated Bolton's movements before this Sonora robbery, and it was not long before Thacker met Bolton in the laundry agency. Without formal introductions Wells Fargo finally faced the man who for eight years had concerned himself so intimately with their express shipments. Black Bart made neither fight nor protest. He just smiled and said nothing.

His arrest was a painful surprise to the city detectives at San Francisco police headquarters. They recognized Bart as a man whom, for years, they had seen almost every day at a bakery in Kearney Street, where they often ate. No linen duster for San Francisco. At times, Bart had sat at the same table with the policemen, and had chatted briskly with them. "You boys are good," he told them. "Those up-country sheriffs are no good. Too bad they couldn't send a few of you up into the hills to get hold of that Black Bart." There were red faces on the detective force on the day Black Bart was arrested.

Gradually the facts about him came out: his name, he first said, was Charles E. Bolton, and he had lived for nearly ten years in the home of a widow in downtown San Francisco. Later he said that he had been born in Jefferson County, New York, as Charles E. Boles. He was a veteran of the Union Army, mustered in at Decatur, Illinois, with a good war record. He had left a wife behind him who was found to be living in Hannibal, Missouri. The widow with whom he boarded in San Francisco said that he was an ideal tenant: "So quiet, so respectable and so punctual about his room rent," she added.

More and more stories developed about Black Bart, Bolton, or Boles, in the early 'eighties. One of the best (which has never been verified) was that Black Bart had been "Professor" Charles Boles in charge of a little one-room schoolhouse in Sierra County. For some years, the story goes, he taught young Californians but suddenly tired of it all. The deadly routine, the uninspiring work of filling young minds with book learning, got on his nerves. One day the sound of a passing Wells

148

Fargo coach filled him with an idea as sinister as it was simple. He knew that Wells Fargo coaches carried treasure: gold, and plenty of it. He had talked with the drivers. They were free with gossip and with information. It all sounded rather easy. And so the teaching profession lost one of its everyday ornaments, and the highway profession gained a highly spectacular one.

This fascinating yarn about Black Bart is stoutly disputed by Joseph Henry Jackson who has made a detailed study of the man and whose *Tintypes in Gold* tells at length of some of the outstanding highwaymen in the California of yesteryear. Jackson says that he can find no proof that Black Bart ever taught school, and attributes the whole yarn to an imaginative reporter on the *San Francisco Chronicle*.

Schoolmaster or not, California never knew another stagecoach bandit like Black Bart.

For all his twenty-seven successful hold-ups (and the one failure) Black Bart was sentenced to San Quentin Prison for not less than six years, a fairly long term for a man of fifty-five. He was released, however, from San Quentin on January 23, 1888, and thereafter disappeared entirely from public sight. It was said that he went back to his profession, that an occasional hold-up here and there was the work of the renowned Black Bart. But Jimmie Hume and Johnnie Thacker never believed those rumors; there was no linen duster; there were no poems; it just could not have been old Bart. Probably they were right. Yet, just as long as the wind rustled through the pines, folks would be saying that it was the restless spirit of the man in the linen duster, old Black Bart, the Po 8, trudging his amazing way through the forest.

A great deal of acrimonious controversy arose between Hume of Wells Fargo and some of the San Francisco newspapers. Particularly the *Examiner*, which seemed to be a bit peeved because Hume had not consulted it in advance before proceeding against Black Bart. Whispers began to go around San Francisco that Hume and Morse had made a deal with Bart to leave Wells Fargo coaches alone in the future. This repeatedly was denied. San Franciscans kept saying: "Of course, Wells, Fargo and Company had to pay him a salary for the rest of his life, or none of their stages would have been safe!"

Joseph Henry Jackson, in his *Tintypes in Gold*, ridicules these statements explicitly, saying:

> Why, if Wells, Fargo was paying Bart a salary to be good, did Mr. Hume spend his company's money on printing an elaborate notice for his agents, complete with Bart's picture? . . .
>
> The fact is that the whole story of a Bart subsidy, flatly denied by everyone who was in a position to know, has no solid foundation whatever. It started no one knew where. It grew as such tales do; it took root and has become firmly fixed as part of the Black Bart legend. But it dies harder than any of the false statements that have been made about Bart. There is nothing people hate so much as having their fairy tales taken away from them.

So the Black Bart tradition persisted. As late as 1897 a man, who had been arrested at Olathe, Kansas, for robbing a store, was said to be the notorious Black Bart. He confessed that he actually was Bart. And Johnnie Thacker went out to Kansas to investigate. One look at the faker convinced the old Wells Fargo policeman. "He is as much like Black Bart," said Thacker, "as a bird's nest is like a mile post." Afterwards Thacker said that he knew Bart was out of the country; that he had gone to live in Japan. Which may, or may not, have been so.

XI   *The Last*
Train Robbery

John J. Valentine has appeared in the foregoing pages from time to time as he fought his way up from the ranks in Wells Fargo. We have seen how, as a Wells Fargo employee traveling dead head on a stagecoach he once fought his way through a raging snowstorm in the Sierras to deliver the mail on foot. Reference has been made to him as he served the company in more responsible capacities through a period of thirty years.

Born south of the Ohio in Bowling Green, Kentucky, in

the 'forties, he first came to work for Wells Fargo as a clerk in its Virginia City office in 1860. Before coming West he had had some experience in the Adams Express Office in Bowling Green. He liked the business and gradually he rose to the top. In 1862, he was Wells Fargo agent at Strawberry Valley; later he was agent and superintendent of the Pioneer Stage Company which Wells Fargo had bought in 1864. Then in turn he was route agent of the company, cashier at San Francisco, Superintendent of Wells Fargo's California & Oregon Stage Company, in 1869 he was made general manager. In 1882 Valentine became general manager, then vice-president. Finally in 1892 he was made president of the firm which he had served for more than thirty years. Thus Valentine was known in all San Francisco as an outstanding man of Wells Fargo, and the city heartily agreed that the honor and responsibility that he had won were well merited.

Valentine was a thoroughgoing expressman. Moreover, he looked the part for the time and region. He was bearded and stood six-foot-four inches in the boots which he always wore in place of shoes. While the company came first in his thoughts and loyalties, his second love was his library in his beautiful Oakland home. He also liked writing and writers. He knew many, among them John Greenleaf Whittier, who dedicated one of his poems to him.

John Valentine handled many cases of train and stagecoach robbery. He was in charge of the last great train hold-up in California—a case which was solved quickly and successfully. But one case of robbery, involving $100,000 was solved *un*successfully. That case concerned Charles W. Banks.

Before we go on, let me set the stage a bit. From 1912 until 1918 I was advertising manager of Wells, Fargo and Company. I had been working for the company a little over a year when a young man came into my office on lower Broadway, New York, and put a manuscript into my hands.

His name was Parker Gilbert and he was the son of a colonel in the United States Army who had once commanded the famous Ninth Regiment of artillery when it was stationed at Madison Barracks, just outside my home in Watertown, New York. Young Gilbert was of a roving nature. Destined for

152

success, he laid a firm foundation for it by becoming an enthusiastic world traveler; round the world trips were his special delight. On one of his trips, on a small steamer bound from New Zealand to San Francisco, he had put in at the South Sea Island of Rarotanga, one of the Cook Islands group. Ordinarily the ship would put in there for a few hours only; the passengers would go ashore at Amara in small boats and return, either thoroughly delighted or thoroughly disgusted.

Gilbert got the urge to stop over and catch the next ship to San Francisco. He spoke of this plan to the captain of the ship who tried his best to dissuade him. Gilbert, however, managed to miss his ship and he remained in Rarotanga until the next one came along, about thirty days later. During his stay he prepared a fairly extensive manuscript on the island. That was the manuscript he asked me to read.

After I read it I asked young Gilbert several questions about the island. I also asked him if he were the only white man on the island. He replied that he was and then, after thinking over the question replied:

"Oh, yes, there was another: an old fellow from San Francisco. His name was Banks."

"Did you ask Banks why he had left San Francisco?"

"Yes, and he told me that San Francisco did not agree with him."

"Mr. Banks was quite right," I answered. So I told Gilbert about Banks and how he came to leave San Francisco.

In the decades before the earthquake, San Francisco was a gay and colorful city and the officers of Wells Fargo played a pleasant part in it. In this brisk coterie there was none more popular than Charlie Banks, the dashing and gay cashier. He moved high, wide and handsome. He belonged to the best clubs, as did most of the younger officers of the company, the Bohemian, the Union, the San Francisco Art Association and he mixed with all the "best" people. But handsome, full-bearded Charlie Banks had a distinction that was not shared by all of his fellow officers. He had a reputation as an "intellectual." In addition he owned the only oil-immersed microscope west of the Mississippi River which he generously lent to the scientific societies up and down the

153

Pacific coast; in return he was elected an honorary member of all of them.

Early in 1887 he went to Lloyd Tevis, president of Wells Fargo, and asked him if he could take an extra day or two off over the coming weekend to do some fishing in the Russian River country.

"Take three or four days, if you wish, Charlie," said Tevis. "You've been working pretty hard of late and the change will do you good."

When, at the end of the week Banks had not returned from his trip, inspectors were put to work on his books. They found that he had got away with somewhere between eighty and one hundred thousand dollars!

Consternation reigned on Montgomery Street. It seemed all but impossible that an honored and trusted officer of Wells, Fargo and Company, financial Gibraltar of San Francisco, should have absconded with funds of the company. Lloyd Tevis and John J. Valentine shuddered, the other officers of Wells Fargo were astounded.

One thing was made clear; there was to be no publicity over the affair. There must be nothing in the newspapers, not even whispered gossip along Montgomery Street. No one must even dream that anything had gone the least bit wrong in the sacred home of the fat cat. Lloyd Tevis, as he did when anything very difficult came up, placed the entire business in the capable hands of John J. Valentine. Valentine in turn sent for James B. Hume.

"This time you have to find your man, and find him quickly," he said to the company detective. "No delay, no publicity. Just get hold of Charlie Banks at once and bring him here. He is somewhere here in San Francisco. He's probably shaved off his beard and must look different. But even so, you can tell him by his eyes and brow."

Hume had the temerity to disagree with his chief.

"We've already searched the whole town," he told the general manager of Wells Fargo. "He's *not* in San Francisco. I'm sure of that."

"Where is he then?"

154

"He's on a ship bound for the south seas," was Hume's quiet reply. "Three of them sailed the day after Charlie was supposed to have gone fishing up in the Russian River. My private opinion is that he might have shipped on the *Star of India* last Saturday and that sooner or later he will turn up in the Cook Islands or some other place where we cannot reach him by extradition."

"Nonsense," said Valentine. "You keep right on trying to locate him here in San Francisco, Captain Hume."

Another week went by, a fortnight, three weeks. Again Valentine sent for Hume, reminded him that it was about time that Charlie Banks, erstwhile cashier of Wells, Fargo and Company's Express, was apprehended and turned over to the police. Hume reddened.

"I'll stick to my statement, Mr. Valentine." But John J. Valentine was not satisfied.

"Do I have to send for Pinkerton?"

Hume's face became redder than before.

"Do you think that he can do anything that we cannot do in our own organization?"

There was silence for a minute or two until Hume spoke again.

"I wish that you would call in your stenographer, Mr. Valentine, and please dictate two letters, written without date. One will be from me to you, tendering my resignation as head of the Wells Fargo police service, a post of which I am very proud. The other will be from you to me and it will be a letter of apology. Give me three months more and then one of the two letters will be dated, signed and mailed."

Valentine agreed. Three months later he mailed Captain Hume the letter of apology. Banks had turned up in Rarotanga. He had not, however, sailed on the *Star of India,* but on a tramp barkentine, the *City of Papeete.* Her skipper, Captain Baruda, when he returned to San Francisco reported that on that memorable Saturday he had had an unexpected passenger, a Mr. Scard, who had come aboard hastily and had sailed with him as far as Australia. "A lovely fellow," added Baruda.

Hume produced photographs of the former cashier.

"That's him all right," said the ship's master. "That's the way he must have looked before he shaved his beard. A good-looking fellow, with or without the beard. He was one of the pleasantest chaps I ever knew. And one of the most generous. He gave every man aboard five dollars as we crossed the equator."

Gradually the whole story leaked out, until it was common knowledge not only in San Francisco but elsewhere. Wells Fargo, badly nettled, sent detectives to get Banks, but they returned empty-handed. Banks had found refuge on the island of Rarotanga, from which there was no extradition. Wells Fargo finally gave up the hunt. For a time it was rumored that any ship captain who could shanghai Banks and bring him back to San Francisco, dead or alive, would receive a handsome cash reward. But it all came to nothing. Charles W. Banks lived the rest of his years in Rarotanga. From his little cottage on the beach he could look out on the same ocean which touched the shores of California and yet he was never to be able to return to the city and people he loved. That was to be his punishment.

From time to time the more sensational newspapers in San Francisco vied with one another in printing lurid and fantastic tales about Banks in Rarotanga. They said that he had married Queen Matea and then, at another time, that he had married one of the princesses. The Sunday *Examiner* delighted in four-column cuts, showing Banks gnawing at a human thighbone. They didn't indicate whether it belonged to the Queen or one of the princesses. At any rate none of these stories was true.

I asked Parker Gilbert about Banks, how he lived, and what were his sources of income. He drew a small pension as South Seas representative of a Bristol, England, trading company and, in addition, he was the British Consul for Rarotanga! He had regrown his beard and remained, as always, an omnivorous reader. He corresponded, at intervals, with some of the Wells Fargo oldtimers who posted him on the news. Everyone liked Charlie Banks. Even John J. Valentine liked him.

In the black hour that immediately preceded the dawn of October 11, 1894, two masked men halted the *Overland Ex-*

press just two miles outside Sacramento. At rifle point they forced the engineer and the fireman to detach the locomotive and the express car from the rest of the train and to move it forward. Then the bandits got into the express car and, catching the messenger off guard, bound him hand and foot. They then looted the car at their leisure. The prize was $51,000 in gold. In all the history of train robbery no one had succeeded in capturing so large a haul. Just in terms of weight, the gold was over 200 pounds. It was a troublesome load and so, after getting the gold out of the express car and sending the *Overland* on its way down the Big Hill they wondered what they should do with it. In a brief time it would be known all over Sacramento that the Central Pacific *Overland Express* had been held up and plundered. Posses would be scouring the countryside for the men and, with their heavy load, it would be an easy matter to catch up with them.

So, as the fog and darkness gave way to the dim early morning, the two men dug a deep hole, not far from the point of the hold-up. Into this hole they dropped their loot and quickly covered it with the soft, fresh earth. They marked the spot in their memory, sprang quickly to their horses and rode away. As they did so, a man crept out of the fog and feverishly began to remove the earth from the hole they had just filled.

If the state of California considered that its reputation for law and order and the protection of property had been violated, how about Wells Fargo whose express lines criss-crossed the entire state? It was the express company that would either have to recover the gold or make up the loss—as it always had. There was, in addition, a matter of reputation. For forty years it had been said throughout the West that there were two institutions dangerous for bad men to tinker with. One was the Federal Government and the other, Wells Fargo. This Sacramento robbery was not the Government's affair but the company's. Moreover, it was the worst of a group of robberies. Within a few months, two of the express company's messengers had been killed in defense of its treasure. This robbery was the last straw.

"It's a job for Jimmie Hume," said John Valentine. "It will be about the biggest job he's ever tackled," he added.

The two men who had held up the train returned to the spot where they had buried the gold. They dug all about the area but didn't find it. When, after repeated attempts to locate the gold, they realized that it was gone, they turned to robbery again. So, a few months later, they held up another train, not far from Redding. This was to be a complete job. The first of the bandits, named Browning, tackled the express car while the other, Brady, went into the sleeping cars. The passengers tumbled out of their berths, held up their hands while Brady removed their watches and wallets. One man, whom novelists might describe as "big and upstanding," said that he would die rather than surrender his valuables to the outlaw. He was the sheriff of Tehama County and he had a reputation to maintain. He maintained it, for he died with his boots on, in the aisle of the Pullman sleeper. But the outlaw who killed him paid the price for his crime right there. The rest of the passengers took courage from the sheriff, fell on the murderer and filled his body with bullets. The other bandit heard the commotion in the sleeping car and quickly rode off into the brake, leaving his booty and dead partner behind.

A telegram was sent to Captain Hume in San Francisco and he hurried up to Redding. He proceeded to the scene of the crime and then he left it and rode off in search of the second bandit. He was gone for three days and, when he returned, it was with Jack Brady's body. He had killed the man when he resisted arrest. But, before he died Brady had made his confession. He also told Hume that the gold from the *Overland* had disappeared and that he and his partner never got it.

Hume had known this fact all the time. By a slow, laborious painstaking method of piecing together clues, Hume had found the man who had stepped out of the fog as the bandits had gone off. This man was a tramp. His name was John D. Harms who had been born Karl Heerman in Hamburg, Germany. He admitted that he was a hobo who slept under the stars and who measured off railroad miles as his daily exercise. He had set up his tiny pup tent at Sheep Camp just outside Sacramento on the night of the first robbery. Awakening just before dawn he had been disturbed by men talking beside the railroad embankment near by. Slowly he crept through the bushes and watched while Brady and Browning buried their gold. In their haste they made a bad job of it and, after they rode off, Harms came over and finished it for them. He made a very good job of it and later he came back and took the gold bars for himself.

There were several things that Harms might have done instead. He *might* have reported the discovery of the gold to Wells Fargo and collected a large reward for his honesty. He might have forgotten what he saw and headed along down the tracks. But dazzled by the size of the haul, he took it and placed part of it in a bank. Then he purchased a fine, new outfit for himself, including three mustache curlers. After that he rode to New York in style and blew in $11,000 on wine, song and a voluptuous blonde from the Tenderloin. When his money was gone he returned to San Francisco and there Wells Fargo finally caught up with him. He was tried but, in the eyes of California justice of that day, his offense was not too bad and he was sentenced to only three years in Folsom Penitentiary.

This case marked the practical end of train robbery in California. The empire by the Pacific had grown up. The Golden Gate had law and order. San Francisco wore spats and it took afternoon tea.

XII Wells Fargo
Rides East

On February 11, 1888, the Santa Fe railway rode triumphantly into Chicago and Wells Fargo rode in with it. Less than a month later Wells, Fargo and Company completed its own through route from San Francisco to New York City by the acquisition of the Erie Express Company which operated between Chicago and Jersey City.

Now Wells Fargo was a transcontinental concern indeed. At last it was in a fair position to do business in competition with its two chief rivals, the American and the Adams Express Companies, neither of whom at that time, nor for years afterwards, had access to California. The business of growing fruit and perishable vegetables in the Southwest was just beginning in 1888 and its market was guaranteed by the swift express cars of Wells Fargo. It was Wells Fargo as a matter of course, because the company had all but a monopoly of express business in the Southwest by virtue of its contracts with both the Santa Fe and the Southern Pacific.

To do business with the Santa Fe, the newly established rival of Southern Pacific, meant a diplomatic handling of S.P. with whom Wells Fargo had maintained an extremely close relationship since 1883, and which was heavily interested in its stock. The Southern Pacific arrangement had always been a most advantageous contract for the express company and also for the Southern Pacific, which took a slice of Wells Fargo stock for itself each time it made a new contract with the express company. Under their agreement the railroad took forty per cent of the gross receipts from the express traffic, Wells Fargo the other sixty. With renewals the relation continued for years and all hands made money on it.

There were never to be such contracts with the Santa Fe. In fact, when the Santa Fe fought its way into California in spite of the Southern Pacific, Wells Fargo had to have an express contract on it to keep rivals out of its territory. And Wells Fargo had to pay richly for that contract. The first contract with the Santa Fe in November, 1888, gave fifty per cent of gross earnings to the railroad; and, besides that, Wells Fargo had to pay in advance $1,450,000 to the Santa Fe against future payments due.

The Atchison, Topeka and Santa Fe started in 1868 at Topeka, Kansas. Originally incorporated as the Atchison & Topeka, Cyrus K. Holliday, the founder, brought about the addition of "Santa Fe" to its corporate name. Having observed the rich traffic by wagon train over the Santa Fe trail, he set distant Santa Fe as the railroad's great goal. With dogged persistence he kept steadily at it until in 1873 Kansas had been crossed, and the line was making money all the way. While helping to develop a magnificent new state of the Union, Hol-

162

liday always kept looking westward. The dream of Santa Fe faded for a bit in favor of a shorter route west and that vision was to be a nightmare.

Holliday and his chief associates, William B. Strong and Albert A. Robinson, looked with favor on the more direct route through the sharp defile of the Arkansas River in the Rockies, today known as the Royal Gorge, and thence across the Continental Divide toward the Pacific Coast.

General William J. Palmer who had a railroad enterprise, the narrow-gauge Denver and Rio Grande, thought otherwise. Building across the Rockies, he also intended to use the Royal Gorge, as this breathtaking thirty-foot-wide canyon was the only notch in the forbidding rampart of the main range through which a railroad might go without seeking an easier pass very much farther south or very much farther north.

Both the Santa Fe and the Rio Grande fought for that gorge. They rushed tracklaying crews toward the narrow pass. The battle that ensued was one of the classics of American railway history. There was actual hand-to-hand fighting by the rival gangs, spurred on by their energetic bosses—and a little bloodshed. Eventually the Rio Grande won and the Santa Fe retired —eventually to win the empire of the Southwest it controls today.

The old dream of Santa Fe returned but with a change. The builders now realized that the ancient city was no longer a logical terminal for their line. The development of California, Arizona and New Mexico had changed all that. The Santa Fe now saw that it had to build its road to the Pacific, where connections with ships in the Pacific trade could be made. But entrance to California was blocked by the Southern Pacific.

To see just how effective that block was, let us see what that wise old fox, Collis P. Huntington, surviving genius of the Big Four, was doing with the S.P.

By 1876 the Southern Pacific tracks reached from San Francisco south to Los Angeles, in spite of the rail spirals, the tunnels and heavy grades which had to be built through Tehachapi Pass.

Then came the push to the East. It must have seemed to the

Santa Fe crowd that from here Huntington was foreseeing with uncanny judgment every move they would make. The Southern Pacific built rapidly eastward through the sandy desert of Southern California, the same desert which, under irrigation, was eventually to become the great citrus fruit garden of the world.

With California behind, it was Arizona, New Mexico, and finally the great pass of the North through which flowed the Rio Grande. This was El Paso, at the boundary of old Mexico, and at the western end of the rails of Huntington's Texas and Pacific.

The Santa Fe, meanwhile, after its defeat in the Royal Gorge, built its line south through and over the saddle-pass of the Raton Mountain to Santa Fe (reaching that city in February 1880), to Albuquerque (a few months later), and through the valley of the upper Rio Grande to El Paso.

But the Southern Pacific blocked the Santa Fe there, so Strong and Robinson (now in charge of the Santa Fe), forced to reach the Pacific somehow, turned their attention to Mexico. The State of Sonora, with its mineral resources, its rich soil for agriculture, its abundant harbors, offered a perfect area for development.

The promoters of the Santa Fe knew all this, and, after studying the profile maps of Northwestern Mexico, finally chose the harbor of Guaymas in the Gulf of California as their western terminal.

The quickest and most practical way for the Santa Fe to reach Guaymas was to extend its line south from Albuquerque to the Mexican border at Nogales. The Santa Fe lines reached Deming in 1882; and in the same year the line from Guaymas to Benson was completed.

But here again was a Southern Pacific fly in the ointment. The 177 miles of existing track from Deming to Benson belonged to the S.P. Strong and Robinson knew that the S.P. would never permit them to operate an efficient railroad of heavy traffic over S.P. track. At best such an arrangement could be an expedient. Eventually it must be Santa Fe all the way.

Strong and Robinson, blocked off from Mexico, now had no

choice but to get their railroad into California in order to sub-
due the powerful Southern Pacific and to work out lasting arrangements with it. They began looking for another route.
They found it in the Atlantic and Pacific railroad.

The Atlantic & Pacific, together with the St. Louis-San
Francisco (popularly known as the "Frisco" to all except residents of the Golden Gate city) controlled a route along the
thirty-fifth parallel of latitude from St. Louis to Needles on the
California border of New Mexico. So far so good. The Santa
Fe, after a battle with Jay Gould, who at one time controlled
the Frisco, bought into the A. & P. railroad.

The line over this route was built from Albuquerque to
Needles. Huntington had already protected his S.P. by building a branch from his main San Francisco-Los Angeles stem
at Mojave due east to Needles. To reach the Pacific Coast from
there the A. &. P. would have to parallel Southern Pacific for
many miles across a dreary desert.

Santa Fe consequently announced that the magnificent harbor of San Diego would be its far western goal instead of
Guaymas. San Diego hailed the announcement with joy. For
years it had been seeking railroad connection with the hinter-
land. Once it had asked Jay Gould to build a road, but Gould had
replied loftily that he never built railroads, he only bought them.

To the San Diego plan Huntington finally grudgingly con-
sented. He sold the branch line of the S.P. from Mojave to
Needles to the Santa Fe, and in return the Santa Fe prepared
to abandon its line to Guaymas. In this complex fashion the old
problem of Santa Fe's trackage from Benson to Deming was
finally ironed out.

Santa Fe now proceeded with seven-league boots. A line from
Barstow in Southern California was quickly built to San Ber-
nardino (forever known to railroad men as San Berdoo),
through to the Pacific coastal plain at Fallbrook, and so to San
Diego. San Diego was wild with joy when the first through
train for the East ran out of the shiny new station in D Street
on the evening of November 16, 1885. It was a truly historic
date for the Santa Fe as well. They had reached the Pacific
with their own track—all the way.

165

By 1888, the Santa Fe had its own track into Los Angeles, leaving its earliest line (the Southern California) at Riverside and going through Corona and Fullerton to the City of the Angels, entering from the southwest.

This line was preceded by another into Los Angeles from the south. In the autumn of 1885 the small Los Angeles and San Gabriel Railroad already had reached Pasadena and was being hurried through to San Berdoo and connection with the Santa Fe. The boom was on! Small new towns sprang up as if by magic for seventy miles east of Los Angeles; the modern miracle of irrigation was being wrought and fortunes were in the making.

The Los Angeles & San Gabriel, like the Southern California, became part and parcel of the Atchison, Topeka & Santa Fe, with the result that the Santa Fe now had two lines from San Berdoo into the City of the Angels.

All of these things mattered much to Wells Fargo, carrying express as it did on the trains of the rival railroad systems. Wells Fargo helped to form a triumvirate that in those days (long before the coming of the improved highway and the motor truck) created a virtual monopoly of transport in California. As such it was not infrequently and bitterly criticized. Out of this bitterness eventually came the San Francisco & San Joaquin Valley Railroad from Oakland to Bakersfield, which was promoted as a "people's railroad" in 1895. But in 1896 this line was taken over by the Santa Fe. This was the line that finally gave Santa Fe its long delayed entrance into San Francisco. Operating west from Barstow on the main stem, it used its own rails as far as Mojave, then those of the Southern Pacific over the Tehachapi Pass to Bakersfield; again its own rails to Stockton and to Oakland. At Richmond, thirty miles north of Oakland, Santa Fe established its own ferry service with the best of Harvey meals on the ferryboats, right into the ferry-house at the foot of Market Street, San Francisco, later to be superseded by a bus connection from Oakland over the Bay Bridge to the downtown heart of San Francisco.

If I have lingered upon this long-continued conflict between Southern Pacific and Santa Fe, it has been to establish the proper background for the vast prosperity that came to all

166

California with the coming of the railroads. Inasmuch as Wells, Fargo and Company had exclusive contracts with both of the roads, it made apparently but little difference to it which of the two transported its high-value freight—the point was that Wells Fargo retained its priceless monopoly in the tremendous state of California.

This maintaining a balance between two rival roads was something that called for a vast deal of tact and diplomacy on the part of the operating heads of Wells Fargo; an increasing problem it became. The two systems were at all times the bitterest of competitors. The battle between them brought to a head a most interesting problem.

When two or more roads ran between two points how should the tonnage of the express be divided between them; in what proportions? The railroads derived their income from the express in direct proportion both to the tonnage and the distance hauled. They were all jealous and demanding. To humor them required no end of patience on the part of the express executives.

It was not until about the turn of the century that other roads alien to Wells Fargo were to enter the Golden State. Back in the late 'seventies rail connection finally was established between San Francisco (Oakland Mole) and Oregon. The line to Portland ran over the steep Siskiyou Pass; many years later a line of far easier gradients was established by way of Klamath Falls and the Siskiyou route was all but abandoned.

Portland itself became a railroad center and a Wells Fargo point of considerable importance. The company maintained a bank there, as well as an express office, and built for itself the splendid Wells Fargo building which still stands. That husky old stager, Ben Holladay, had joined forces with a pioneer river-steamboat man, Captain James C. Ainsworth, and a railroad system, at first pushed up the valley of the Willamette, was begun in the pioneer American state upon the West Coast. It was at first known as the Oregon Railway & Navigation Company and eventually it reached south to the California line and joined forces with the Central Pacific, reaching north from Sacramento.

It was this small line that a traveling journalist, Henry Villard, stumbled upon on his first trip into the rich Oregon country. He was so impressed that he secured control and prepared to use it as the terminal of the transcontinental line struggling to find a pathway for itself across the northern tier of the United States all the way from Duluth, at the head of the navigable Great Lakes, to Puget Sound.

This was the Northern Pacific, an enterprise conceived by a dreamer in Boston in Civil War days—Josiah Perham. The Northern Pacific had had a gift of 47,000,000 acres of superb land dropped into its lap by charter from a magnificently mad United States Congress. Perham soon was eased out of the picture. The "express crowd"—the Fargos and the Barneys and William B. Dinsmore and the Vermont Central's Smiths—took over the budding railroad. That highly picturesque financier, Jay Cooke of Philadelphia, came into the scene, and had it not been for the panic of 1873, for which Cooke was partly responsible, they would have built it at once through to Tacoma, the terminal city first chosen by its founders.

It took the indomitable Villard to complete the road, even though it nearly bankrupted him to do it. As a pioneer terminal for Northern Pacific he chose Portland, where he was already in control of the Oregon Railway and Navigation line; at a later time it was to extend north to Tacoma, first from Portland and then, at a still later time, Seattle, which until the days of the Klondike rush was a sleepy fishing village. Still later Northern Pacific built a direct entrance to Seattle, across the newly formed territory of Washington.

The Oregon Railway and Navigation Company south of Portland was given to Southern Pacific when that road took over and absorbed the Central Pacific. Its line up in the south bank of the Columbia, from Portland through the Dalles and well beyond became known as the Oregon-Washington Railway & Navigation Company; later, in connection with the Oregon Short Line, it became the far western extension of the Union Pacific railroad up into the Pacific Northwest. At about the same time Union Pacific finally invaded sacred California by taking over the Los Angeles-Salt Lake Railroad which Senator William A. Clark of Montana finally succeeded in building between those two cities. Not only that but the shrewd Montanan had established trackage rights for his new road for just an even 100 miles over the Santa Fe through the difficult Cajon Pass from a point just east of Barstow. At Riverside the Union Pacific went again upon its own tracks into Los Angeles.

Wells Fargo never operated on the Union Pacific, although as will be seen in due course, it was of supreme aid in financing the rebuilding of that key railroad of the Union. For a time, at the outset, it had the express contract on Northern Pacific, but lost that shortly after the completion of the Villard transcontinental road. There was a bitter fight over the matter which went into the courts, but the powerful Wells Fargo lost, and it was not until a quarter of a century later that Wells, Fargo and Company had its own express route across the northern tier, and then it was over the remarkable extension to Puget Sound of the Chicago, Milwaukee & St. Paul Railway. Wells Fargo in 1909 rode the Milwaukee from Chicago and St. Paul into Seattle and so rounded out its western coverage in the Northwest.

At about the same time that the Union Pacific took over the Los Angeles & Salt Lake and entered Los Angeles rather dramatically, another free-booting railroad forced itself into San Francisco from the East. This was one of the final Gould enterprises—the Western Pacific, all the way from Salt Lake City across central Nevada and through the Feather River pass to Sacramento, Stockton and its own ferryhouse at Oakland. This road, built as a sort of western extension of the Denver & Rio Grande, was the pet hope and pride of Jay Gould's son, George. It was supposed to have had the support of the Hill roads, although James J. Hill himself once bitterly denied this to me. Western Pacific finally made traffic arrangements with Southern Pacific, so that the two single-track roads across Nevada were operated as a double-track line, to their mutual advantage. Wells Fargo never operated on that line. To the contrary, one of the company's competitors, the American Express Company, finally reached into San Francisco over it (it had entered Los Angeles a few years before on the Union Pacific), and the Wells Fargo monopoly in the city by the Golden

169

Gate, extending for more than half a century, was finally broken, although Wells, Fargo and Company still retained the vast bulk of express business of the town. San Francisco was a Wells Fargo town—its sympathies and its interests were with the company that had grown up there. When San Franciscans wished to send parcels, they lifted their telephones and said, "Wells Fargo, please." Even after Wells Fargo had expanded to a vast system with many thousands of employees, extending all the way across the continent, it still did thirty-five per cent of its business in California.

In the early spring of 1888, as I said at the beginning of this chapter, the Santa Fe rode into Chicago, Wells Fargo with it.

For some years Santa Fe had been itching to get itself into the chief railroad hub of North America. The three railroads already in operation between the Missouri and the Great Lakes, the Rock Island, the Burlington, and the Chicago & Alton, fought for the traffic from this territory for the 500-mile haul up to Chicago. Yet the first two of these roads began to invade Kansas, and this the Santa Fe resented. More than this, the Santa Fe very well knew that if it remained with its eastern terminal at Kansas City it would continue merely as a "bridge road." This, to William B. Strong, would be an unthinkable predicament for his road.

Strong, for a long time its dominating force, became president of the Santa Fe in 1873. An aggressive man always, he sought to bring his line, at last secure in its entrance to California, right into the great metropolis of the Middle West.

Strong was the sort of man who, once he had made his decision, did something about it. Rejecting a suggestion to buy the Chicago and Alton (at that time both rich and proud) he decided that Santa Fe would build its own direct line from Kansas City to Chicago. Decision gave way to immediate action. At once surveying parties went into the field.

With the exception of the first hundred miles out of Chicago where Santa Fe picked up at a bargain the struggling little Chicago & St. Louis line, it was to be all new track. As nearly airline as possible (when finished it was 450 miles long), it would be the shortest route between Kansas City and Chicago. Intermediate towns were not essential to the new road which was to be, in effect, a "bridge" between Chicago and Kansas City, designed chiefly to handle through traffic rather than local. Two enterprising towns, Galesburg, Illinois, and Keokuk, Iowa, fought to be on the new line. Galesburg, with a proffer of a handsome new station and a right of way, won.

Never was a line more rapidly or better built than that extension of the Santa Fe into Chicago. Despite the fact that five great bridges had to be erected for it and much other heavy construction done, the 350 miles of brand-new line were finished in nine months of 1887, in addition to the rebuilding of the rickety Chicago & St. Louis. Final opening of the line was delayed awaiting the completion of the 4000-foot bridge over the Missouri at Sibley, twenty-five miles east of Kansas City. But this delay was inconsequential. On February 11, 1888, Wells Fargo rode the first through Santa Fe train into Chicago. On March 11th, a month later, it at last was in its own great goal—the city of New York, just in time for the Great Blizzard of 1888 which raged into the city·one day later.

Tremendous advance preparations had been made for that arrival. Wells, Fargo and Company had taken over the plant of the erstwhile Erie Express Company and it already was placing its signs and its call-cards along the entire length of the New York, Lake Erie & Western Railway, as Erie was then known.

The invasion of New York and of Chicago meant that a large and aggressive new Wells Fargo organization had to be built up at once in each city, including local and depot offices and the operation of a great fleet of horses and wagons (all this was before the coming of the motor truck) requiring many shops, warehouses and stables. In New York the street flotilla was to consist eventually of over four hundred trucks and wagons and nearly twice that number of horses; in Chicago it came to more than half that number. Yet when the first Santa Fe passenger station was established in Chicago, December 1, 1887, at a point not far from the crossing of South California and Blue Island Avenues, Wells Fargo agent Anson Gordon had to get along as best he could with a street equipment of six wagons and eight horses.

Wells Fargo grew rapidly in the unfamiliar East. By May

of the following year the handsome new Dearborn passenger station, close to the downtown Loop, had been opened as the Chicago terminal of both the Santa Fe and the Erie systems, as well as of the Wabash, the Monon and the Grand Trunk. Gradually, Wells Fargo was installed on the first three of these railroads and the fact that they shared a common terminal in Chicago was of vast assistance in the swift operation of through transcontinental express. Horses and wagons aplenty came to supplement the original equipment. The Wells Fargo tradition of acquiring fine horseflesh started by the McLanes was splendidly maintained.

Over the Erie each night out of Jersey City ran two of the fastest trains on the road, Number Nine and Number Thirteen. At Dearborn Station, to old expressmen always "Polk Street Station," they made close connection with Santa Fe Seven, lately named the Fargo Fast, one of the swiftest and best-named railroad trains in all the land.

Anson Gordon was General Agent of Wells Fargo at Chicago for seven busy years. On his death in 1895 he was immediately succeeded by his assistant, Bernard Wygant, who for thirteen more years was an outstanding figure in the commercial life of Chicago. In the meantime the operating headquarters of Wells Fargo for the central portion of what was becoming a real express empire were being established in Chicago; while the local headquarters of the company were at 154 Dearborn Street, general headquarters were finally located in the Harris Trust Company in West Monroe Street. Here reigned for years the genial and efficient Emory A. Stedman, who, as assistant superintendent of Wells Fargo, had ridden into Chicago in the spring of 1888 and who remained there for thirty years, rising to be the vice-president and general manager for the entire central and eastern sections of Wells Fargo.

When Wells Fargo's entrance to Chicago was limited to the Santa Fe and to the Erie, its depot operations were concentrated at "Polk Street," but in later years, with the company's acquisition of express rights on the Milwaukee, the Chicago Great Western, the Wabash and the Baltimore and Ohio, it

172

expanded into two other passenger terminals, the Union Station and the Grand Central.

Wells Fargo's route to New York City on the Erie was not the most direct route between New York and Chicago, but the Erie was then, as now, a well-operated, dependable railroad, and the affiliation between it and Wells Fargo, once established, continued for many years.

The situation in New York itself was complicated by the fact that the Hudson River was a barrier between the passenger terminals of the Erie in Jersey and Manhattan. But the swift and efficient operation of a large fleet of ferryboats across the Hudson to terminals at the foot of Chambers Street and West Twenty-Third Street on the west side of Manhattan largely overcame this barrier.

The chief Wells Fargo city office in New York had been established for a number of years at 63 Broadway (long years before that at 84 Broadway) until finally it was moved a few doors further down that street to Numbers 49 and 51. Manhattan and Brooklyn also were served by a number of city branch offices.

New York was a city of tremendous potentialities for Wells Fargo and it worked vigorously, once it had arrived in the metropolis, to build up a large traffic. Against long-established competition it put up a stiff and successful fight. The company had only one road into New York, the Erie, but west of Chicago it could offer its customers transport on a number of lines, not the least of them the tracks of the Santa Fe, now "all the way" to Wells Fargo's home city of San Francisco.

XIII   *A Proud Company and a Railroad King*

Throughout the entire final quarter of the past century and well into the beginning of the present one, Wells, Fargo and Company continued to expand its express activities. At the same time the banking department of the company prospered mightily. These two major activities of the company had grown to be pretty much disassociated since the 1860's. As the business of the company grew, the stoutly built castle of Chinese stone that John Parrott had erected long ago at Montgomery and California Streets became outmoded, and the bank moved to

175

Sansome Street, where under the skillful guidance of Homer S. King, it continued its operations.

Four years after the Santa Fe contracted with the company for exclusive express privileges over its line, Wells Fargo was operating, among others, over the following rather extensive system of railroads in the United States and Mexico:

St. Paul & Omaha	Sioux City & Pacific
Southern Pacific System	Atchison, Topeka & Santa Fe
Denver & Rio Grande	Atlantic & Pacific
Mexican Central	Sonora Railroad Company

A good many of these names have long since disappeared from the railroad guides but in their day they were enterprising roads. Most of them, as can be seen from their names, were headed for California.

This vast expansion was recognized by president Lloyd Tevis when, on March 13, 1884, he made E. N. Cooper general superintendent of the western department of Wells Fargo Express with headquarters at San Francisco, and W. J. Hancock general superintendent of the eastern department with his headquarters at Omaha. The title of general manager for these departments had not yet been adopted. But a little later John J. Valentine was made general manager of the entire Wells Fargo Express enterprise with Cooper and Hancock reporting to him.

The company continued to pay its eight per cent dividends annually and, after that, to push its huge undivided profits into the vaults of the company bank. Homer King took good care that these were properly protected.

The contract, dated November 1, 1888, which Wells Fargo secured with the Atchison Topeka & Santa Fe established a fifty-fifty division of gross earnings. There was a guarantee of not less than $150 a mile annually for express earnings on the main line of the Santa Fe and $60 a mile on branch lines. The contract also applied to the various subsidiary Santa Fe lines, including the Gulf, Colorado & Santa Fe operating in Texas and which, under the laws of that commonwealth, had to be incorporated as a separate railroad system with headquarters in the Lone Star State.

176

The company in 1892 owned and operated 2,829 offices and agencies. The annual dividends were beginning occasionally to drop from eight to six per cent a year.

In the autumn of 1893 a new contract was made with the Southern Pacific for all the lines of the system and the San Antonio and Aransas Pass, which was brought into the S.P. system at a slightly later date. The terms of this important contract were that Wells Fargo was to pay forty per cent of the gross earnings. For such a juicy prize the company put up $1,750,000 in stock. Earlier that year Wells Fargo had renewed its old contract with the Santa Fe at fifty per cent of the gross, but that contract called for an advance of $1,450,000 on the part of Wells, Fargo and Company. The fat cat of Montgomery Street must have groaned a bit that year as he gave up so much of his hoardings.

In 1897 Wells Fargo began a ten-year contract with the St. Louis & San Francisco—better known as the Frisco, which brought Wells, Fargo and Company for the first time on a through route into the important city of St. Louis. A superintendent's office was established in the Continental Bank Building, and Grover B. Simpson, whose name was to be identified with Wells Fargo for the next quarter of a century, was placed in charge. Later Simpson went to Chicago to become a general superintendent of Wells Fargo and was succeeded in turn by C. R. Teas and H. B. Calkins—names also to become well known on the roster of Wells, Fargo and Company.

Meanwhile, the company decided to pull out of the old Montgomery Street building entirely and to erect a modern office of its own. A convenient site was chosen at the corner of Second and Mission Streets, almost within a stone's throw of the Palace Hotel, and there, in 1898, it moved its activities. Wells Fargo at last had a home of its own of which it might be proud.

On August 11, 1892, Lloyd Tevis retired as president and John J. Valentine assumed the responsibility for which he had trained so long and so arduously. Tevis remained on the Board of Directors with Leland Stanford, James C. Fargo, Charles C. Crocker and others. Valentine had been a long time getting the post of presidency, but he was to hold it only a little more than eight years. But all of the last forty years of his life he worked faithfully for Wells Fargo, and, on December 21, 1901, he died. It had been in very many ways a hard world for him—a world of many disappointments, of robbers and of highwaymen, not all of whom toted guns. But through all of it he kept his faith and his honor.

John Valentine at his death was only a little over sixty-three years old, a man retaining still his fire and his energy if not his physical vigor. In his passing Wells Fargo suffered an almost irreparable loss. He was mourned in San Francisco and far beyond as were but few men of his day and generation.

The West was coming to maturity. The wave of banditry was subsiding. Occasionally there was a sporadic outburst, but always it was short-lived. Picturesque sheriffs were becoming story-book idylls. Wells Fargo had played its full part in subduing these criminals and it was entitled to more credit for the job than it sometimes received. Jimmie Hume and Johnnie Thacker knew it and so did their fine and grizzled chief, John J. Valentine.

The growth of the West and the Southwest, which we have sketched in by noting the extension of the railroads through the country, brought immense opportunities for the growth of the express, which we have given, by necessity, pretty much in terms of new contracts for Wells Fargo. Back of each of these, however, there is a story of hard work and toil, of the people who settled and built up the great West and Southwest and of the agents of the express who made that growth possible. Take as an example of the whole story the tremendous agricultural growth of Southern California and Arizona following the development of irrigation; and take as example of the part Wells Fargo and its men played, the story of Dudley T. Mervine.

Mr. Mervine is one of the oldest Wells Fargo officials still living, at present writing well and happy. He is a typical old-time Wells Fargo man. I shall not embarrass him by giving his age, but will mention the fact that but a short time ago in his pleasant home at La Grange, Illinois, Mrs. Mervine and

178

he celebrated the sixty-fifth anniversary of their marriage. He is one of the very few Wells Fargo men still living who remembers John J. Valentine. He knew Dudley Evans, Aaron and Nathan Steins, Homer King, William Pridham, Andrew Christeson, Emory Stedman and Charlie Gardiner, all those gallant knights of the old Wells Fargo days. He remembers when Elmer Jones (whom we shall hear much about later) first came to work for the company. He was Elmer's first employer.

Dudley Mervine came originally from a small town in Northern Pennsylvania. He started work in a Pennsylvania railroad signal tower, took up telegraphy, pounded brass for Western Union and later for the West Shore Railroad.

"I guess I got that Horace Greeley feeling about 'Go West, young man,'" he told me a few years ago. "I read how they were building the Santa Fe and I made up my mind that the best thing to do was to marry the sweetest girl in the world, and take her out with me. Which was the very thing I did. I wired the Santa Fe and they told me to come on out and work for them.

"We arrived at the brand-new town of Carbondale, Kansas, and within twenty-four hours I was tapping the key in the Santa Fe station there. Not long after that I was the night agent at Carbondale and somehow I felt as if I had been working for the Santa Fe all my life. I was that proud of the road. As a side job I held down the Wells Fargo agency.

"One night, when I was alone on the trick, a man came in and sent a bundle of bills wrapped up in a sheet of heavy brown paper to some town out in Ohio. I received it and issued a receipt for it. But when the package was received back East there was nothing in it but a bundle of newspaper clippings, cut to the same size as paper money. Wells Fargo got pretty excited about that. Mr. Valentine heard about it and sent Captain Hume out on the job. Hume never found the thief or the money, but he was convinced that the theft had occurred on the line somewhere and apparently he liked the way that I had behaved in the matter. Anyway pretty soon Wells Fargo superintendent Campbell up at Kansas City asked me if I did

179

not want to give *all* my time to Wells Fargo and be a route agent, which was a job pretty much coveted in those days."

Mervine took that job in 1888. A little later he was chief clerk, then assistant to the superintendent at Kansas City. With a passion for hard work and detail, within four years he was sent to Omaha where Dudley Evans was general superintendent.

All this while John J. Valentine, back in San Francisco, was watching young Mervine and finally Valentine wrote him that he wanted someone who was observing and responsible to make a general investigation of Wells Fargo conditions in the United States, Cuba, Mexico and Alaska. Mervine accepted the post gleefully and made a thorough job of it, with the result that in 1895 he was made superintendent of Wells, Fargo and Company at Kansas City, where he remained from 1895 to 1911.

But by 1911, as presently will be seen, a good many things had happened at Wells, Fargo and Company. John J. Valentine was ten years gone and so was Dudley Evans. There was a new president of Wells Fargo, William Sproule, a shrewd, upstanding and very able man. A man of vision, Sproule decided that the time had come for Wells Fargo to have a transportation department. He also decided that D. T. Mervine was the man to head that department with jurisdiction over all the widespread system.

There was good reason why Mervine had this fine post offered to him.

As I have said, it was a long time after the development of the Southwest that it became self-supporting. Before the day of widespread irrigation the country could not raise the food it consumed and most of the green vegetables and the fruit for New Mexico and Arizona had to be shipped in. In ordinary transport (none was swift) in such a hot climate, there was much spoilage. The railroads had already adopted the refrigerator car for their freight service, but it was notoriously slow and undependable.

D. T. Mervine had an idea and put it into effect. He worked with the Santa Fe operating people and got them to set aside

180

a baggage car, fit it with large refrigerators and then to place it in service in passenger trains, which could be relied upon to make their schedules. The idea was an instant success.

The new car went into service between Kansas City (then the eastern terminus of the Santa Fe) and Phoenix and Tucson. From the beginning it did a land-office business in meats, poultry, eggs, perishable vegetables and fruit. Soon it was doing over $1,000 business a trip, of which a generous $500 went into the coffers of Wells Fargo.

Soon the Santa Fe, and then the Southern Pacific, were rigging up still more baggage cars for Wells Fargo passenger train service. The plan was extended to Southern California for citrus fruits, to Rocky Ford, Colorado, for melons, to Arkansas for peaches and strawberries, and to the vast growing areas of Southern Texas and of Louisiana. A vast new field for the express had been created. For the regular and high-volume movement of meats and poultry and fruit and perishable vegetables, the refrigerator car in freight-train service would continue to carry the bulk of the traffic, but for out-of-season produce there was plenty of room, and still is, for the express.

The railroads were in many instances unable to finance the large quantities of new and expensive refrigerator cars, properly equipped for handling in fast passenger trains and so Wells Fargo, always with plenty of capital at its command, began building these cars itself and leasing them to the roads on a mileage basis.

By 1918 Wells Fargo had 175 refrigerator cars of its own and they were the finest in the land.

I have mentioned several times before the fact that Wells Fargo always had plenty of capital on hand for financing expansion and for purchasing the lucrative contracts of so many Western railroads.

With the express and banking departments moving hand in hand, they formed a perfect team for the work of building a mighty business. Not only that but, as we have seen, that team took its part in developing the resources of the country through supplying fast and reliable transportation for its products. Yet there was a young broker in Wall Street whose

181

shadow was in due course to fall across Wells Fargo and make profound changes in its destiny. That young man was Edward H. Harriman.

We must go back a decade or so before the turn of the century to get the sequence of such far-reaching events. The son of an Episcopalian minister, Harriman married into a well-to-do family in Ogdensburg, New York, and became interested in the railroads of that district, among them a little line not sixty miles long which ran from the terminus of the old Northern Central (long since become part of the Pennsylvania system) from Stanley in Ontario County, straight north to Sodus Bay on the south shore of Lake Ontario. Harriman obtained control and went down to Broad Street Station, Philadelphia, to see President A. J. Cassatt.

Here was a fine chance, said Harriman, for the Pennsylvania to develop heavy tonnage for its Northern Central line. There was a magnificent, protected harbor at Sodus, and it would be easy enough to develop a fine export coal traffic right across Ontario and down the St. Lawrence to Canada, which was an increasing market for bituminous coal. Cassatt got the picture, and he got the road. Harriman cleaned up a neat profit and launched one of the most spectacular careers of American finance.

At an early age he was able to buy a seat on the New York Stock Exchange and immediately immersed himself in the financial network of American railroads. Through his friendship with Stuyvesant Fish, he became vice-president of the Illinois Central in 1883 and twenty years later gained control of that railroad. This was his first great triumph as a financial manipulator, and from that it was a short step to his predatory dream of empire.

With the aid of Kuhn, Loeb & Company, he formed a syndicate to acquire the Union Pacific, then in receivership and looked upon as a hopeless failure. This was in 1898 and his plans were well made. He saw the Union Pacific as the key railroad for his transcontinental system from the Atlantic to the Pacific. The Illinois Central would link Omaha and Council Bluffs with Chicago. For the link to the Atlantic he contemplated either the Erie or the Baltimore and Ohio; possibly, with luck and an extension of his wizardry, the New York Central.

However, before he could engage in the titanic battle for Eastern supremacy, he had to consolidate the Western link from the Missouri to San Francisco. Having under his control the Union Pacific which ran as far west as Ogden, the next job was to acquire the Central Pacific from Ogden to San Francisco. That line, by this time, was a part of the Southern Pacific system controlled by Collis P. Huntington. The latter's death in 1901 gave Harriman his opportunity.

Huntington had left to his widow and a nephew, Henry E. Huntington, 475,000 shares of Southern Pacific stock, the chief single interest in the company, representing forty-seven per cent of the entire outstanding capital stock. Gradually Harriman acquired this stock and gained control. Now he held both the Union Pacific and the Southern Pacific and therefore had his transcontinental chain complete from Omaha to San Francisco. However, Harriman's operations did not stop here because, not satisfied with one transcontinental line, he entered into a contest with James J. Hill for mastery of the Northern Pacific. This led to a Wall Street crisis and Harriman was defeated.

He turned his attention again to the Union Pacific-Southern Pacific. He actually wanted only the Central Pacific section of the latter railroad, but so far as federal statutes permitted, this whole complex of Western roads was merged. Later, after Harriman's death, the Union Pacific and Southern Pacific systems became independent of each other with traffic arrangements acceptable to the Interstate Commerce Commission. But during his reign Harriman controlled 18,500 miles of railroad west of the Missouri and immediately entered upon a campaign of rehabilitation for the rickety Union Pacific. It had an ideal route for a transcontinental road, but its original line made too many detours with too many sharp curves and wicked grades.

It was at this point that the preacher's-son-become-railroad-magnate fell upon Wells Fargo.

The fat cat of Montgomery Street, San Francisco, had never

183

been fatter. Three decades of unexampled prosperity had filled its coffers to overflowing. In its strongboxes were nearly $30,-000,000 in gold and liquid securities. Month after month with surplus profits of from $100,000 to $250,000 had invested Wells Fargo with a Midas-like quality.

Harriman used to boast that he could control any company with an ownership of thirty-five per cent. Now the S.P. controlled Wells Fargo and Harriman controlled the S.P. With the aid of Southern Pacific, he moved in quietly and swiftly on Montgomery Street. The men who had been there for years suddenly realized that a new boss was in the saddle. With the S.P., Harriman controlled Wells Fargo with even less than his usual thirty-five per cent!

The president of Wells Fargo at that time was Colonel Dudley Evans, who had succeeded John Valentine at the latter's death. He definitely was a gentleman of the old South, handsome, courteous and courageous. He knew fully his exalted position in the world and demanded not only respect, but deference, which eventually was to be his undoing. He was to meet more than his match in one Edward H. Harriman.

The new president of Wells Fargo heard about Harriman's coup, of course, and calmly waited for Harriman to send for him. There was much to be discussed. For instance, that matter of the express contract with the Union Pacific.

In order to supplement properly its operations on the Santa Fe and Southern Pacific, particularly the latter, Wells Fargo needed the express contract on the Union Pacific. The Colonel smiled pleasantly as he contemplated the fact that the new power in control of Wells Fargo was the man who was also in control of Union Pacific. It would all be easy now.

While he was waiting, Dudley Evans ordered the sign painter to prepare Wells Fargo signs to go up on the U.P. stations all the way from Ogden to Denver, Omaha and Kansas City.

But Harriman never sent for Dudley Evans. The president of the proud firm of Wells, Fargo and Company grew more and more restive. Days passed. And still no word from Harriman. Finally Evans broke down, swallowed his pride and

184

went direct to the magnate, which he should have done in the first place. He was received coldly.

"We have given the express contract on the Union Pacific to the American Express Company," was all that Harriman said.

That was a bitter pill for the president of Wells Fargo. Soon the American would not only be in Ogden, but in a matter of months it would be in the Wells Fargo strongholds of Los Angeles and Portland.

On the heels of this blow was to follow the loss of the bank.

The new captain of the ship did not particularly care for the banking operation of Wells Fargo. He felt that what had been in the early days of the company a great aid to the miners and the other colonizers of the modern California had, by the turn of the century, become an anomaly. For one thing the bank was far too rich. There were not nearly enough deposits or liabilities in comparison with its capital. Its vast surplus far outbalanced its deposits. It should have had more depositors and less surplus. Of that E. H. Harriman was certain.

Another factor worried Harriman: he did not like some of the loans that the banking department of Wells Fargo had been making. Lloyd Tevis had been entirely too generous with his friends.

Long before the end of the last century agriculture had supplanted mining as the chief industry of California; manufacturing on any large scale still was more than sixty years away. But the superb Central Valley already was in full development. Wine grapes, wheat, other cereals and vegetables were beginning to flow out of it in fullest measure. To the farmers of these crops Wells Fargo was a godsend.

All of these crops were highly seasonal. Wells Fargo financed these agricultural enterprises by the millions of dollars, so they could meet payroll and other year-round expenses.

While banking never was his end of the business, John J. Valentine, even before Harriman's advent, had felt that Lloyd Tevis overdid that sort of banking. And so did E. H. Harriman.

Harriman was not dissatisfied with the quality of the loans so much as with their size. He was used to banking in New

185

York where the banks did not take too large a proportion of any one corporation's paper. Wells Fargo had two loans of a million-and-a-half dollars each to two big corporations. Both were perfectly good, but Harriman felt they were entirely too big. He felt that he was running into a liability and consequently prepared to sell the bank.

He found a purchaser in Isaias Hellman, president of the Nevada Bank of San Francisco. Thus, in 1905, the Nevada Bank purchased from Wells Fargo the banking department of the business in exchange for 200,000 shares of stock paid by the new bank (which was called the Wells Fargo-Nevada National Bank) to Wells, Fargo and Company. This represented the value of the assets that Wells Fargo turned over to the new bank.

The rest of the huge surpluses which had been piling up from the express business were retained by Wells Fargo and at last, Harriman, as head of the express company, was in control of these huge sums. He was now free to go ahead and distribute most of the assets gradually in the form of cash and stock dividends and so to finance the complete reconstruction of his Union Pacific railroad.

With Wells Fargo's surpluses as a starter* and the best brains and experience of United States railroading in executive control of his system, Harriman began the physical perfection of his holdings. He straightened the road west of Omaha, relocating, realigning and reconstructing it over Sherman Hill, Wyoming, building new stations and new terminals, double tracking the entire main line of the U.P. and buying a tremendous amount of rolling stock. And on the Central Pacific he shortened the main line west of Ogden by forty miles by the thirty-two mile Lucin cutoff straight across the head of the Great Salt Lake.

The plans he had for his railroad empire were magnificent indeed, but on September 9, 1909, he died. It marked the beginning of the end of the close alliance between the Southern Pacific and the Union Pacific. It also meant, so far as Wells Fargo was concerned, that the company would never have the

* The projects eventually cost over $240,000,000.

186

operating contract on the U.P. On this score the company missed out completely.

So it was that Wells Fargo was changed by a railroad king. From 1905 on Wells, Fargo and Company was devoted wholly to transportation and express. The independent Wells Fargo Bank assumed an important role in the history of California business and finance.

Free enterprise indeed! We shall not see its like again.

Harriman died before he could complete his transcontinental network. Even so, had he lived, times were changing. Theodore Roosevelt was President, and his trust-busting program, which included the revitalizing of the Interstate Commerce Commission, was in full swing. His denunciation of "malefactors of great wealth" and "big business" applied alike to the Standard Oil, the United States Steel and the great railroad manipulators. A new concept of the responsibility of the enterprisers was coming into being and, whether they liked it or not, the corporate giants were being forced into regulation which recognized not only their obligation to stockholders and investors but also to the people as a whole. The day of the ruthless old free-booters was done—finished.

Had Harriman been delayed just a few years in his absorption of Wells Fargo, the new regulations of the Interstate Commerce Commission, which were being enacted into law, would have made a different story and the history of the Fat Cat of Montgomery Street would certainly have taken another course. Or to look at it another way, had Harriman's ruthless dream of empire ever brought him to the place where he was willing, as a pawn in his gigantic game, to give Wells Fargo a contract on the Union Pacific, things would have been different in another way.

XIV The Wells Fargo Bank

Historically, Wells, Fargo and Company, Banking and Express, were one and the same. As in the case of most human institutions the need dictated the nature of its organization and brought forth the men to make it work. In the rough days of the gold rush the treasure which the miners unearthed required both safekeeping and transportation. Wells Fargo supplied them steadfastly and swiftly. As we have seen, the company set up banking offices at convenient points in the Mother Lode country and the other great diggings of the state where

189

it received from the miners the nuggets and gold dust, gave receipts for the precise number of ounces and dispatched it to the Assay Offices in San Francisco. When Uncle Sam had established the exact value of the gold, that sum, minus a carrying charge, was placed to the credit of the miner at the branch bank nearest his claim. It took ingenuity, brains and guts to build up such a system in a frontier land—not to say the highest integrity. The result was to create good will for Wells Fargo with the early settlers (who became the financial leaders of the West) which was to last throughout the life of the company.

As Wells Fargo grew, so grew the Wells Fargo Bank. It came to the point where the banking department demanded, and received, its own management, quite apart from the transport functions of the company and in due time separate quarters were established for the bank in Sansome Street.

It was there that Frederick Lockwood Lipman first saw the Wells Fargo Bank with which he was to be prominently associated for so many years of his long life. He first came to Wells Fargo in 1883, when he was but seventeen years old, but he has memories of the company that go at least ten years back of that time. He recalls going with his father before he was seven years old to the Union Club, then in Montgomery Street, and hearing of the terrific nitroglycerine explosion in the old Wells Fargo building next door.

Mr. Lipman joined Wells Fargo when the company was only thirty-one years old as an assistant note clerk. Ten years later, in 1893, he was appointed assistant cashier, and, after another decade, became cashier. In 1906, after Wells Fargo's merger with the great "Bonanza Bank" of the Big Four, the storied Nevada National, Mr. Lipman was elected vice-president. He became president in 1920. In 1935, in the midst of the fourth depression his financial career has spanned, Mr. Lipman became Chairman of the Board of the Wells Fargo Bank and Union Trust Company.

Commenting on his resignation as Chairman of the Board, the San Francisco *Argonaut* concluded an editorial with the following words: "Even after his resignation as Chairman of the Board, Mr. Lipman will not relinquish his full burden of duty to the bank's depositors. He will continue to serve as director. In San Francisco's banking and business circles, that means that the top-floor office of the Wells Fargo building will remain a source of good sense and sound advice, backed by sixty-six years of Mr. Lipman's brand of sanity and devotion."

Son of a former resident of Philadelphia who came to San Francisco not long after the gold rush and engaged for a time in the real-estate business, and grandson of a distinguished Prussian army officer, the younger Lipman, born in San Francisco, was reared in the then fashionable Rincon Hill section, now entirely disappeared. The family suffered reverses and, at twelve, young Fred Lipman went to work. He recalls his mother taking him by the hand and walking with him down to Market Street and seeing him safely across that busy, broad thoroughfare with all its traffic and carriages, before there were any of the new-fangled cable cars. After that he found his way to the brokerage house of Latham & King, both names identified with Wells Fargo, where he had his first employment. He remained with Latham & King some four or five years. During this period he grew to realize that he did not want to be in the mining stock-brokerage business. He wanted to be a banker and perhaps some day to work for the Wells Fargo Bank, or perhaps Ralston's great Bank of California which then was the shining financial light of all San Francisco. But in the meantime he stuck by the brokerage job, and evenings at night school he studied bookkeeping.

Finally he found that the wholesale paper house of Bonestell, Allen & Company was looking for a bookkeeper and having completed his course he got the job. Latham & King had been giving him $50 a month, and Bonestell would not raise that figure. However, young Lipman had decided that he was going to be a bookkeeper rather than an office boy so he took the job anyway. In the course of but a few days he found the books of the concern badly in arrears, but he worked hard and finally got them up to date and in good order. Mr. Lipman has told me a great deal of those days, both in personal interviews and by letters. I quote parts of his account herewith:

"Homer King had let me go to take this job as bookkeeper,

but had not lost sight of me. So when Mr. Wadsworth [cashier of the Wells Fargo Bank at that time] told him that they wanted an assistant note-teller, one who had had some experience in the mining stock-broker's business, he called me into his office.

"The Bank offered me $75 at the outset. There was nothing glamorous about any of it. I didn't think of it as a lot better than the job I already had, but I was much influenced by Mr. King's advice. At that time I was seventeen; four and a half years had gone by. So I went to see Mr. Wadsworth and he took me in to see Mr. Lloyd Tevis and they gave me the 'once over.' I remember that Tevis went to Bonestell and Bonestell gave me a good sendoff. In fact, Mr. Bonestell offered me a $10 raise to stay."

Frederick Lipman went to work for the Wells Fargo Bank May 10, 1883. In 1892 Homer King became manager of the bank. He had been treasurer of Wells Fargo, succeeding Calvin Goddard in that post March 18, 1873. In after years when the Wells Fargo Bank became affiliated with the Nevada National Bank, under the aegis of the Hellman family, Homer King became president of the historic Bank of California of San Francisco, and there he continued his successful career.

At the time Mr. Lipman first went to work for the Wells Fargo Bank it had branches in New York, Salt Lake City, Carson City and Virginia City. With its $2,000,000 in deposits in San Francisco it ranked as about the fifth in the town. The Bank of California, N.A., was the most important, then came in succession the Nevada Bank, the Anglo-California Bank, Ltd., Lazard Frères (afterwards called the London, Paris & American Bank) and finally the Wells Fargo Bank. The Giannini Bank of America was not to come until many years afterwards.

The Wells Fargo Bank at the time that Lipman came to it was situated on the northeast corner of California and Sansome Streets where the Alaska Commercial Building now stands.

Mr. Lipman continues his recollections of the bank in those days:

"The entrance to the bank floor was up a flight of steps so there were offices below—which happened to be an insurance

192

office. I remember looking down those steps to see my first typewriter."

A little later the Wells Fargo Bank was to get its first type-writer—one typewriter. And a little after that its first telephone —just one telephone. The nearest person at hand answered the calls.

"But that was before I went into the bank," continues Mr. Lipman. "The lobby was around the window section. To the left of that, as you went in, was the note desk. That was where I was located. Then, as the counter extended itself around the corner, was the paying teller. On the California Street side, at the side of the paying teller, was the exchange teller. In front of the note desk was the open space of the lobby. Behind the lobby you went into a glass enclosure where the officers were. The officers of the Wells Fargo Bank then consisted of the cashier and the president. You went into the president's office by staying at the side of the windows and you went into the cashier's office by entering a door on the right, just as you went in.

"The president was quite separated from the bank. He did not have much to do with the handling of the ordinary affairs of the place, although he was the head of the institution, the man who passed upon all matters of difficulty. The place furthest away was the vault. Between the vault and the Exchange Department were the bookkeepers. In the alleyway behind the paying teller were the people who dealt with the counter checks—checks being paid over the counter by the paying teller or being received by the receiving teller. It all was quite simple. The paying teller, the receiving teller, the exchange teller, and the note teller, the three other than the note teller, were men working singly who represented the whole department. The man who was assistant to the cashier had a desk in the cashier's office."

Young Frederick Lipman was always observant. He laughs when he says that he came into the Wells Fargo Bank at the age of seventeen as an "expert" just when the average boy to-day is getting ready to go to college. He got the job on account of his "experience." He says:

"I had to go to work when I was twelve, so I had been made

193

assistant note clerk when I first came into the bank and the word 'routine' hardly suggests the job that was given to me."

The note clerks in those days, as at present, attended to the Bank's loans and to collateral for them. But in addition to that, in 1883, young Lipman and his associates also had to make the collections and care for the bullion. In those days all the collections were registered. The bank had a big book and in it one item would run all the way across the page—the date, the name of the maker of the check or whatever it was, the payee, the endorsers, the bank that it was drawn on and finally the amount—a lot of work for just one entry.

Lipman used to let these items accumulate during the day. Then, at about a quarter past two, he would start work upon them. He worked swiftly, and generally they were done by a quarter to four. Today this sort of accounting in a modern bank is all handled by machinery.

"Later," he adds, "we kept no individual record of anything under $100 and the items under $100 each would be three foot thick at the close of the day—some fifteen or twenty thousand of them. I had to make a summing up record of them all. Also I had to tend to the registering of the notes.

"In those days we also had mining stocks on our hands. Of course they belonged to our customers, but they all had to be taken care of and registered. We had a huge wallet that we put in the vault every night that held these certificates. No one ever seemed to take the time to audit. Finally I took that task upon myself; every so often I made a proof."

There came a day when young Lipman found that he was a hundred shares short on a mining stock, and he says that his hair nearly turned gray that night. Afterwards he found that it had been sent on to the Wells Fargo Bank in New York, but without record. That was the sort of thing that used to occur every so often in those rough-and-ready days. No wonder so many bank officers went gray.

Early in Mr. Lipman's career paper bank notes were hardly considered real money. This was in full accordance with the San Francisco tradition which used to abhor "folding money." Such currency items were then considered by the Wells Fargo

Bank as checks, and were so handled. All *payments* were made in gold. The paying tellers had trays for the $20 gold pieces and each paying teller had a gold shovel. They all became expert in handling $20 gold pieces. These were stacked, twenty pieces to the pile or $400 worth. Then other stacks were measured to precisely the same height, all in multiples of $400. A customer presented a check and took away gold.

But paper money, despite a popular thought to the contrary, always was known in San Francisco. It had been handled at a discount until the resumption of payments in gold by the United States Treasury in 1879.

"With a steadily increasing influx of Easterners into San Francisco," says Mr. Lipman, "paper money became more and more tolerated. Lots of individuals would not accept it, but the stores would. San Francisco merchants gradually got in the habit of taking it and the banks were handling both gold and paper until 1914. Then the first World War broke out and a terrific problem had to be solved at once—with San Francisco the only place on earth where gold was actually and freely handled, the question became how to get rid of that San Francisco habit."

The Federal Reserve Bank there finally hit upon an ingenious device that worked. It left the banks in a position where although they *had* to pay gold on demand, they *could* pay in gold when asked for it, and yet put something of a stopper upon the free distribution of the yellow coin. This was the plan:

The banks of San Francisco paid out gold freely upon demand, *but only in $20 gold pieces*. The $5 and $10 gold pieces were withheld and this gradually killed the circulation. The $20 gold pieces were being used mostly for bank reserves, but the gold in the steadily lessening circulation was practically all in $5 and $10 pieces. Gradually these were turned into the Federal Reserve Bank of San Francisco and then they were taken out of circulation. At first on the small coins the government stood the abrasion losses, which were heavy. Later the holders were compelled to assume the depreciation.

The banking situation in San Francisco in 1883, when Mr. Lipman first went to work for Wells Fargo, had settled down

195

considerably from the old days of boom and bust which the city had known. The leading bank then, as previously stated, was the reorganized Bank of California, the history of which is a book by itself. This was the institution which was organized in 1864 by the picturesque William G. Ralston and which failed spectacularly in 1875. It was housed in a magnificent marble Italian palace that Ralston had built at Sansome and California Streets.

Dr. George D. Lyman's book, *Ralston's Ring,* gives a vivid picture of perhaps the most vivid character in the entire history of San Francisco. Ralston, it points out, was more than merely a promoter and bank president, builder and financier. He was the vortex of the most sensational decade in the city's history— a decade that was to end by his swimming out into the waters of the Golden Gate at sundown, to his own death.

Just before the Bank of California closed in 1875, the Bonanza Quartet of Comstock Lode fame, Flood, O'Brien, Mackay and Fair, had formed their Nevada Bank. It at once became one of the most important financial institutions in San Francisco. However, when a few months later the Bank of California was reopened under circumstances highly creditable to its management, it resumed its old position at the very head of all the city's banks.

The founders of the Nevada bank fixed its capital at $10,-000,000, which created a sensation as it was the largest capital of any bank in the United States at that time. The Bonanza Quartet was not in the habit of doing things by halves. It was said that once the bank had been chartered, its owners drew a check for $10,000,000 against it. It is not clear for just what purpose, but there was nothing illegal about such a transaction. A little later the capital of the Nevada Bank was reduced to $3,000,000. Louis McLane, the former president of Wells, Fargo and Company, was made its first president.

Z. S. Eldredge in his *History of California* (Vol. IV) said that the Nevada Bank opened on October 2, 1875, with a paid-up capital of $5,000,000 which was increased about a year later to $10,000,000 and later reduced to $3,000,000. In 1883 Flood and Mackay engaged in an attempt to corner the world's wheat supply and the deal, carried on through the Nevada

196

Bank, was so disastrous in its results that, but for the interposition of James G. Fair, who put a large amount of cash into the bank, it would have been obliged to close its doors. Fair, who had withdrawn sometime before from the bank and from the "Bonanza firm" took the presidency of the bank until it reorganized with new capital and new people who brought it into the first rank.

Frederick L. Lipman does not believe that this is categorically true. He says:

"I felt perfectly sure that Flood and Mackay were not the sort of men who would go into a speculation. They had a bank of high standing. The great losses that they made in wheat speculation were of a later day. I never heard anyone speak as if the Nevada Bank was not good. The fact of the matter was that those big Nevada magnates who were behind it put up the money when Brander [George L. Brander] in his administration of the bank had speculated with its money. In other words, in banking you are depending upon individuals and their character and no one had any reason to doubt that those men were not good for their money—no matter what the bank did. It was because of that difficulty that I. W. Hellman first came into the Nevada Bank."

Isaias W. Hellman came to San Francisco from Los Angeles where he had long since established the firm of Hellman, Temple & Company, which later became the Farmers' and Merchants' National Bank. Hellman, born in the small Bavarian town of Reckendorf in 1842, had come to America in 1859 and soon afterwards came to the little town of Los Angeles, where he clerked in a store, speculated in real estate— Los Angeles fashion—and laid the foundations of a great fortune. He was shrewd, capable, honest—and successful. His sons and his grandsons were destined to follow in his steps.

Hellman had worked with E. H. Harriman in the financing of the Los Angeles Street Railway Company and had won the respect and admiration of that Wall Street wizard. As has been seen in the previous chapter, Harriman, when he came into Wells, Fargo and Company in 1901, was not satisfied with conditions in the banking department. He asked Hellman to take entire charge of the Wells Fargo Bank. For a long time Hellman hesitated. He already had come into command of the Nevada National Bank, and he felt that that was enough San Francisco banking responsibility.

The step that Harriman proposed would have meant the complete elimination of the much-loved Homer S. King from Wells Fargo. No one liked that idea, King least of all. He had been with Wells Fargo for many years and he always had been one of its most trusted and respected officers.

He went east and tried to talk Harriman out of replacing him, but Harriman had his own plans and said bluntly that he could not and would not do it. Finally he relented to the extent of suggesting to King that he go to Isaias Hellman and talk the matter over with him. King found Hellman at his summer home at Lake Tahoe.

Hellman was friendly, but definite. He told Homer King that while he no longer was a young man—he now liked to spend much of his time at Tahoe—he still went east often, was away much of the time, and that he would like to have King take general charge of the Nevada Bank. But when King suggested that he would like to become president of the Nevada Bank Hellman said there could be only one president. It was only a little after this that the Wells Fargo and the Nevada banks were finally merged. Homer King then said good-bye to the Wells Fargo that he loved so dearly and went to the presidency of the California Bank with which he was strongly identified the rest of his life.

All this anticipates. In 1883 Lloyd Tevis was in the eleventh year of his long term as president of the company; John J. Valentine, who later was to succeed Tevis, was in charge of express operations, and Homer S. King of the bank.

The capital of Wells, Fargo and Company at this time was $3,180,000. But that was not the whole story. The strength of the Wells Fargo Bank was in those monthly deposits of cash earnings that steadily were poured into it from the operations of the express. The banking department held the bag—literally. It carried on its books about $1,000,000, which represented chiefly physical assets, such as buildings, wagons, horses and

198

the like. When Wells, Fargo and Company put up its own handsome new building at Second and Mission Streets, this figure was raised to $2,000,000. Also a few years later Wells Fargo acquired a new office building in Portland, Oregon. It would have been far wiser if the company had invested some of its surplus funds in railroad equipment—as later experience in rate cases was to prove.

The express business was continuously profitable and the profits were all turned into the bank and added to its working capital. Prosperity ruled.

Although John Valentine's chief interest always was in the express end of the business, he had taken notice of Frederick Lipman in the Wells Fargo forces and it was not long before he was sending for this new man and was discussing with him the banking situation up in Portland.

Portland was a growing town and it seemed that Wells Fargo had interested itself in the purchase of the Commercial National Bank up there. Frederick Lipman was sent up to investigate the situation and report. This he did, favorably, and Wells Fargo bought the bank. But the investment did not turn out as well as had been expected, and for a long time John J. Valentine held that against Lipman.

Portland seemed almost to have been Lipman's undoing. The Commercial National which had had a hard time of it in the great panic of 1893 had approached the rich Wells Fargo Bank of San Francisco, to which panics—even the great one at the beginning of the 'thirties—hardly ever were more than incidents, to see if it did not wish to buy and make it a Portland Branch. The proposal looked interesting and Lipman, at the suggestion of Homer King, went up to Portland and looked into the assets of the Commercial National. Mr. Lipman told me what happened as follows:

"I listened to what those people said and I passed on a lot of assets that never should have been passed. The reason that I made that kind of error was that I laid too much stress on their good faith. I didn't allow for the fact that a man of good faith might lack something of good judgment. In my investigation I would ask them about this or that or the other thing and they would tell me and it would appear to be all right. Homer King came up after I had been there some weeks; he took my results and Wells Fargo purchased the bank. The result was that we lost everything that we put into it. Mr. Valentine was so annoyed over the whole transaction that he then took hold of the place and ran it his own way, which much increased the loss. Mr. Valentine was not a banker. He was essentially an expressman, and there was none better."

It all was a very bad bargain. Wells Fargo put $300,000 into the Portland Bank and stood a fair chance of losing at least half that figure, but in the long run it lost all of it. The Wells Fargo Bank of Portland ran as an entity until 1905 when, at the time of the Wells Fargo-Nevada National Bank merger in San Francisco, it was sold to the United States National Bank, long since become an outstanding bank of Portland.

John J. Valentine became president of Wells, Fargo and Company in 1892 and that was about the time that things began to happen in the banking department of the company.

The big spree up at Virginia City was over. No longer was that wild vortex of money-making, of work and of pleasure, of good eating and fast drinking, revolving at its old pace. The streets of the little town that clung so precariously to the steep slope of Sun Mountain no longer were crowded night and day. The mines of the Comstock Lode were not inexhaustible. They had begun to peter out. The completion of Adolph Sutro's great tunnel under Mount Davidson had been like a shot in the arm to them. There still was gold and silver in "them thar hills" but they were becoming increasingly difficult to mine, and operations were being abandoned. The little trains of the Virginia & Truckee still made their stiff climb up to Virginia City—the "crookedest railroad in the world" they used to call it—but the trains that went up there were fewer and farther between.* The huge brick International Hotel burned and was

* The Virginia & Truckee Railroad still operates one train a day between Reno and Minden, through Carson City, but the difficult line up the mountain into Virginia City with all its grades, curves and tunnels long since has been abandoned. At the time of going to press an application was pending before the State Public Service Commission and the Interstate Commerce Commission for the abandonment of the whole line, with considerable opposition from the residents served.

not rebuilt. Virginia City was on its way toward becoming the ghost town that it is today. The pretentious Piper Opera House no longer housed a succession of opera and of drama, and began to fall to pieces. That once brisk newspaper, the *Territorial Enterprise,* gave up the ghost as did much of the rest of the doomed town.

Since the supreme days of the Comstock Lode, the branches of the Wells Fargo Bank at Carson City and at Virginia City had prospered, but to a steadily decreasing extent. When the mining operations in Nevada ceased almost entirely, there was no further use for them and in 1891 they were closed.

In that year the manager of the Wells Fargo Bank at Carson had come to San Francisco to confess a shortage in his accounts, and Lipman was sent up there to investigate. A few days later Lloyd Tevis joined him and it was decided then and there to end the banking operations of Wells, Fargo and Company at Carson City and to sell the building to the Bullion & Exchange Bank. This was done in June, and the local bank carried on the banking business of the pleasant capital town of Nevada.

From Carson young Lipman went up to Virginia City to inspect the situation there. The manager of the Wells Fargo Bank at Virginia City was an old and trusted employee of the company. However, Lipman found that the books did not balance, and he uncovered the fact that the accounts were short some $150,000 to $200,000.

These men were not inherently dishonest. But with large amounts of ready cash in their possession, in a time when speculation ran rife twenty-four hours a day and new fortunes were being created each turn of the clock, the temptation to take part in it was too much to overcome. Seemingly they all were doing it, but most of them managed to make good on the amounts that they "borrowed." Of one thing you may be sure—John Valentine never speculated. Once when he had caught his superior officer in that sort of thing he forced his resignation. But that was John Valentine. You do not find integrity of that sort every day.

The Wells Fargo banking branch at Virginia City was at once closed and sold to the Nevada Bank which, in July, 1891, sent one of its most trusted officers, J. F. Bigelow, from San Francisco up there to arrange the purchase.

It was said that both the Wells Fargo and the Nevada Banks had been directly interested in the development of the fabulous Comstock Lode. The Bank of California also maintained a branch office in Virginia City and it had major mining interests up there. I asked Mr. Lipman if the Comstock mining securities had ever represented any considerable portion of Wells Fargo's investment up there. He replied, "Decidedly not. The Bank never would put its money into such stuff as that. Even a badly run bank would not do anything like that—and we were not badly run. The trouble that we had was in loaning on those mining securities—as well as with the falsifications of the books on those loans—for which the branch managers were responsible; although in the long run the parent bank had to make good on them.

"Remember that Wells Fargo and Company was always express and banking and that the most picturesque part of the business was the express. It went into the mining districts and it offered various services to the miners. The miners sometimes would make deposits of gold because the metal was too heavy to carry in their pockets—not always because they wished it shipped away. Wells Fargo took their gold and if the miner wanted us to keep it there it was a banking operation. If he wanted to ship it somewhere it was an express operation. In Carson City and in Virginia City in 1891, both banking and express were run under the same roof. The Bank of California and the Nevada Bank were only banking, but Wells Fargo was both banking and express."

There also was a banking branch of Wells, Fargo and Company at Salt Lake City. It ranked almost as important as the home bank in San Francisco. John E. Dooly was its manager. He was a man of independent means, shrewd and likeable. Lipman tells of one of his first visits to Dooly at the Wells Fargo Bank in Salt Lake. He says:

"I got into town in the morning of my arrival. I hurried to the bank to get there before it opened, but the teller's cash already had been distributed to the tellers so I had to count that first and take the vault cash afterwards. The cash was $9,000 short. I never found it. While I was counting the tellers' cash, the assistant cashier went down the street to the T. R. Jones Bank and said: 'I wish you would let me have $9000 in $20 bills.' They gave him the $9000. He wrote out the check form they had there, which afterwards was cleared and paid, came in with the $9000 under his coat while I was with the paying tellers. When I counted it, in a final count, the $9000 was there."

The Wells Fargo Bank in Salt Lake City was sold out to the Walker Brothers of that community, who immediately added it to their already successful banking institution. The four Walker brothers of Salt Lake were Mormons who early made their mark in the community. At every turn they were successful.

There still remained the New York Branch of the Wells Fargo Bank. It was located in lower Broadway, cheek by jowl with the express office of the company. Before 1905 the laws of the State of New York had been changed so that the Wells Fargo Bank in New York had become a state bank corporation. At that time it was not literally a branch bank of Wells, Fargo and Company; it was an independent bank with Dudley Evans, president of Wells, Fargo and Company, as its president. H. B. Parsons ran the New York Wells Fargo Bank and ran it very well indeed, but it was too small for the situation there and, finally, after the Wells Fargo Bank of San Francisco had been merged in 1905 with the Nevada National, the Wells Fargo Bank of New York was sold to the stronghold of the Delafields, the National Park Bank, at Broadway and Fulton Streets, which later was merged into the Chase National Bank.

It was in 1905 that the Wells Fargo Bank of Portland was sold to the powerful United States National Bank of Portland, the stronghold of the Ainsworths, which for years proudly advertised upon its plate-glass windows the fact that it was the successor of the Wells Fargo Bank.

In January, 1905, the long-anticipated merger of the Nevada

National Bank and the Wells Fargo Bank of San Francisco finally came into being. Harriman and Isaias Hellman had engineered it quietly. There had been a time when Harriman had considered the idea of closing the Wells Fargo Bank, but bitter protests had arisen. There still remained the problem of making money with a bank with $16,000,000 capital and only $11,000,000 in deposits. Yet to throw away the name of Wells Fargo with all its vast prestige was unthinkable. As we have seen in a previous chapter, it was in the beginning years of the present century that the idea of a merger between the Wells Fargo and the Nevada Banks first began to be seriously discussed.

In January, 1905, Homer S. King accepted the invitation of the Bank of California to become its president and resigned the post of treasurer of Wells Fargo and Company, nominally "president of the Wells Fargo Bank" which he so long had held. Lipman was made president for the few months preceding the merger. That move precipitated the news of the merger of the Wells Fargo and the Nevada Banks, which had been kept secret up to that time. Isaias W. Hellman was then in Europe and the merger could not be brought about until his return.

When the news of the approaching merger had become public property, Frederick Lipman received a telephone message from Isaias Hellman's son, I. W. Hellman, Jr., asking him to come and see him, which Lipman did, in the very room that he now occupies as chairman of the Wells Fargo Bank. Young Hellman stated that Lipman was to become cashier of the merged bank. In the following April, 1906, however, San Francisco was visited by the earthquake and fire, in the confusion of which J. F. Bigelow, vice-president of the Wells Fargo-Nevada National Bank, became so worn that he resigned the position. Frederick Lipman was then made vice-president of the Wells Fargo-Nevada National Bank, and Frank B. King, son of Homer S. King, was made its cashier.

The deposits of the Nevada Bank at the time of the merger were, roughly, about $9,000,000; those of the Wells Fargo Bank were about $6,000,000. Despite the efforts of competitors to pull its business away, the newly merged Wells Fargo-Nevada National Bank opened April 24, 1905, with $16,000,000 in deposits, and it never went below that figure.

Here is the way that the merger actually was accomplished:

The Nevada Bank had a capital of $3,000,000 and a surplus exceeding $1,500,000, and it paid its stockholders a dividend sufficient to reduce the combined amount to exactly $1,500,000. That gave its shares a book value of $150 each. Wells, Fargo and Company qualified with assets of $2,000,000 capital and $1,000,000 surplus by putting in a mass of assets exceeding the deposit liabilities by $3,000,000. There was a new issue of stock sold to the public at $200 a share—$2,000,000 all told—thereby contributing $1,000,000 to the capital fund and $1,000,000 to the surplus. It all worked out to $9,000,000 capital and $3,500,000 surplus and a book value at the start of $158.33 on each of all the shares due to the two banks that had made the merger.

"Nineteen hundred and five was a time of great financial activity in San Francisco," said Mr. Lipman in recalling those days. "The railroads were very busy buying properties, and many other things were going on, so that between April, 1905, and April, 1906, our deposits grew from over $16,000,000 to $24,000,000. That was where they stood at the time of the San Francisco Fire, April 18, 1906. After we reopened, following the fire, we had a good deal of insurance money to handle. The Spring Valley Water Company's financing came on so that we reached a high point on September 1, 1906 of about $35,000,000 in deposits. We realized, Mr. Hellman and I, and discussed the fact that the high point could not last and we did not expect it to do so. In December, 1907, with the panics of that year to come into reckoning, it fell off—back to $16,000,000 again. In this fall we lost $1,000,000 a week in the final six weeks. Pure life-blood. And yet at the end of that gruelling time we had more cash resources than we had before that last $6,000,000 went out."

In the first set-up of the new Wells Fargo-Nevada National Bank, Isaias W. Hellman was president, I. W. Hellman, Jr. and F. A. Bigelow vice-presidents, Frederick L. Lipman cashier, and Frank B. King, George Grant, William McGavin and John E. Miles assistant cashiers. After Mr. Bigelow's retirement, Frank B. King became cashier of Wells Fargo-Nevada.

In all these years, E. H. Harriman was a director of the Wells Fargo-Nevada National Bank. He already was a tremendous figure in American business and he was on the board of the National City Bank of New York, but he had refused to go on the board of any other institution. At Hellman's suggestion, however, he joined the board of the Wells Fargo-Nevada, representing the interests of Wells, Fargo and Company. Also representing Wells Fargo were W. F. Herrin, prominent in Southern Pacific affairs, and Dudley Evans, its president.

From the outset, the new Wells Fargo-Nevada National Bank proceeded to make its influence firmly felt, not only upon San Francisco but upon the entire West Coast. San Francisco itself had settled down to a conservative prosperity long before the earthquake and fire. Days of the Argonauts and the Vigilantes and of the swollen fortunes and the excitements of the Comstock Lode were slipping far into the past. San Francisco was developing as a world city of metropolitan proportions, a great seaport set to serve the seven seas in the chief port of the United States upon the Pacific Coast.

After the fire, the Wells Fargo-Nevada Bank moved into the building in which it is now located, at the northeast corner of Market and Montgomery Streets. It was designed and built for the Union Trust Company as a fireproof building, and it stood the test of the great fire very well indeed. For a time the Union Trust Company, another Hellman enterprise, occupied the Market Street frontage of the building and the Wells Fargo-Nevada was down the Montgomery side. A little later the Union Trust Company built its present building at Market and Grant, and Wells Fargo-Nevada moved into the entire structure at Market and Montgomery believing it to be the best banking corner in all San Francisco.

Eventually the Wells Fargo-Nevada took over the Union Trust Company and merged it into the parent company which then dropped the words "Nevada National" from its title, becoming the Wells Fargo Bank & Union Trust. Many in San Francisco hope that some day it will drop the Union Trust from its corporate name and become just the Wells Fargo Bank.

XV The Great San Francisco Fire

San Francisco slept soundly in the early morning of the eighteenth of April, 1906. A gay and vivacious city much given to late hours, it went to bed late and awoke late. San Francisco in 1906 was the coquette of five continents. She was rich. Everything that the tips of her slender fingers touched seemed to turn to gold. Her great merchandise marts were unequaled by any city in the world—Chicago, New York, even Paris. In fact, one of the most outstanding, the smart shop founded by the old French family of Verdier in the very early days of San Fran-

207

cisco, proudly bore, and still bears, the name of the *City of Paris.*
Contemporary with it was Raphael Weill's *White House,* still
white and still outstanding. There were many others. San
Francisco women were reputed to be the best dressed in the
world. Its shops, oriental and occidental, were known across
the country.

What other city on the whole North American continent
could offer such magnificent opportunities for pleasant living?
It was the hey-day of the road companies and the theaters held
their own among those of all American cities. No great actor,
no great play failed to have a long run in San Francisco. Light
opera at the Tivoli was an unforgettable experience. San Francisco had acquired culture; she always had charm. She had lost
much of the boisterous spirit of the gold rush days and a period
of gracious living was in full swing.

On that eventful night of April 18, 1906, the Metropolitan
Opera Company of New York was in town, Caruso having
sung *Carmen* the night before. The night of the 18th he was
to sing Tonio in *Pagliacci.* Again, all San Francisco, dressed to
the teeth, would be at the performance. There would be din-
ners in the great homes before and suppers after the opera in
the vast variety of restaurants that made the city an eternal delight to the gourmet. The great, four-square Palace Hotel
would be aglow. There was no other hotel like it in America;
it had a great galleried courtyard eight stories high to the roof
which a coach-and-four could enter with ease. There were other
great hotels in San Francisco at the beginning of the century;
the new St. Francis on Union Square was among the best. It
bore the name of the city and there seemingly had never been
a time when there had not been a hostelry by that name. But
in all the world there was only one Palace Hotel. William C.
Ralston had erected that huge place, with its brick outer walls
eight feet thick, and had gone to the extremes of building fac-
tories all over San Francisco to make the carpets and the furni-
ture and fixtures for it. It was the pride of the city, although
Ralston never lived to see it finished.

Frederick L. Lipman liked music and he planned to attend
the Opera that evening of April 18th. On the preceding night
208

he carefully packed his evening clothes in a small suitcase. The Lipmans lived across the Bay in Berkeley and, in the morning following his custom, Lipman planned to take his suitcase across to San Francisco on the ferry and, after business, commuter style, he would change his clothes at the bank. Mrs. Lipman would join him and they would go to dinner in town before the Opera. It was all arranged, but it never came to pass.

The Lipmans were awakened that morning of April 18th rather earlier than usual. Their house was rocking violently. Another earthquake, thought Fred Lipman. They were all used to earthquakes, only the one that morning seemed a little worse than usual. Lipman could hear the brick chimneys falling on the houses all the way up and down the street. Then after a minute the clatter and rumble ceased and all was quiet again. The Lipmans got up and dressed. It was a chilly morning, with a trace of fog in the air and so they hurried. The plumbing in the house was not damaged and the Chinese cook prepared breakfast on the gas range just a little earlier than usual. After breakfast, Lipman took his suitcase containing his evening clothes, kissed his wife and started for the little train that took him down to Oakland Ferry. As usual the train was crowded with other commuters, headed for the city and the day's work.

Lipman stood on the front lower deck of the big, white ferryboat as it finally rounded Goat Island (in those days it was called Yerba Buena). San Francisco appeared through the lifting fog to greet him. At the extreme right, Telegraph Hill loomed above the portal to the Golden Gate and the open sea: the gaunt semaphore whose blades in other years had telegraphed the news of incoming ships to the people in the streets of the town was long since gone. On the foreground the highly fashionable Nob Hill, with the magnificent Fairmont Hotel that James Fair's daughters were building to their father's memory; in the distance Russian Hill with barracks-like wooden houses clinging precariously to its precipitous sides; the Twin Peaks at the far end of Market Street rose back of all; Rincon Hill, once the habitat of the San Francisco aristocracy, where Fred Lipman had lived and played had long since been leveled; at the foot of this great city, the Embarcadero with docks and

209

ships and architect Page Brown's Ferry House with its dominating clock tower and the many white ferry boats clustered
at its feet; the stout red-brick tower of St. Mary's Cathedral on
California Street; the lofty Synagogue on Bush; the immense
Palace Hotel; San Francisco in all its glory, for the benefit of
the waterbound commuters.

Frederick Lipman studied it all intently as the ferryboat
came closer to the slip as he had done every morning for years.
But this morning something was wrong. At two or three places
in the town smoke was rising from behind the buildings. Fires,
thought Lipman, there must be several of them. The thought
worried him.

When the ferry docked and Lipman and his fellow commuters had passed through the main door of the Ferry House,
there was much confusion in the streets. Fire engines were
dashing through the streets, people rushing hither and yon in
great confusion. Lipman waited for a few minutes at the foot
of Market Street for a cable car. None came. His suitcase was
growing heavier. Finally he set out on foot for the new banking
house of Wells Fargo-Nevada at Pine and Montgomery Streets.

All was in its usual good order at the bank, although the
street outside was a scene of noise and turmoil. San Francisco
that morning had suffered the greatest earthquake in its entire
history. The whole Peninsula, in fact, had been badly shaken.
Worst of all, fires were breaking out all over the city. The efforts of the fire companies were almost useless because the
earthquake had snapped the water mains of the city as if they
had been tubes of brittle glass. There was no water! That was
the tragedy that faced the helpless firemen as the flames spread.
At the beginning there must have been twenty fires and gradually they united to make one horrifying conflagration which
raged until the night of the third day, destroying or gutting
the buildings in nearly three-quarters of the city.

Frederick Lipman remembers that morning well:

"I carried my suitcase up to the bank, which was at Pine and
Montgomery then, and I could see that the fire was spreading. I
came up California Street and I could see where the fire was
burning in places, but there was nothing in the way to keep
me from getting through, although there were fires not so far

away. I went to the telegraph office and sent the last telegrams that went through Western Union from San Francisco to our New York correspondents, instructing them to call loans that we had out and to send us $3,000,000. They sent that $3,000,000 through the United States Mint and through that whole period we had that $3,000,000 lying in the Mint; it was quite a luxury for us to have, for it cost us $9,000 in interest. We never used it."

The Wells Fargo-Nevada opened its doors promptly at nine that morning. Most of the staff were at their desks. Lipman went into the vaults and all was in good order. The vaults were fireproof and, if worse came to worst and the fire swept the bank, it was certain that the vaults would come through safely. They all had faith in those stout vaults.

At ten-thirty the firemen came and ordered all hands out of the bank. The great fire was coming closer; already it had attacked the rear corner of the Palace Hotel whose eight-foot walls had withstood the quake. One of the first guests to leave the hotel when it was evacuated was the incomparable Caruso, a wildly excited Italian in his pajamas, rushing down the main stair with his most prized possession, an autographed photograph of Theodore Roosevelt tucked under his arm. There would be no opera that night, nor for many nights to come in San Francisco.

"As the fire got nearer and nearer [Mr. Lipman resumed] we were chased out by the firemen, and we put our working books into the vault. When I left my desk I opened it just as any person might easily do, without any specific purpose in mind, and I saw in the top drawer my father's old watch that my mother had worn from the time of his death until she gave it to me. I took it up, looked at it for a minute, and placed it in my pocket. Right after that I left the room, never to reenter it. We had to get out of the bank at once and that was the last of that. During the day the bank burned. There was nothing else to do, the ferryboats were still running, and I went home. I suggested to Mrs. Lipman when I got home that we might buy a little food—no telling what might happen. But the cities on our side of the Bay were not badly upset by the quake."

Down the Peninsula, though, it was very much different.

The earthquake had wreaked havoc all the way to San Jose. Perhaps the greatest disaster of all on the Peninsula was the destruction of the magnificent group of buildings of Stanford University. It took years to restore the huge murals made of thousands of small bits of colored stone.

Frederick Lipman did not go back to San Francisco on Thursday, the 19th. No one went across the Bay, for the ferryboats had ceased carrying the public. Idle people were not wanted in the badly torn streets of San Francisco. There were no street cars, electric or cable, nor cabs. The homeless survivors either helped in the fire fighting or huddled in parks, vacant lots or other places of safety. Fire companies came on special trains from many miles around to reinforce the gallant San Francisco Fire Department. However, the destruction of the water mains throughout the city was an all but overwhelming handicap.

On the following day (Friday, the 20th) Lipman returned to the ravished city. The once proud and beautiful town that rose from the sea was a terrible sight. Most of the better-built structures had survived the quake but almost none escaped the holocaust of flame that followed it. High above the town the new Fairmont Hotel towered like a death's head; windowless, like eyesockets with no eyes, its white façade blackened. Most buildings met a similar fate; the huge and curious-looking new City Hall, out toward Van Ness, had been sacked by flame and smoke. The vast Palace Hotel still stood, its outer wall intact but within it was a blackened mausoleum, filled with debris and charred wood; its great court was a shambles. The hotel would have to be torn down before it could be rebuilt.

Among the older buildings of San Francisco was the old stone building at Montgomery and California Streets that John Parrott had built with cut stone imported from China; apparently nothing could shake it down. It came through the explosion of 1866 that had killed Wells Fargo's superintendent, Sam Knight, along with ten other men, and it came through the fire of 1906 a frightful wreck, but still intact. When, some twenty years later, it was torn down to make way for a towering skyscraper, the wreckers found it almost impossible to tear it down. Parrott and the Chinese had worked better than they knew.

On the Thursday when it had been impossible to get to San Francisco, Lipman busied himself by forcing his way into the crowded telegraph office in Oakland and sending to New York, London, Paris and other far corners of the world, a single message which read:

WELLS FARGO BANK BUILDING DESTROYED
VAULT INTACT CREDIT UNAFFECTED.

On Friday Lipman went up to the ruins of the bank at Pine and Montgomery. The sight saddened him. There was no getting into the place; faint flames still licked the charred embers. Somewhere, under the rubble, was the fireproof vault. I hope that it really *is* fireproof, was Frederick Lipman's constant thought.

There was no place for him to go. No club. No hotel. Nothing! Finally, he went up to Van Ness Avenue and beyond. E.S. Heller, assistant teller of the bank, had a house at 2020 Jackson Street. His family still has it. The staff of the Wells Fargo-Nevada Bank went there and resumed the bank's business.

It was a crude arrangement, but presently the bank was functioning again. There was no stationery, and stationery is a pretty important thing in the operation of any business. All the big stationery stores downtown had been burned and Lipman and his fellows went out to all the little neighborhood shops and purchased composition books and paper blocks that children used in school. With this paper they proceeded to carry on the affairs of the great Wells Fargo-Nevada National Bank. The staff sat around the dining room table in Mr. Heller's home and there they handled what mail was received and other immediate affairs of the institution which never officially closed its doors.

There were a great number of silver quarters in the vaults of the United States Mint in upper Mission Street that had escaped the holocaust and these quickly became the chief medium of exchange in the city of a half million. The various banks in town joined in effecting payments of every sort and

213

the commercial life of the city was resumed. Mr. Lipman recalls:

"Each bank was in some private house, as we were, and the checks that bank were permitted to handle had to be drawn by that bank or permitted by that bank. Each had a paying teller but he did not pass upon the propriety of the checks. You had to go to the bank to get a certification and present that in order to cash the check."

Seldom has American honor been put to a sterner test. The Wells Fargo-Nevada Bank, as were all other banks in San Francisco, was entirely without books or records of any kind. They could only trust their customers as to the amount of money due each of them. The banks of San Francisco paid out hundreds of thousands of dollars on the strength of their depositors' integrity. In the case of the Wells Fargo-Nevada, Lipman estimates that the total loss, due to possible lapses of memory on the part of its depositors, did not exceed two hundred dollars.

A few days after the fire had subsided, came the question of the vaults and the notes, securities and other valuable and irreplaceable papers. Frederick Lipman and a few others went down to the once-handsome banking house:

"It was the longest trip I ever took in all my life [Lipman said]. It happened that when we put the working books into the vaults on the tragic morning of the 18th, some were just thrown in on the floor.

"The vault which held the books was built on the bank floor, which was just one floor above the basement; built on the framework of the building. The vault did not go down to the ground, so the fire had run along the ceiling of the basement and it just *cooked* the vault. What we found on its floor was but a floury ash. That was the worst part. After that things began to get better. In the first place we found that only one of the great Boston Ledgers was entirely destroyed. And that was but one of fifteen or sixteen. Then we found at the bottom of the vault the lower part of each book—and that gave us the footing on each page. By that footing we had proof of what the limit was on that page. We felt better when we saw that.

214

We now had the footing of each page and the statements, and we proved up within a hundred dollars. It was all a most dramatic affair—and it saved us."

The Union Trust Company owned the fine structure at Market and Montgomery Streets in which the Wells Fargo Bank is located today. It is a fireproof building and withstood the fire very well. The Wells Fargo-Nevada moved down to it from Mr. Heller's house early in May, 1906. The Union Trust retained the Market Street frontage; the Wells Fargo-Nevada took the Montgomery Street side.

That was the arrangement that prevailed throughout the panic times of 1907 and Lipman recalls how busy he was kept, running back and forth to the Clearing House during that panic. Shortly after the Wells Fargo-Nevada National Bank bought the entire building from the Union Trust which then moved farther up Market Street to Grant.

The express department of Wells Fargo was far from asleep during the tragic days of April, 1906. You could trust Andy Christeson for that.

He was the head of Wells Fargo in San Francisco for two busy decades and by 1906, had become manager of the company on the West Coast. He was a powerful man in physique with tremendous energy and he caught hold of the great emergency with all his vigor.

The United States Army, under edict of the President, had placed the stricken city under martial law. Major General Frederick G. Funston of Spanish-American War fame was commanding officer of the entire Western area with his head-quarters at the ancient Presidio in San Francisco. Order was restored at once in the ruins of the city, and the Army helped tens of thousands to get out of their ruined homes and to places of safety. Many left the city entirely; some found haven in the great Golden Gate Park. A few went all the way down to Sutro's Gardens by the historic Cliff House which the earth-quake had tumbled into the ocean.

Emil La Forest was superintendent of the extensive Wells Fargo stables over on Folsom Street where three hundred horses and nearly as many wagons were kept. As the flames approached, La Forest started to move out the horses and movable property. It was a good idea. He had a better one. He phoned Andy Christeson and suggested that the company let people use its wagon equipment to get their household goods out, and to places of safety. Christeson agreed that the idea was a good one and told La Forest to go ahead with it. Within the hour the mobile equipment of Wells Fargo in San Francisco was at work, doing its own large part in the evacuation of the lower section of the city which was in the direct path of the oncoming flames. The fleet of dark blue-and-gold (the familiar livery of Wells, Fargo and Company) wagons and trucks was turned over to volunteer drivers. Heavily laden with beds, mattresses, tables, chairs, trunks and even the inevitable family cat and dog, the wagons evacuated people to safety.

They drove far and wide. They camped out in the vast acres of the Presidio, in equally large Golden Gate Park and far beyond. Wells Fargo equipment carried them. And it is a matter of record that none of their horses and wagons failed to be returned promptly after the crisis was past.

Wells Fargo needed those horses and wagons, for, once the flames were conquered, there was the gigantic task of rebuilding the city that had become an all but impenetrable morass of smoking ruins and tottering walls, rubble and rubbish. Streets were choked and impassable. Railroad tracks were twisted and torn and it was months before the noisy and quaint cable cars operated again up and down the steep hills of the city.

Even before the flames that destroyed the city were entirely extinguished, tents and small wooden shacks bearing the hastily printed names of commercial firms well known in San Francisco were thrown up. Workmen built a temporary St. Francis Hotel in Union Square in front of the ruined remains of the old one. It would be many months before a fine new St. Francis— and a brilliant, new Palace Hotel—and the finally completed Fairmont on Nob Hill—would be ready to dispense magnificent San Francisco hospitality to the world.

Courage ruled San Francisco in those grave days. The disaster—the greatest in the history of any American city—had been relayed in detail by telegraph and cable to the whole world. The reply was instant. Help came from every corner of the country. The Red Cross, with its trained workers and equipment, jumped into the breach. And so did the railroads and steamships. In the evacuation of San Francisco, the Southern Pacific railroad brought out 224,000 evacuees and charged them not one cent. It brought in 1300 carloads of relief supplies— free. The express companies brought in supplies. Food and every other necessary commodity began pouring in from far and near.

At first, the Army, acting under martial law, received and distributed all foodstuffs. Gradually channels of distribution became normal. Wells Fargo, its wagons and horses safely returned, was hard at work. It commandeered a circus tent and set it up at Franklin Street and Golden Gate Avenue, in the district west of Van Ness which had not been scorched by the flames. The familiar sign, Wells, Fargo and Company, Express, appeared on the tent. The company was again doing business.

As soon as lumber could be rushed in, the tent was replaced by a crude, one-story building. Farther down Franklin Street, at Bush, a two-story wooden flat, so characteristic of San Francisco, was taken over as the temporary headquarters of Wells Fargo for the Pacific Coast. Andy Christeson had his office in the front parlor downstairs. Clifford R. Graham was rushed down from the Northern Pacific Express in Portland to set up again the express traffic out of San Francisco. He used the dining room and kitchen on the second floor as his headquarters. He did his job so well that he became the company's general superintendent at San Francisco. Today, Graham is operating vice president of the Railway Express Agency for the entire Eastern part of the United States and he is regarded as one of the outstanding expressmen in the entire country.

The fine six-story building that Wells Fargo had erected at Second and Mission Streets for its general headquarters on the Pacific Coast (Harriman already had moved the president's office and a few other top offices to New York) had remained standing through the earthquake. But, like so many other buildings, it was completely gutted by fire. All the records of the most picturesque of all the oldtime companies were completely destroyed. Another temporary Wells Fargo building was put up next to it. This two-story, wooden structure became the downtown city office of the express. A year later the permanent building was restored with two more floors added. Wells Fargo was prepared to grow greater than ever before. Like the city, it rose from the ashes.

To complete the record of those tragic days, mention should be made of the temporary adjustment of express rates to San Francisco and adjacent points that followed the holocaust. Transportation rates, of the express companies as well as the railroads, had been for years a moot and unhappy question up and down the California coast. But, at the end of April, 1906, they were slashed. Extremely low rates, in many cases hardly more than nominal, were set. The rates were lowered by Wells Fargo to facilitate the restocking of merchants' shelves. Wells Fargo again proved itself a good neighbor.

XVI Wells Fargo—
A Mighty Giant

The Wells, Fargo and Company to which I came as advertising manager in 1912 was, even without the Union Pacific express contract, a business of impressive proportions. The railroads over which it operated by a variety of routes from the Atlantic to the Pacific covered over 80,000 miles. In addition, there were many routes over steamship and electric inter-urban lines. In mileage, Wells Fargo was the greatest in all the land. The company maintained its own extensive services, not only in the United States, Mexico and Cuba, but also in Hawaii, Alaska and the Yukon, the Philippines and China—and it was preparing to invade Europe. Even without the Bank in which it still held a $3,000,000 interest, it was stronger and richer than ever before in all the sixty years of its history. In addition to its paid-in capital of $24,000,000, it had a surplus of nearly $7,000,000, and no debts.

Yet it was not immune to criticism.

There was a growing feeling, gaining ground in the public press and in various legislative halls, against all the express companies, based largely upon their tariffs and charges, and their vast surpluses. The shadow of the oncoming parcel post was drawing closer and closer. The Hearst newspapers and the muckraking magazines were becoming more and more vociferous in their outcries against express charges and prices. "There are just four reasons for the failure to establish the parcel post," shrieked Honest John Wanamaker of Philadelphia in the New York *Herald,* "and they are known as Adams, American, Wells Fargo and United States Express Companies."

In February, 1911, Albert W. Atwood, one of the leading journalists of the period, wrote in the *American Magazine* of Wells Fargo and the other express companies under the title of "The Great Express Monopoly":

> For many years before his death, E. H. Harriman dominated Wells, Fargo & Co., long one of the richest of the express companies, as one man has rarely dominated any business. But the Harriman estate was hardly less ambitious than Harriman himself and early in 1910 the American Express Company acquired a large interest in Wells, Fargo & Co. Originally known as the Holladay Overland Mail & Express Company and capitalized at $5,000,000 in 1872, Wells, Fargo & Co. was one of the few express carriers to take the corporate form. . . .
>
> With $5,000,000 stock, whose original value none living knows, as a starting point, Wells, Fargo & Co. increased its share capital to $6,250,000 in 1878 and to $8,000,000 in 1893. This $3,000,000 of new stock was issued solely for securing a contract from the Southern Pacific Railroad. Part of the stock was sold and the proceeds given to the Southern Pacific; the rest was given directly to the railroad company. . . .
>
> On its $8,000,000 of stock, only a part of which represented

cash or property, Wells, Fargo & Co. was able to pay dividends ranging from 6 to 8 per cent a year from 1872 to 1902, in which latter year 9 per cent was paid. From 1903 to 1905 9 per cent was disbursed and from 1907 to the present time [1911] 10 per cent has been the rate.

Early in 1910 Wells, Fargo & Co. declared a 300 per cent dividend, 200 per cent in new stock and 100 per cent in cash. Upon the increased stock of $24,000,000, which represented no new capital or investment, the company has been paying 10 per cent as before [in 1912 this was reduced to 6 per cent annually], and has not suffered. For the year ended June 30, 1910, more than 20 per cent was earned on $24,000,000 of stock, of which $16,-000,000 was a dividend, $3,000,000 a bonus given to a railroad company [Southern Pacific], and only the remaining $5,000,000 even partly representative of any paid-in capital. At this rate there should be another large extra dividend ready before many years have passed. Finally it may be noted that this glittering business success is based on an investment in real property and equipment of but $6,000,000. Is it in the least surprising that E. H. Harriman should have given his closest personal attention to the affairs of Wells, Fargo & Co.?

Atwood was accurate in his facts and figures. He quoted a statement in *Harper's* Magazine of 1875, which said that the express business had created by then over fifty millionaires in the United States. Atwood closed with the comment that when Wells Fargo had but $4,000,000 invested in the business it took in over $66,000 in cash over the counters each day, so that only two months were required to turn over its entire investment.

Articles like this did not tend to make friends for the express companies. Shippers and even their own employees were beginning to line themselves up against the companies. Lacking any form of public-relations services, they found themselves beleagured and alone. The astuteness of a Robert Young in public relations was not found in Harriman, or in the estate which took over his affairs after his death in 1909. The express companies apparently were deaf to criticism and they were to pay dearly for their failure to understand the changing times.

There had been many shifts in the Wells Fargo organization. As we have seen, one of the first things that Harriman did was to move the general headquarters back to New York. There were anguished cries in San Francisco, for people there had come to regard Wells Fargo as their very own. But Harriman was accustomed to having his way and the protests of the San Franciscans were unheeded. Harriman merely followed the policy that he had used in setting up the general headquarters of his combined Union Pacific and Southern Pacific systems in lower Broadway, New York. He had his own offices near by and he demanded that he be kept in constant touch with his properties.

While Harriman did not like Dudley Evans, he had retained him as president of Wells Fargo. In 1908, Emory A. Stedman, R. A. Wells and Andrew Christeson—all Wells Fargo veterans—were elected vice-presidents and general managers, and were located respectively in Chicago, Kansas City, and San Francisco. Even though Wells Fargo Express was now a nation-wide institution, it still did over thirty-five per cent of its business in the state of California.

Harriman died in September, 1909, and eight months later Dudley Evans died. H. W. De Forest represented the Harriman interests on the Wells Fargo board and on February 3, 1910, Charles A. Peabody, an outstanding Harriman lawyer, also was elected to the board to succeed his deceased client. The distribution of the assets was about to begin.

On the 10th of February, 1910, Wells Fargo declared its fabulous 300 per cent dividend, a total of $24,000,000: $8,000,000 in cash and $16,000,000 in stock, all in one lump sum. I saw, myself, a dividend check of over $2,400,000 made out to a single member of the Harriman family. This was a big melon cutting. In addition, there were three five per cent dividends in that memorable year of 1910. Within twelve months the treasurer's office of Wells, Fargo and Company, Express, had paid out exactly $26,796,740 in dividends. Fortunately for the Harriman estate, there was no income tax in those pleasant days. What a joyous time the United States Internal Revenue offices would have today with such a melon cutting! Yet in 1910, outside of Wall Street there was not much attention paid to it. The Wells Fargo vaults were being emptied and that was all there was to it. It no longer was a fat cat—be quite assured of that.

The period between the passing of Dudley Evans and the coming of the next president was a hectic one for Wells Fargo. For a time there actually was no president in the company, while various interests fought for its control. In this interim a sort of regency had been established for it, and the extremely capable Frederic D. Underwood of the Erie acted as regent; he "doubled in brass." When he had closed his ancient desk in the Erie offices in the old Hudson Terminal Building each afternoon, Underwood would stroll down to the Wells Fargo building at 51 Broadway and work until late at night handling the important matters of the express company. It was an awkward arrangement that could not last. There was a good deal of relief at 51 Broadway when it came to an end. The directors of Wells Fargo finally composed their differences and William Sproule was elected president of the company in November of 1910.

This administration lasted less than a year, in all. Sproule, an able and aggressive man, was needed by the Harriman interests for bigger things. It was a pity that he could not have remained longer with Wells Fargo, but on October 1, 1911, he resigned his post as president and was immediately elected president of the Southern Pacific Company with headquarters in his beloved San Francisco.

The official roster of Wells Fargo at the beginning of 1910 was as follows:

President	William Sproule
Vice President	Emory A. Stedman
Vice President	R. A. Wells
Vice President & Assistant Secretary	Andrew Christeson
Secretary & Treasurer	A. W. Zimmermann
Assistant Treasurer	B. H. River
General Auditor	Richard Burr

The number of express offices at that time was 5,204.

In the midsummer of 1911 long-term contracts were made, enabling Wells Fargo to replace the historic and once-powerful

223

Pacific Express Company on the so-called Gould system: Missouri Pacific-Iron Mountain, Wabash and the Texas & Pacific. Shorter term contracts were made with the Wheeling & Lake Erie, the Ann Arbor, the Missouri, Oklahoma & Gulf, a group of electric interurban lines in Ohio, and a number of minor roads.

All in all it was quite a formidable array of railroads that faced Burns D. Caldwell when he succeeded Sproule as president of Wells, Fargo and Company October 1, 1911, and the end was not yet in sight. Within three years the oldtime United States Express Company would go out of business and Wells Fargo would take over its contracts on the far-reaching Baltimore & Ohio system, thus gaining much needed entrances into Washington, Baltimore and Philadelphia, and on the St. Louis and San Francisco. All of which would bring its mileage, in the United States, to nearly 80,000 miles. The number of offices increased to 9,108. There still was much money in the treasury, and the company, even with its capital stock tripled to $24,-000,000, paid its ten per cent dividends with the greatest of ease. And there still were no debts.

Burns D. Caldwell came to Wells Fargo from the Delaware Lackawanna & Western, where he had been vice-president in charge of traffic. He had been well schooled in St. Louis and elsewhere and had for a time served successfully as head of various traffic bureaus. He was a handsome man with a great shock of snow-white hair, a million-dollar smile and invariably a white carnation in the lapel of his coat. I have never known a kinder, more considerate man. He and his wife lived in East Orange, New Jersey, and twice a day he telephoned to make sure that all was going well with her.

He tackled his new job with gusto. He aimed for the first time in all history to give an express company a thorough-going traffic organization like a railroad. He found Fred S. Holbrook, a former traffic officer of the Vermont Central, and made him vice-president in charge of traffic of Wells Fargo. John W. Newlean, a most able man, was brought in from the Union Pacific and made comptroller, later vice-president. The veteran Charles W. Stockton was general counsel. There was a foreign traffic manager; at the beginning another Wells Fargo veteran, Davis G. Meller, was chosen for this post that was to come to large proportions. Dudley T. Mervine had another newly created position, that of general superintendent of transportation. There was an efficiency manager and an advertising manager, the writer of these pages being chosen for the latter position, and it was by all odds the finest job that he ever was to hold.

Out on the line were two vice-presidents and general managers, the genial Emory A. Stedman at Chicago, and at Second and Mission Streets, San Francisco, Andrew Christeson. Chriseson and Stedman as operating heads divided the whole vast territory of Wells Fargo lines between them. Around them were grouped a remarkable group of general superintendents: F. J. Hickey at New York, Grover B. Simpson and H. B. Calkins at Chicago, Gerrit A. Taft at Houston, Elmer R. Jones at Los Angeles, and Clifford R. Graham at San Francisco.

Under the stimulus of an untiring executive like Burns Caldwell the men he hired produced magnificent results. New methods which had long been needed were introduced. New ways were devised to promote the use of the express.

For instance, down in the swift-growing Southeast, especially, merchants were being told that they need not stock their shelves as extensively as they had in the past. Methods in the women's clothing industry had changed radically. Women, at least the greater number of them, no longer made their own dresses. Ready-mades were now the thing, from one end of the country to the other. Shrewdly the industry developed the new order of things. It flooded the shelves and the hangers of merchants with ready-mades. It all took capital. Even the country storekeeper had to keep a considerable amount of capital tied up in stock, which did not always move too quickly.

Wells Fargo came to the rescue.

It said to the merchant in the little town in Texas, or Colorado or Oregon, far distant from New York, the chief center of the ready-made garment industry:

"You do not need to tie up a lot of capital in stock. You do not need to carry every type of woman's frock in every color and every size. Just a representative lot—one size in one color and one style, another style in a different size and color. Your customer comes in; she knows her size and perhaps she knows the color she wants. She picks out the style. You do not have that particular garment in stock. What of it? That evening you send a telegram to New York and in a matter of hours, the gown, the size, style and color that milady wants is ready for her."

The scheme worked well. The merchant saved money and Wells Fargo profited.

Ever since Dudley T. Mervine had refrigerated that old Santa Fe baggage car for shipping meat, poultry, butter and eggs, seasonal fruits and perishable vegetables, Wells Fargo had enjoyed a swiftly increasing business in foodstuffs. In the top season when these ran high in volume they traveled by refrigerator cars in fast freight service. Wells Fargo was content to take the pre-season and after-season business which demanded the very swiftest service.

The business swept into an astounding volume.

The George Apley sort of Bostonian who sat at his breakfast table and talked proudly of the halibut that came from the Newfoundland banks down to the markets of the Hub little dreamed that the fish on his table probably had been caught five thousand miles from Boston, brought by fast steamer to Seattle or Tacoma, and then sent east by Wells Fargo. Wireless from the steamers still hundreds of miles at sea had informed Wells Fargo men at the ports of entry, and refrigerator cars, all ready and iced, stood at the wharves to take the cargo east.

The kosher markets of the eastern cities demanded absolutely fresh *live* fish from the Great Lakes; Wells Fargo, co-operating with the Baltimore & Ohio, provided cars filled not only with fresh-water tanks but with apparatus for the constant changing of the water. The fish had to be in perfect condition when they arrived from Sandusky.

There were strawberries from Sacramento, asparagus from Jersey, prunes from Santa Clara, garden truck from almost anywhere in the great Central Valley of California; oranges, grapefruit, lemons, dates and figs from Southern California;

226

the rich food outpouring from the lands of the Imperial Valley; from the newly irrigated fields of the Valley of the Sun, in and around Phoenix; the vast productive terrain of the lower valley of the Rio Grande and the rich marginal lands all along the rim of the Gulf of Mexico. There were melons out of Rocky Ford, Colorado, peaches and strawberries from Arkansas, Missouri, Southern Indiana and Ohio, all coming in a mighty volume; oysters and fish from the Chesapeake Bay and Louisiana; apples, grapes and other fruits from Western New York and Northern Ohio. The variety was almost endless. This was the gold of the twentieth century. In swift-moving quantities it ran into millions of dollars of revenue for Wells Fargo.

The company also operated outside the United States.

For a good many years Wells Fargo had been active in Mexico—of which much more in another chapter—and in Cuba.

Alaska was within operating range of the company, and it was not long after the Klondike gold strike in 1896 before Wells Fargo was bringing oranges, bananas, other fresh fruits and vegetables up into Dawson, Nome and St. Michael. It is 2,487 miles from Seattle to St. Michael (Nome is near by) but all through the summer Wells Fargo, using the coastwise steamers, managed to get fruit from Seattle to Kennecott in six days, to Dawson in ten days and to Fairbanks in sixteen.

There was also gold in those hills of Alaska, and gold has always been Wells Fargo's specialty. So when, in December, 1911, the company first began the operation of dog sleds over the tops of the snow drifts of Alaska, it merely was keeping pace with its oldtime traditions. That pioneer run became typical. A 479-mile trek in the dead of winter from Iditarod to Seward was but a part of the day's work for Wells Fargo.

For the initial run two teams of sixteen dogs, under the charge of two noted mushers, Norton and Griffith, were selected. In two Yukon basket sleds rested a shipment of $558,-963.44 in pure gold. A responsibility, but nothing new for Wells Fargo.

This dog-sled shipment of gold was a long trek, a run of

fifty-four days from Itadarod to Seward. On the 6th of February, 1912, they arrived at Seward and their shipment was placed immediately on the S.S. *Alameda* of the Alaska Steamship Company. Five days later it was in a bank in Seattle.

This shipment compared with one made on sleds from Fairbanks to Valdez before the railroad was built from Cordova. Horses were used instead of dogs for a 376-mile run which carried $600,000 gold in eleven days.

Of course there were products other than gold that came out of Alaska in those stirring days. The Wells Fargo superintendent at Seattle, Jim Hill (no relation to the empire builder), was kept pretty busy looking after the shipments to and from the Arctic Circle. He constantly went back and forth to Alaska. It used to fascinate him to see the little kayaks, the comiaks and the bidarkas bring small fortunes in walrus ivory, furs and other trophies of the hunt into the port of St. Michael. The most fearless men sailed all the way from Port Barrow in the Arctic Sea down through the Bering Straits, a passage only possible in the summer months. Sometimes as much as a half a million dollars in furs were brought down in a small vessel, itself hardly worth $10,000.

Across the Pacific Wells Fargo by 1911 was well established with offices in Hawaii, Shanghai and Manila. Also, a start was being made in Europe.

For a long time Wells, Fargo and Company had maintained a commercial office in Threadneedle Street, London, but by 1912 President Caldwell was planning to invade England, France and Germany to provide real competition for the allpowerful and immensely successful American Express Company. Bertram Lord, a former American Express executive in its foreign service, was chosen to inaugurate tourist services in London and Paris. Wells Fargo already had inaugurated a comprehensive system of money orders and travelers' checks of its own, and these were meeting with ready favor.

For the Paris office of Wells Fargo and Company a roomy store was chosen on the Rue Scribe, close to the Opera and a bare stone's throw from the historic Paris quarters of the American Express Company. In the new office in London at

228

10 Charles Street, just off Haymarket, American Express again was a neighbor and friendly competitor. Both of these new offices, handsomely fitted out and staffed for the comfort and the pleasure of the American tourist, were already doing a good business when World War I flamed over Europe.

The coming of World War I in the summer of 1914 found thousands of American tourists stranded in continental Europe and in England frantically trying to get home at once. It so happened that F. S. Holbrook, the traffic vice-president of Wells Fargo, was in Germany at the time. Holbrook watched with dismay the efforts of the tourists to struggle their way back to the United States. In the mad rush luggage was left behind and forgotten. As soon as the worst of the excitement was over, Holbrook took upon himself the task of getting together the abandoned trunks and other luggage. On his own responsibility he caused 400 trunks to be shipped to New York where in the course of time they were claimed and picked up at the Wells Fargo warehouses by the original owners. No charge was made for this service, but Holbrook's quick action brought Wells Fargo many thousands of new and enthusiastic friends.

The new offices in London and in Paris remained open for the duration of the war and were of great service to the men and women of the American armed forces. Offices that had been planned for Hamburg, Berlin, Brussels and Rome never were opened. World War I ended Wells Fargo's European enterprises.

Burns D. Caldwell, sitting in his comfortable office overlooking New York Harbor, swelled with pride at the strides that Wells Fargo had made under his leadership. The company still was making money hand over fist. Despite the vast increase of its capitalization it continued to pay its six per cent dividends each year.* More important was the rise in Wells Fargo prestige. The old company was making a world-wide reputation for efficient and friendly service.

* On December 28, 1916 Wells Fargo declared a dividend of 33⅓% on $24,-000,000, payable January 20, 1917.

But there were those who said that express as a business was dying, that there soon would be a newcomer in the field of handling packages large and small in the United States that would put the old line companies completely out of business.

Although Caldwell refused to accept defeat, he watched nervously as the United States Post Office Department established a parcel-post system just prior to the beginning of World War I. The government had support behind it from many quarters. The old line express companies had set themselves firmly against the parcel post, already well-established and well-liked in Great Britain and other European nations. [We have already seen what John Wanamaker had to say about the parcel post.] In the period of changing times the advantage to the whole people of the parcel post was recognized and soon it was put into being.

Its immediate effect on the express companies was a reduction of their rates for handling small packages. The long-range effects are not so easily stated, but it is certainly true that the parcel post has been doing pretty well ever since its inception; and so has the express.

The *Wells Fargo Messenger,* the company paper of which I was the editor, carried an editorial on the question of the parcel post in February, 1913, which well reveals the attitude of Wells Fargo to their new competitor:

> The new-born year brought to the express a competitor worthy of its mettle—the new parcel post. This country has had a parcel post for many years. The new plan is, however, a radical enlargement of the old, both in raising the weight limit of packages from four to eleven pounds, in establishing a lower scale of rates through a zone system and requiring the issue of a special series of stamps. A great many Wells Fargo men have hardly known just how to view this new competitor. There should be no hesitancy as to their attitude. They should treat this newcomer as worthy of respect, realizing that he represents governmental policy and is an experiment of national interest. And they should consider that the express, vital to the commercial life of the nation, gains growth and strength not by opposing competition, but by rendering a service which best meets public necessity and convenience.

This editorial, which was widely circulated, brought many expressions of approval.

Compared with the express, the parcel-post business was easy to handle. There was no pick-up service and, save in the case of registered packages, for which a special charge was made, no receipts were issued. Throughout the years the express had worked up a rather complicated and costly system under which a receipt, which was practically a waybill, was issued for every single package that it accepted for transport. A package going across the continent might easily traverse a half dozen different railroads. That meant that each of the six railroads was entitled to a proportion of the charges. To figure out the earnings of all the packages of all the railroads on, say, 100,000 waybills, was no small bookkeeping job. When William Sproule transferred the accounting department of Wells Fargo from New York to Chicago in 1911, it meant the removal of 1100 employees with their families and their personal effects, all at the expense of the company.

As time went on, the tariff sheets of the express companies had become increasingly difficult and complicated. They were in effect a vast structure with many ramifications to meet a variety of emergencies. The final result was a patched-up structure with very little order or consistency.

At the beginning of the second decade of this century there sat on the all-powerful Interstate Commerce Commission in Washington a man of unusual brilliancy and ability, Franklin K. Lane. Later Woodrow Wilson chose Lane as his Secretary of the Interior, in which capacity he added to his record of public service.

In the course of his thorough investigations of the entire transport picture of the United States, Lane had come across the ancient tariff structures of the expresses. He was horrified by their confusion and their lack of efficiency. He sought to create a new schedule of equitable express rates, understandable to the average user.

After many months of patient work he evolved a tariff sheet, essentially simple in its working. Lane divided the entire United States into several thousand blocks or zones uniform in size. All express rates were divided into two classifications and the amount of the charge on any package depended on the classification and the number of blocks crossed. There was some slight variation in the rate scale per block in various portions of the country but in general the new scales reduced express rates on an average of fifteen per cent. The express executives did not particularly resent that, for rates on the new parcel post had been put so far below those of the express that they felt there must be some reduction to meet the new governmental competition. Even so there was opposition in some quarters.

A few of us in Wells Fargo saw the folly of obstruction. I went to the president of the company, although it really was none of my business, and begged him to accept the Lane plan as graciously as possible.

"Don't you see," I told Mr. Caldwell, "that those Washington boys have you licked, no matter which way you turn? If you find definitely that you cannot beat a man, why oppose him needlessly? Let Wells Fargo refuse to be bogged down by the fears and the silly traditions of its fellows in the business; let it be the first to accept the new order of things, so much, much better than the old, and accept it graciously."

He took my advice. I went down to Washington, saw Lane, and told him that Wells Fargo felt that he had done a fine job and that the company would go along with the new plan. Lane turned to me and said:

"Fine, that sounds like the old Wells Fargo. There's plenty of life in the old fellow yet. . . ."

And so there was. The new plan went into effect early in 1914, and within the year there was hardly an expressman the whole land over who was not blessing it.

There was indeed a new order of things.

In midsummer of 1914 came the spark that set half the world afire and Wells Fargo and its fellows were in for it. A tremendous burden was placed on the express. Shipments for the armed services and for civilians increased by leaps and bounds. Men worked night and day. The volume of traffic rose to astounding proportions as trains across the land carried the goods of war.

232

Number Nine went out of the ancient Erie terminal at Jersey City each night freight-laden to the roofs. Always a pet of Wells Fargo, Number Nine was the fastest train on the Erie, just as the Fargo Fast was the fastest train on the Santa Fe. Her departure from the Jersey City Pier each week-day evening was something of an event.

After the close of the business day, the 400 wagons of the Wells Fargo fleet in New York and Brooklyn were ferried to Jersey City. All of the packages from these hundreds of wagons were dumped on a great revolving platform at the Wells Fargo pier in Jersey City and sorted for their hundreds and thousands of destinations.

At 7:40 each evening the sorting was over. Eight o'clock was Nine's rigid departure time. Ten minutes before that hour its various through cars were locked and sealed: the Texas car, the St. Paul, the Los Angeles, the "San Fran," the "K.C.," the Wisconsin, the Buffalo, and still others. Through the still open door of the forward car (the "messenger car"), the messenger and his helper could be seen buckling on their holsters. No monkey business for a train with perhaps a million dollars of valuable freight aboard.

At just 8:00 P.M. the last door slammed shut and was locked. The depot agent raised his hand and the Wells Fargo Pony Express of the twentieth century was off for Chicago. It was always a thrill just seeing Number Nine make its evening "depart."

Three thousand miles across the continent in San Francisco veteran city agents, Tol Elliott and Bill Kiefer, daily prepared their eastbound express for the Overland at the Wells Fargo pier close to the Ferry House. All the rest of the way up and down the West Coast and far inland Wells Fargo would be setting out on its nightly treks to Chicago and the Atlantic seaboard. War and its necessities also but a part of the day's work, of the unending work of the express.

On a pleasant day in June, 1918, we were told that Wells, Fargo and Company was going out of business forever, on the final day of that very month. The three great operating companies of the express in the United States: Adams (which in-

233

cluded the Southern), the American, and Wells, Fargo and Company were to be merged into a single agency to be called the American Railway Express.

It was a bitter pill to Wells Fargo men. That the name of their disliked competitor should be chosen, and that of their own beloved company ruthlessly thrust aside, was bad enough. They were all promised jobs with the new company, but some of them refused to accept them. They preferred to remain Wells Fargo men in spirit if not in fact, until the end of their days.

As will be recalled, W. G. McAdoo was Secretary of the Treasury under President Woodrow Wilson, and later director-general of the United States Railroad Administration. The suggestion was made that the three big express companies be merged "in the interests of winning the war."

McAdoo is credited (or discredited) with having been the active force behind the idea. It was being said freely in Washington that he was using the proposed express merger for his own political advancement. The express business in the United States at that time was absolutely non-union. The companies had not been too progressive in their personal relationships with the rank and file of their employees. It was not until 1915 that the highly prosperous Wells Fargo came forth with a comprehensive, modern and extensive pension and benefit plan for its workers. The pay in the express as compared with other businesses of a like nature was not high. Yet the conditions of general employment were such in those days that Wells Fargo men not only worked hard, but generally retained a loyalty for the old company that was translated into splendid morale.

But McAdoo, so it was said, subtly spread the idea of unionism among the rank and file of all expressmen. Come together into one company, was what he said in effect, and I will see to it that you get the protection of the union system.

Whoever was responsible, the merger was made. Adams, American and Wells Fargo merged to form the new American Railway Express, to cover with one exception the entire railroad map of the United States.

That one exception was the important Southern Railway,

234

whose brilliant president, Fairfax Harrison, did his own thinking and went his own way. Soon after the beginning of World War I he had quarreled with the White House and had withdrawn into his shell. He refused to accept the ill-considered dictum of the express merger. For the Southern, Harrison created the independent Southeastern Express, which covered effectively the entire southeastern part of the United States and which remained in business until after Harrison's death when it finally was merged with the American Railway Express.

The details of the merger were engineered by the extremely capable George C. Taylor, who, in 1914, had succeeded the aged James C. Fargo as president of the powerful American Express Company. He became president of the new American Railway Express. Burns D. Caldwell was made chairman of the board of the new company. The rest of the executive offices were parcelled out among the executives of the three companies.

There was much bitterness. Once the new combination had been made, the Wells Fargo signs and insignia were torn down all the way across the land to be replaced immediately by the signs and insignia of the American Railway Express. Wells Fargo disappeared from the telephone listings everywhere; the name was apparently never even to be whispered. When I went out to San Francisco in 1922, one of my old Wells Fargo pals there caught me by the sleeve and pointed to the roof of the handsome old Wells Fargo building at Second and Mission. There, outlined against the sky, stood a modest sign reading, "Wells, Fargo & Co., Express."

"They haven't discovered it as yet," Bill Kiefer whispered to me. "We haven't told them and they are not smart enough to find it. When they do, it will come down."

Bill Kiefer was right. When it was discovered, the sign was torn down. Only the raised lettering in the great lintel stone over the door, "Wells, Fargo & Co., Express Building," remained. That lintel was a sort of a shrine to good Wells Fargo men. They would look at it, shake their heads sadly, and go away, thinking of the company that was.

After the merger, Wells, Fargo and Company retained its corporate existence and some of its assets. It received $10,075,400 in stock of the American Railway Express, a part of which was offset by its contribution of automobiles, horses, wagons, office equipment, etc. It still had its precious twenty-thousand shares in the rich Wells Fargo-Nevada Bank in San Francisco. It also had its interests in Mexico and in Cuba, but it was not an encouraging picture. One of the finest trade names in all America had been thrown into the discard—and with it the faith, loyalty and ambition of 25,000 men and women employees.

The other companies adjusted themselves to the change. Long since the American Express had built up a magnificent overseas organization. What Thomas Cook & Sons was to the Britisher away from his native land, the American Express Company had become to the traveling American. It was his banker, his forwarding agent, his post office, his travel agent. It had built up for itself a highly profitable traffic in travelers checks, money orders and the like.

All this business it chose to retain as it continued its operations with headquarters in its great building in lower Broadway, New York. The Adams Express Company decided to remain in business as an investment company, and as such it has been successful. Only Wells Fargo chose to give up the ghost. It sold its 20,000 shares of Wells Fargo-Nevada stock. Its own shares, which had never dropped below the par of $100 a share, were reduced through distribution to stockholders to a par value of $1.00 per share. The New York Stock Exchange removed the name from its listings, where it had been for so many years.

A few Wells Fargo men did not go to the American Railway Express. One of these was Davis G. Meller, expert in foreign affairs as well as in the food-handling ends of Wells Fargo's vast activities, who replaced Burns D. Caldwell as president of the corporate Wells, Fargo and Company. Another was Elmer R. Jones of whom again more in a moment. Also remaining in the Wells Fargo family were James O. Ellis, who joined the organization in 1903 and is Vice-President of the company and its subsidiaries, and the editor of the *Wells Fargo Messenger*. In its final issue (June, 1918) I wrote this editorial:

FAREWELL

In the transfer by Wells Fargo of its domestic express operations to a new company which is to handle the express business of the country under a contract with its Director-General of Railroads, the nation loses an institution, hardly less distinctive than the great Capitol down at Washington. For sixty-five long years our company has kept the faith. Its task has been trust, and no man has ever trusted it in vain. From the stirring California days in which it was born down to the stirring times in which we move this day and hour, Wells Fargo has been synonymous with honor and energy and ability.

Wells Fargo men!

What a regiment they have made! And before this company of the present, the serried ranks of those who are dead and gone—back, back to the generation of the pioneers. What a mighty army, moving forward in eternal step and cadence! And above the shuffling of the feet, the clatter of the lumbering stages and the crack of a whip in the silence, the calls of the dust-enshrouded boys who raced their ponies across the plains, the echoes of the first locomotives, the splash of the sea against the bows of swift ships bearing precious burden to and from San Francisco—and the honorable young firm of Wells Fargo & Company.

Wells Fargo men! And steadily marching feet—in perfect time and good order. In good order Wells Fargo marched in —back in those stirring days of 1852—and in good order Wells Fargo marches out—in these stirring days of this year of grace, 1918. Marching out of an unsullied page of American history and into a new and glorious career of service to our country in its hour of greatest need.

We live in a material age. Around us boil and seethe the cauldrons of material things. And in the confusion it is easy to forget. But some of us are not going to forget—this world or the next. In the quiet moments that are given to every man for reflection and retrospection we are going to remember the days of our past—the days and months and years that come to the mind when the lips breathe those ardent blessed words— *Wells Fargo.*

237

A great many people wrote me because of that editorial. They saw, as I did, the supreme tragedy of the passing of Wells, Fargo and Company, Express.

It was pathetic to see the way older Wells Fargo men clung to the ancient institutions. In every possible way they sought to keep the company alive in their hearts. They retained the honorable name in the telephone directories of the western cities in which it had operated. They behaved as a beleaguered people. Wells Fargo could not die easily. Men wondered why it should die at all. It was quite beyond their comprehension.

XVII Elmer Jones— Modern Expressman

Wells Fargo did not die. Elmer Jones didn't let it.

There was, of course, the bank in San Francisco, which long ago passed out of the hands of the parent company and perpetuated the ancient name in an institution vitally associated with the financial and commercial life of the whole Pacific coast. But more important to Jones was the Mexican Wells Fargo.

He saw an opportunity and he grasped it. He gathered together some of his close associates among the officers of the

239

old Wells Fargo and proposed that they buy the Mexican company and the Cuban interests of Wells, Fargo and Co. George C. Taylor, who was president of the American Express Company, and who was to become president of the new American Railway Express, gave his full approval to the idea. Thus the good name and reputation of Wells, Fargo as a common carrier was to go on. At one time it was suggested that the Mexican and Cuban business be turned over to the new American Railway Express, but that suggestion was almost immediately rejected. The name "American" still was none too popular in Mexico, while that of Wells Fargo had long since attained very great popularity.

So, in 1919, Elmer Jones, as an individual, with the American Express Company, bought the Wells, Fargo and Company Express of Mexico and Wells, Fargo and Company in Cuba for $640,000. In 1924, Jones and the American Express bought Wells, Fargo and Company in the United States from the Harriman estate with the agreement that other stockholders who cared to sell their stock could do so at the same price. Eighty per cent of the remaining stockholders accepted the offer.

After careful study and with full approval of George C. Taylor and Frederic P. Small of the American Express, Jones made the arrangements with Charles A. Peabody and Robert W. De Forest, executors of the Harriman estate.

Under the new ownership the shares of the original Wells, Fargo and Company acquired, were divided, 51 per cent to the American Express Company and 49 per cent to a group consisting of officials of American Express Company and Wells Fargo & Company, headed by Mr. Jones. Headquarters were established at 65 Broadway, New York, where they have since remained and where the parent company operates under the Colorado charter of Wells, Fargo and Company. In this way the legal as well as the sentimental continuation of the original company was brought about. While it was deprived of its package express service upon the railroads of the United States by the merger, it had plenty to do.

Wells Fargo had been in Mexico since the very beginnings

of the company. I very well recall going into the Acapulco office in 1940. The old office there had been opened in 1852 and it had changed but little since then (a few years ago the old building was torn down and Wells, Fargo and Company moved into modern quarters in the swiftly growing resort town). The old office had great charm. I recall the large mechanical fans up against the high beamed ceiling (in the Far East they call them *punkahs*) moving listlessly backward and forward but seemingly forever. It was a fascinating old place: in ninety years it was practically unchanged, typical of a land which has never lost its old Spanish colonial charm.

In Wells Fargo's earliest years it had operated on the lines of the Wilcox and Pacific Mail Steamship Companies between Panama City and San Francisco: only the Wilcox ships operated into the Mexican ports of Guaymas, Mazatlan, Acapulco and Salina Cruz. From the outset Wells Fargo opened offices in each of these four ports on the West Coast of Mexico; it is still doing business in all of them.

In the early 'seventies British capital completed the stoutly built Mexican Railway from Vera Cruz on the Gulf side up to Mexico City, one of the most remarkable pieces of railroad construction in the entire world, and in 1880 Wells Fargo moved on it into the Mexican capital over which they operated until 1943 when service was stopped by mutual consent. The road was acquired by the Mexican Government in 1948. The express company also operated on the Mexican Central that had come south to the capital from El Paso.

The company opened offices on the Calle Donceles, in the stone palace built by the Spanish Duke of Albuquerque. It still stands in the very heart of Mexico City, although Wells, Fargo and Company is no longer quartered in it. This old palace is even today regarded as one of the architectural gems of this continent.

About fifty years ago the ambitious Southern Pacific system decided that the time had arrived for it to thrust a long arm down into Mexico. Down the West Coast of Mexico, from Nogales, Arizona, on the border to Tepic, more than 700 miles to the south, it built a fine modern railroad, the Sud Pacifico de

241

Mexico. Threading Hermosillo, Guaymas and Mazatlan, it opened up the magnificently rich states of Sonora and Sinaloa to development; it finally reached Guadalajara, the important capital of the province of Jalisco, where connection was made with the Mexican National Railways leading to Mexico City and most of the other important cities of the country.

Colonel Epes Randolph, of Virginia, was the master-mind of this stirring project. In his day Randolph was considered one of the outstanding railroaders of the North American continent. He was the engineering genius who threw the first single-span railroad bridge across the Ohio at Cincinnati. At the beginning of the century, when the Colorado River went on rampage, Randolph succeeded in doing the impossible, in damming the onrush of waters and so saving millions of dollars in valuable Southern California property. E. H. Harriman thanked him warmly for his feat.

If Epes Randolph had been possessed of even ordinary good health, he would have gone even farther as a railroad builder, but he was a consumptive and was forced to live in the thin, dry, sunshiny air of southern Arizona. When he accomplished the dramatic feat of damming the runaway Colorado River by dumping whole trainloads of material, cars and all, into the river, he commanded the job from a litter in his car, the Pocahantas, named after his well-known ancestor. The Pocahantas was his home on wheels. When Harriman finally recognized his genius, he made him president of the Sud Pacifico de Mexico and Randolph, terribly sick man that he was, went right ahead and built the road. I used to see him sometimes in his old upstairs office in Tucson; a mere wraith of a handsome man, sitting close to an ancient wood stove, a shawl gathered around his thin shoulders, a man dying by inches, living and still realizing his magnificent dreams.

Epes Randolph lived long enough to see the road built through to Tepic. There it halted for a long time. Between Tepic and the golden city of Guadalajara, just a little way to the east, were ninety miles of high mountains with deep gullies or *barrancas* between them—one of the toughest construction problems that ever confronted any railroad builder.

242

In 1925 Randolph was dead and Harvey Titcomb was president of the Sud Pacifico de Mexico. Titcomb, long schooled as an engineer on the Southern Pacific, accomplished the seemingly impossible. He built the railroad straight across the *barrancas*, and it was a good railroad every foot of the way. No matter if there were thirty-five tunnels in the ninety miles of its course, between them fills and trestles of tremendous height.

It came as a matter of course that Wells Fargo operated the express on the Sud Pacifico de Mexico. It had operated on the Southern Pacific ever since the days of Lloyd Tevis when the parent road had first been completed. Wells Fargo operated on the Sud Pacifico de Mexico from Nogales to Guadalajara until December of 1944, when the express function was taken over by an administrator appointed by the Mexican Government as the result of a strike for higher wages. The case was still pending at the time of going to press.

When I first met Elmer Jones in 1911 he was a tall, lean, positive individual, retaining all the vigor of his youth. He looked more like a New Yorker than the native Missourian that he is. As a matter of fact, among his forbears was the Culpeper family of Virginia whose ancient courthouse in the old Dominion still bears the family name. There was also much Kentucky blood in his veins. In 1911, Elmer R. Jones was general superintendent of Wells Fargo at Los Angeles. Already he had made many friends, for himself and the company.

Wells, Fargo and Company was more than a mere employer to Elmer Jones; it was, and still is, his life. For it he was prepared to die if necessary, and once or twice he nearly did. There was no crusader for any cause more ardent, more loyal than Elmer Jones.

As a small boy in Webb City, Missouri, he had sold the *Kansas City Star,* down at the railroad station evenings. He watched the little Missouri Pacific trains come and go, and then and there transportation caught his imagination. At fourteen he worked as helper for the depot agent at Webb City. The agent, Grant Wilbur, handled the express for the town. In those days it was the Pacific Express, and presently Elmer Jones was in the express business in one of its lowlier roles, handling freight. It was a rough job, and not suitable for a weakling. But Elmer never was a weakling.

He didn't wrestle with heavy boxes of the express for long. He had not nearly enough education, and he was determined to get more, and yet college seemed beyond his reach until one day in 1890 when the state of Missouri announced a competition for scholarships for a two-year course at the University of Missouri that would specialize in military training. He won a military scholarship hands down, and at once headed for the state university.

General Enoch Crowder, who afterwards was to come to fame as the general in charge of the draft during World War I, and who became our Ambassador to Cuba, was in charge of the students' military regiment at the University of Missouri. West Point trained, he was a martinet and a soldier, and the training that he gave the boys was most thorough. Afterwards he was succeeded by Captain Beaumont B. Buck, also a West Point man, and also destined to become a general of distinction in the United States Army.

Elmer Jones knew Buck better than Crowder, although he retained his friendship with both these men for many years. He showed an aptitude for military work and sports and to his two years at the university he attributes the strength and good health that have been his all his life. But it was the military training that appealed to him most. With the student regiment he traveled the entire state. The drill that the boys put on one autumn at the historic old Fair Grounds at St. Louis was a memorable one.

Young Jones wished he could have had two additional years at the University of Missouri, but he could not afford it. He had to get back to work. He took courses in English and oratory in the Cumnocks School of Northwestern University at Evanston. Later in his life he took a four-year law course at the University of Southern California, going to class at night after his regular work was done, and studying at every possible moment in the long day that began for him promptly at six o'clock in the morning. He was graduated with honors from U.S.C.

244

in 1914 and soon after he was admitted to the California bar. Jones's thirst for education has never ceased.

When he went his rounds of the express—as messenger and as general superintendent—and later as assistant general manager—he carried his books with him and was forever at them. By nature an inveterate reader, and a deep thinker, he always has found his best love in books of substantial character. His special tastes are in law, the Bible, Shakespeare and the standard classics.

In October, 1893, when he was nineteen years old, Jones became a full-fledged express agent at Webb City, Missouri. He spent two years there and two years at the much larger town of Pittsburgh, Kansas. Then Superintendent D. T. Mervine called him up to Kansas City. A short term as a messenger out of Kansas City, a boyhood ambition, was finally realized and then Jones was made a route agent, one of the most responsible jobs of the express. The route agent is a sort of traveling superintendent who sees that the work of the men out on the road is kept right up to snuff.

It so happened that when Superintendent Mervine and local manager R. A. Wells summoned Elmer Jones to give him the responsible route agent's job, the distinguished president of Wells Fargo, John J. Valentine, happened to arrive in Kansas City. He beamed approvingly upon the newest route agent of Wells Fargo, shook hands with him warmly, and said:

"I see that you are an ambitious fellow, Elmer. You keep right at it and some day, who knows, you may be president of Wells, Fargo and Company."

Which classifies John J. Valentine as a good deal of a prophet.

Route Agent Jones worked first out of Joplin and then out of Hutchinson, then through Southern Kansas, all the while developing new business for the company. In 1906, he went to Los Angeles, always one of the key points in Wells Fargo territory, as assistant general agent. Three years later he first became identified with Wells Fargo activities in Mexico. And from July, 1909, to the present he has been associated with Mexican transportation. Early in 1912 Jones was sent to the Argentine and arranged contracts with the British railroads there, but before operations could begin, the war clouds of World War I prevented the extension of Wells Fargo into South America.

In 1912, Jones became general superintendent at Los Angeles and a little over a year later he was assistant general manager and assistant to the vice-president and general manager, Andy Christeson, up at San Francisco. He was succeeded at Los Angeles by L. O. Head, who recently retired as President of the Railway Express Agency. Jones's progress was steady. In 1916, he was appointed assistant to the president, Burns D. Caldwell, of the parent Wells, Fargo and Company in New York. He remained in that post until the express activities of Wells Fargo in the United States were absorbed by the war-born American Railway Express.

Jones, as we have seen, came to Mexico in 1909. He had gone there against his will because he had planned to leave the company to establish a law practice. However, his knowledge of Spanish as well as his broad experience in all branches of the express business, made him immediately invaluable to Wells Fargo's Mexican business.

When Jones first went to Mexico, L. L. Ward, a veteran Wells Fargo man who had been with the company in Mexico City for a number of years, was president of the Mexican organization. Unfortunately Ward was not destined to hold the post many months. He fell seriously ill, went to Rochester, Minnesota, for a major operation, and died there.

He was succeeded by Elmer R. Jones, in 1910. Jones has been president of Wells, Fargo and Company, Express, S.A., ever since.

When Jones went to Mexico City in 1909 he rented an apartment near the castle of Chapultepec, took a corner office on the upper floor of the fine old house of the Duke of Albuquerque and set to work further to develop Wells Fargo's Mexican business, which at that time operated not only on the lines of the British-owned Mexican Railway but on those of the Mexican National Railway system and some smaller roads.

Those were the final days of President Diaz' regime. Mexico City at the time of Jones's arrival was a pleasant, sleepy national

246

capital, situated on a level plain 7,300 feet above the sea, and cupped in by magnificent mountains, forever snow-capped, chief of all Iztacchiuatl, "The sleeping woman" and Popocatepetl.

With the Mexican Revolution of 1910 Diaz and the things for which he stood collapsed. Wells Fargo held firm, and Elmer Jones remained on the scene. At the risk of his life he went everywhere in war-torn Mexico, seeing to it that the many interests of Wells, Fargo and Company were protected.

Once in the days when Pancho Villa ruled the *mesas,* Elmer Jones was traveling with two or three companions on horseback across the northern state of Durango. They suddenly came face to face with a little group of men also mounted. Hardlooking customers, these were obviously guerrillas. They gave no pleasant salute, but at once raised their guns.

"Viva Villa?" they queried. "Viva Estados Unidos?"

Elmer Jones thought quickly. It was no moment for the wrong answer. He smiled at the guerrillas.

"Viva Wells Fargo," was his instant reply.

They dropped their guns and came forward, smiling, to shake hands with the gringos. Once again Wells Fargo had averted a crisis.

But the situation in Mexico grew no better. The revolution became a series of revolutions. President followed president: Madero, Huerta, Villa, Obregon, Calles and others, an all-but-endless succession of names. At one time there were no fewer than three armies in and around the capital: Huerta, who was in the capital; Pancho Villa, who was battling to get in from the north; and Guitterez, who finally joined forces with Villa. In all this hubbub and confusion Wells Fargo kept on the job and Jones found it necessary to spend more and more time in Mexico City.

Despite the revolution, the company continued to make money, but what to do with the cash, gold and silver bullion became the problem in these constantly recurring crises. Jones looked around headquarters in the ancient palace of the Duke of Albuquerque. In the second, or inner, patio, he found what he thought would be a safe resting place for the company's

247

treasure. He lifted the paving stones, dug a deep hole, and in it placed the safes with gold, silver, bank-notes and valuable papers of all kinds, and then replaced the paving stones.

At one time in 1913 during the Huerta regime he had buried $756,000 of company funds under the pavement. He did the job himself, with the aid of two or three trusted assistants. Even so word leaked out. A day or two later he was summoned to the president's office in the National Palace. The *Presidente* smiled and said that the government was to issue bonds the following day and that he should like Wells Fargo to subscribe for $756,000 of the $13,000,000 issue. Jones smiled too. He bought the bonds; they were good, and the company has them to this day.

Always in those days it was a struggle to retain the profits that were made. Elmer Jones recalls the time when two baggage cars carrying almost a million dollars worth of silver bars were being rushed on the railroad to Vera Cruz, in those days generally under the protection of American warships.

The two baggage cars, with their silver freight, did not get through to Vera Cruz. Word came finally that there had been a wreck down the line in a rough and unpopulated region of the country; just one of those nasty wrecks that Mexican railways always seemed to be having. At the time Wells Fargo had its own good secret service man in Mexico, Captain Giacamino Canotti, a former officer of the Italian Army, who in the Diaz days also had been a captain in the Mexican forces. Canotti went to work on the case. He scoured the entire line and finally reported to Elmer Jones that he had located the two cars. They had been wrecked, surely enough, and thrown from the tracks halfway down the line. And they were empty.

At the time General Emiliano Zapata was in command of the armies in that part of Mexico. Jones found Zapata seated before a campfire wrapped in an Indian *zarape* (blanket) near the little San Lazare station on the outskirts of the capital where the railroad had its terminal. Zapata was cordial, and said that he would help *el presidente* of Wells Fargo. He put a whole company of troops at Canotti's disposal and they found all the missing bars; all save two which later were found under

248

the body of a dead burro upon a mountainside not far from the peak of Orizaba.

One thing remained. There had been a single bar of pure gold, valued at about $45,000, American money. To find that single missing nugget in a land as vast and with as many unpopulated areas as Mexico was no easy task. But Jones and George A. O'Brien of Wells Fargo and Canotti went at it. Eventually they unearthed it in an hacienda shed near San Luis Potosi, 300 miles north of Mexico City. Gradually the men who had stolen the bullion were apprehended and punished.

Wells Fargo never forgets!

The episode that Elmer Jones most clearly recalls today is the one that nearly cost him his life. It was in December, 1914, when Pancho Villa was rapidly closing in on the capital. Villa was in his headquarters in a private car on a railroad siding at Tacuba about fifteen miles out of the city and had telegraphed the president of Wells Fargo that he wished to see him. Jones, with O'Brien, went out to Tacuba at once.

Villa received the two Wells Fargo officers graciously. He smiled and reminded Senor Jones that he, too, had once worked for Wells Fargo. He had been a muleteer for the company, bringing the silver down out of the mines back of Durango. He smiled again. It occurred to him, he said, that it was high time that Wells Fargo operated on the railroads in the northern states of the republic that he had—to use a pleasant word— taken over. He repeated the suggestion.

Jones again did some quick thinking. He said that he would have to consult with the directors of the company in Mexico City. Villa dismissed the two Wells Fargo men, saying that he would see them again in three days. A hurried meeting of the Wells Fargo directors was called. The directors—all save Jones —were against the Villa suggestion. Villa had not yet entered the city which was still occupied by Vittoria Huerta. They did not see how Wells Fargo could work for two opposing governments at the same time.

Jones and O'Brien returned to General Villa—Jones says frankly that he was now in great fear—and reported that Wells

249

Fargo could not operate over the railway lines that had been seized by Villa in the north.

Pancho Villa was enraged. He turned to the aide near by and commanded:

"Call the guard."

Elmer Jones turned to O'Brien and said in English: "They'll shoot us, George!"

Villa ignored that remark. He spoke no English. He turned to Jones and roared:

"You have bought Huerta's bonds. The bankers have bought Huerta's bonds. I am going to shoot all of you."

"I told you so," said Jones to O'Brien, again in English.

Villa's rage now knew no bounds. His face grew purple. He stamped his feet on the floor. In Spanish he shouted:

"No English spoken in this car. You men are to be shot. Call the guard."

Six rough soldiers strode into the car. Elmer Jones could feel his heart pound. George O'Brien was having none too happy a time of it.

Each man was seized by three soldiers, taken to another car and placed at opposite ends of it. No communication was permitted between them. Some time in the course of the evening the car began to move. Blinds were closely drawn and it would have meant death to touch them. But the two Wells Fargo men knew the territory pretty well, and after the car had stopped on the very outskirts of the city and six more prisoners placed inside, it was shunted over to the Cuernavaca line, the steep little railroad that leads up past the chief cemetery of the city.

The chief cemetery! The Dolores Cemetery! That was an appropriate place for executions. Saved a lot of work with hearses or camions.

One by one the six poor devils, accused of one crime or another—most of them were counterfeiters—were taken out of the car. Jones and O'Brien counted six shots and awaited their turns.

For some reason they were not taken out. Toward dawn they were hauled right into Mexico City. The car came to a halt in the yard of the old Buena Vista station: Jones and O'Brien were taken to a near-by barracks where they were locked up in the feed room for the burros and horses. And for long hours they wondered what their fate would be.

In the meantime, Leon J. Canova, President Wilson's personal representative, telegraphed to the President that Jones and O'Brien of Wells Fargo had been executed. Jones's aged mother in Hollywood read the news in the morning paper and collapsed. In Washington Wilson demanded that the State Department immediately investigate the entire affair.

In Mexico City there was much indignation. Finally, during the night, the second day after their disappearance, Jones and O'Brien were traced to the feed room of the barracks.

Canova found genial Mexican Colonel Fierro who was giving an all-night party for a group of his women friends. The colonel was gay and in his cups when Canova came to him to plead for the release of Villa's prisoners.

To Canova's amazement Fierro issued a pass allowing him to pick up the prisoners on the condition that he would guarantee their delivery to the Minister of War in the morning. Canova with Burton Wilson, an American lawyer and friend of Jones, rushed to the Buena Vista station and, with the pass, had Jones and O'Brien released. The two men with Canova went up to their own apartment near the castle, bathed, had a good sleep and a good breakfast, and then went to the Ministry of War.

They were accompanied to the Mexican Minister of War by Canova. The Minister, Carlos Robles, also a former Wells Fargo employee, had been cashier for the company up at Chihuahua. But he was a Villa man and he was afraid to go against the orders of his chief. For a time he stuck it out. Then argument and friendship had their way and Minister Robles handed Jones a *salvoconducto* (a safe conduct) to leave the country at once. Tragedy, close at hand, had been averted. Jones and O'Brien took the evening train for El Paso. Nothing ever looked better to the two men than the International Bridge across which their train finally rolled after its slow progress from Ciudad Juarez to El Paso, Texas.

Elmer Jones believes to this day that he and O'Brien owe

251

their lives to an unknown French girl. Villa, on the evening that the two men were to be executed, had gone to a small restaurant where he saw a charming and beautiful French girl working as a cashier.

Villa, being what he was, insisted that the girl leave the restaurant with him. She did, and Villa promptly forgot all about his two prisoners whose execution awaited his final orders.

Those strenuous days in Mexico are over now. Gradually the country regained balance.

The tourist business, next to the express itself, has remained Elmer Jones's greatest love. He has always sought new opportunities for its expansion. Back in 1925 one of the best of them came to his far-seeing mind and he proceeded to take instant advantage of it.

He was in New York on a ferryboat and chanced to pass the White Star piers on the North River close to the foot of West Twenty-third Street. The White Star liner, *Calgaric,* was moored at one of the piers. He saw her again and again. She was moored there a long time. That interested Jones. It was a shame, he thought, to let as good a ship as that stand idle all these weeks and months. Think of the money that she should be earning all this while. Ever of a curious, investigating mind, he inquired about the ship. She was idle simply because there was no place for her to go. Jones thought again, asked more questions: what did it cost to tie up a large ship like that week after week, month after month? He got the answers.

Then Jones went to the White Star offices. At that time the historic British company was owned and operated by the United States Lines (later it was sold to the Cunard Company and merged with it). Philip A. S. Franklin and P. V. G. Mitchell—shrewd and experienced shipping men—were operating it. Jones went to Mitchell.

Mitchell was not receptive to his suggestion that the *Calgaric* be put into the tourist trade between New York, Havana and Vera Cruz. Jones, who is never easily daunted, kept at it. He argued that it would cost little more to operate the ship and

252

let her bring in revenue than to have her standing idle, month after month, at her pier in New York.

"I will join her in Havana each trip, ride with her to Vera Cruz and tell the tourists what they ought to see in Mexico," Jones told Mitchell. "We will have a special train on the Mexican Railway to take them up to Mexico City. I will ride the train and see to it that these people see Mexico in the proper way."

Gradually Elmer Jones began to wear down Mitchell's resistance. He won Franklin over also when he said that Wells Fargo would participate in any operating deficit. They accepted the offer and Jones went to work.

Five trips were planned for the spring of 1925. The *Calgaric* was booked almost to capacity each trip. Jones or one of his capable assistants, vice-presidents O'Brien or Darnielle, met the ship each trip at Havana, became acquainted with the passengers and talked to them about Mexico and the wonders it had to offer.

The *Calgaric* didn't make the five trips that were scheduled. It made but three. Politics, in the form of the flare-up of revolution under Huerta, intervened; and the *Calgaric* was hastily withdrawn from the new service and sent to Europe. But Jones was satisfied. He had made his point. There was a tourist demand for Mexico and in future years this demand would continue to grow. He was a prophet, far ahead of his years.

Not long after the end of World War I, a popular tourist route was developed between San Francisco and New York through the Panama Canal. The United States Lines built three splendid ships for this trade, the *California*, the *Pennsylvania* and the *Virginia* for operation by its subsidiary, the Panama Pacific Lines. They were fine modern ships and Jones watched their coming with keen interest. In his restless mind he conceived a plan that would give the jaded tourist a fresh road to travel. He would include the port of Acapulco with a side trip to Mexico City on this San Francisco to New York route.

Because Wells Fargo had an office in Acapulco, Jones had been in that town many times. He had been impressed, not only with its great beauty but with its practical advantages as a deep-water harbor. Had it been given a railroad in the old days, it might easily have become the chief Pacific port for all Mexico.

Wells Fargo awakened it. Many times Jones had ridden the stone road that Cortez had built out of Acapulco harbor, up through Taxco and Cuernavaca, right over the 11,000-foot ridge of the Sierra Madres—the backbone of the continent—and down into the ancient capital of the Aztecs, 300 miles away. It was a difficult road but a much-traveled one. Wagons and coaches used it and their drivers boasted that they could make the trip from Acapulco over the mountains to Mexico City in two days and a night.

In recent years the ancient highroad of Cortez had been relocated and repaved. It is now more sinuous than it was. There are many more curves but the grades are far easier. Today you can easily make the 300 miles from Mexico City to Acapulco in ten or twelve hours by motor. Airplanes cover the distance in little more than an hour.

The more Elmer Jones thought of the plan of making Acapulco the western portal of this new trans-Mexican tourist route, the better he liked it. He went to Philip A. S. Franklin, of the United States Lines. Franklin didn't think much of Jones's plan. But Jones, never one to be discouraged, got Franklin to let his right-hand man, P. V. G. Mitchell, make a study of the proposal. Mitchell, a shrewd and experienced traffic man, studied the plan in his New York office and decided against it. Jones kept at them. Would Franklin please send Mitchell down to Mexico to take a look? Mitchell went. They reconsidered and agreed to stop at Acapulco if Wells Fargo would guarantee them at least nine passengers a voyage. Wells Fargo agreed to this and the arrangements were made.

The success of this plan was instantaneous and it was continued until the outbreak of World War II. The ships were then transferred by the United States Government to the South American service and were renamed the *Brazil, Uruguay* and *Argentina.*

Percy Mitchell became an Acapulco enthusiast and has

254

remained one. It was he who insisted on my visiting the town, which I did on a special trip of the trans-Atlantic liner *Washington* in December, 1940. Tourists by the thousands were coming to Acapulco. Modern hotels were springing up on the hillsides that faced the deep, blue waters of the Pacific. And the Wells Fargo office in Acapulco was torn down in 1943 to make way for a new modern building.

Corollary to the problem of getting travel-minded Americans from the Caribbean to Mexico City was the matter of getting them from Mexico City west to Acapulco where the California-bound ship would pick them up. Before the present smooth road was built, the only way to travel the old stone road was to take two days for it. But the only suitable stopping place was Cuernavaca and that was only one-fifth of the way from Mexico City to Acapulco.

Elmer Jones sensed the situation and envisioned the lovely, old hill town of Taxco, just a hundred miles from the capital, as the most suitable overnight stop for the through traffic. But Taxco, lovely as it was, had no hotel facilities. Jones made up his mind quickly. Wells Fargo would build an inn at Taxco, and use it not only for the overnight guests going through to Acapulco, but for tourists who wanted a longer stay in one of the most graceful of all Mexican mountain towns. Travelers came for many miles just to see the church that Jose Borda— the old Frenchman who first developed the great silver mines in the region—built with his own funds more than two and a half centuries ago. That church, in rare baroque, has never been permitted to deteriorate. In recent years it has been thoroughly renovated and redecorated. Its great organ is famous. And it is, itself, with its two high and ornate towers, the outstanding sight of lovely Taxco.

Now Wells Fargo was in the hotel business. Jones had succeeded in getting hold of an old ranch house, standing in a commanding position on the brow of the great hill overlooking the valley and he proceeded to make a first-class inn of it. He named it after his wife, Marion Telva, a distinguished contralto of the Metropolitan Opera Company. "Hotel" is hardly the word to describe the Rancho Telva. Even though it possesses

255

all the features of a modern hostelry, it retains all the patios, terraces and simple charm of an oldtime Mexican inn. I was so carried away when I first saw Rancho Telva that I wrote:

Taxco the unbelievable . . . not since I left Amalfi have I seen sheer beauty such as this . . . Here is the rarest and most exotic of communities—an Italian hill town transplanted in the rugged mountains of North America. I am going to return to it— again and still again. I am caught and held captive by its sensuous charm, its delicacy of outline, the repose that only long years of peaceful life can give a town. Taxco has something more than the serenity and dignity of old age. She is venerable, but time has touched her lightly; in some way time has permitted her to retain her virginal beauty.

Wells Fargo has expanded its field of activities, but it is still very much in the business of carrying express. In January, 1947, its vigorous and alert president, at the request of the Mexican government, arranged for the shipment of thirteen tons of gold (worth these days $35 an ounce) from Canada to Mexico. The entire shipment was made in three planes. Elmer Jones, happy as a lark in his oldtime role as express messenger, accompanied the first plane on its entire trip. News of the movement, which was intended to be a tightly held secret, leaked out and Jones was besieged by newspapermen when the gold-laden plane reached Newark from Ottawa. The stories released to newspapers throughout the country reminded the old-timers of the early days when Wells Fargo shipped millions in gold bullion from the Sierra Nevada and the Comstock Lode. The second and third planes carried, in addition to the gold, pianos and baby chicks from San Antonio to Mexico City. Baby chicks, pianos, and gold! What a cargo! It would have taken 85 ponies at least 121 days, a third of a year, to carry that cargo of gold, and yet the trip was made in twenty-two hours. Wells Fargo has kept abreast of the times.

In Mexico, today, Wells Fargo maintains the largest tourist agency in that country in co-operation with the travel and financial departments of the American Express Company.

Today Wells Fargo also owns ten great stores in Mexico handling huge quantities of farm equipment and supplies and

256

carrying a line of automobiles and trucks. It has joined with two other great and old American institutions, the John Deere Company which, for over 100 years, has made plows and all other modern farm implements, and the Studebaker Corporation which has been manufacturing vehicles for more than a century and now turns out one of the finest lines of automobiles and trucks made in the United States. Thus, Wells Fargo and these two fine old American concerns are serving the Republic of Mexico as they have served our own country for decades.

In New York City, Wells Fargo, under Jones' guidance, has developed a fleet of more than fifty armored cars. Painted bright red, they are a familiar sight in the city streets. These armored cars, serving the Federal Reserve Bank, the National City, the Corn Exchange and other banks and important financial institutions, handle a great percentage of all the gold and silver that moves into and out of these institutions.

Although it no longer carries express in the United States, the Wells Fargo Carloading Company operates extensively on the nation's railroads with great transcontinental movements of consolidated fast freight. Jones, with the company's present enterprising directors, R. L. Clarkson, R. T. Reed, Lynde Selden, F. P. Small, Howard A. Smith, J. K. Livingston and James O. Ellis, are still expanding the services of Wells Fargo. Plans are afoot for Wells Fargo to carry air express between the United States and Mexico via the planes of the American Air Lines. At the same time the company's offices in Cuba (where they have been open for seventy-five years) are growing, serving that country both as express and travel agencies.

Wells Fargo has indeed changed since 1852. Its role in the development of the country has been considerable; and it appears that this company which has survived financial crises, mergers and consolidation, will continue to expand. The days of Hank Monk, the Concord Coach, and the Pony Express are gone. The boisterous and adventurous forty-niners are dead; it is no longer necessary to cross Panama by mule to get from New York to San Francisco; transcontinental mail and freight no longer depend on an Overland Stage vulnerable to Indian attack. Today we have the finest trains and air service in the world. We have come a long way, and Wells Fargo's role has been an impressive one through it all. Speed, safety and dependability are still its watchwords.

Bibliography

Alta California (newspaper), Sacramento, 1850, 1852, 1854, 1855, 1856.

American Magazine, February, 1911.

Anonymous: *A Brief History of the Mail Service, Settlement of the Country, and the Indian Depredations* (pamphlet), (publisher and place and date of publication not known).

Appleton's Railway Guide to the United States and Canada (periodical), 1870.

Bancroft, H. H.: *Chronicles of the Builders of the Commonwealth,* The History Co., San Francisco, 1891-1892.

Banning, Capt. William and George Hugh: *Six Horses,* The Century Company, New York, 1930.

Bates, D. B.: *Incidents on Land and Water or Four Years on the Pacific Coast,* E. O. Libby & Co., Boston, 1858.

Boggs, Mae Helene Bacon: *My Playhouse was a Concord Coach*, An Anthology of Newspaper Clippings and Documents Relating to Those Who Made California History During the Years 1822-1888. Printed at the Howell-North Press, Oakland, Calif.

Bowles, Samuel: *Our New West*, Hartford Publishing Company, Hartford, 1869.

Bradley, Glenn D.: *The Story of the Pony Express*, A. C. McClurg, Chicago, 1913.

Bulletin (newspaper), San Francisco, 1855, 1860.

Burnett, Peter: *Recollections and Opinions of an Old Pioneer*, D. Appleton & Co., New York, 1880.

Butterfield, D. A.: *Prospectus of Butterfield's Overland Despatch* (pamphlet), W. L. S. Harrison, New York, 1865.

Calaveras Chronicle (newspaper), Calaveras, California, 1871.

Chapman, Arthur: *The Pony Express*, G. P. Putnam, New York, 1932.

Clemens, Samuel Langhorne (Mark Twain): *Roughing It*, 2 vols., Harper & Brothers, New York, 1899.

Daily Placer Times and Transcript (newspaper), Placerville, California, 1855.

Dana, Richard Henry, Jr.: *Two Years Before the Mast*, Harper & Brothers, New York, 1841.

Downie, Major William: *Hunting for Gold*, Press of the California Publishing Co., San Francisco, 1893.

Driggs, Howard R.: *The Pony Express Goes Through*, Frederick A. Stokes, New York, 1935.

Eldredge, Z. S.: *History of California*, Vol. IV, Century History Co., New York, 1915.

Enterprise (newspaper), Virginia City, Nevada, 1883.

Frederick, J. V.: *Ben Holladay, the Stagecoach King*, The Arthur H. Clark Co., Glendale, California, 1940.

Glasscock, C. B.: *Bandits and the Southern Pacific*, Frederick A. Stokes Company, New York, 1929.

Glasscock, C. B.: *The Big Bonanza*, A. L. Burt Company, New York, 1931.

Greeley, Horace: *Autobiography of Horace Greeley*, E. B. Treat, New York, 1872.

Greeley, Horace: *An Overland Journey*, C. M. Saxton, Barker & Co., New York, 1860.

Harlow, Alvin F.: *Old Post Bags*, D. Appleton and Company, 1928.

Harlow, Alvin F.: *Old Waybills*, D. Appleton-Century, New York, 1934.

Harte, Francis Bret: *A Night at Wingdam*.

Head, L. O.: *History of Wells Fargo & Co.*, Joint Stock Association, Express Co., 1852-66.

Hittell, John Sherster: *The Commerce and Industries of the Pacific Coast of North America*, A. L. Bancroft & Company, San Francisco, 1882.

Hittell, Theodore H.: *A History of California,* Occidental Publishing Company, San Francisco, 1882.

Hunt, Rockwell Dennis, and Sanchez, Nellie Van de Grift: *A Short History of California,* Thomas Y. Crowell, New York, 1929.

Jackson, Joseph Henry: *Tintypes in Gold: Four Studies in Robbery,* The Macmillan Co., New York, 1939.

Johnson, Allen, and Malone, Dumas: *Dictionary of American Biography,* Charles Scribner's Sons, New York, 1930.

Johnson, Theodore T.: *Sights in the Gold Region and Scenes by the Way,* Baker and Scribner, New York, 1849.

Lang, Walter B., ed.: *The First Overland Mail: Butterfield Trail* (Waterman L. Ormsby and William Tallack), privately published, 1940.

Lyman, George D.: *Ralston's Ring,* Charles Scribner's Sons, New York, 1937.

Lyman, George D.: *The Saga of the Comstock Lode,* Charles Scribner's Sons, 1946.

Marshall, James: *Santa Fe: The Railroad That Built an Empire,* Random House, Inc., New York, 1945.

McLeod, Alexander: *Pigtails and Gold Dust,* Caxton, Caldwell (Idaho), 1947.

McNeil, Samuel: *McNeil's Travels in 1849, To, Through and From the Gold Regions in California* (pamphlet), Scott & Bascom, Columbus (Ohio), 1850.

New York Times (newspaper), New York, May, 1852.

Ormsby, Waterman L.: (Lyle H. Wright and Josephine M. Bynum, eds.), *The Butterfield Overland Mail,* The Huntington Library, San Marino, 1942.

Paine, Albert Bigelow: *Mark Twain, A Biography,* Harper & Brothers, New York and London, 1912.

Paine, Swift, and Orrum, Eilley: *Queen of the Comstock,* A. L. Burt Company, New York, 1929.

Rascoe, Burton: *Belle Starr, "The Bandit Queen,"* Random House, Inc., 1941.

Richardson, Albert D.: *Beyond the Mississippi,* American Publishing Co., Hartford, 1867.

Rocky Mountain News (newspaper), Denver, 1860.

Sacramento Union (newspaper), Sacramento, 1868.

San Francisco Chronicle (newspaper), San Francisco, 1870, 1904.

San Francisco Examiner (newspaper), San Francisco, 1873.

Sanchez, Nellie Van de Grift: *Spanish and Indian Place Names of California,* A. M. Robertson, 1930.

Schaffer, John G.: *The Early History of the Wells Fargo Express,* University of California Press, Berkeley, 1922.

Sonora Herald (newspaper), California, 1855.

Soule, Gihon and Nisbet: *Annals of San Francisco,* D. Appleton and Company, New York, 1855.

Stimson, A. L.: *History of the Express Business,* Baker & Godwin, New York, 1881.

Truman, Major Ben. C.: *Knights of the Lash: Old Time Stage Drivers of the West Coast, The Overland Monthly,* XXXI, 218-26, 308-18, 1898.

Villard, Henry: *The Past and Present of the Pike's Peak Gold Regions,* Sutherland & McAvoy, St. Louis, 1860.

Visscher, William Lightfoot: *The Pony Express,* Rand, McNally & Company, Chicago.

Wells Fargo Messenger (newspaper), New York, 1913, 1918.

Wells, Henry: *Address to the Buffalo Historical Society* (misc.), 1863.

Wells, Henry: *Letters* (collection of Wells College, Aurora, New York), (misc.)

Wilson, Neill C.: *Treasure Express,* The Macmillan Co., New York, 1936.

Wiltsee, Ernest A.: *The Pioneer Miner and the Pack Mule Express,* California Historical Society, San Francisco, 1931.

Winther, Oscar O.: *Express and Stagecoach Days in California,* Stanford University Press, Palo Alto, 1935.

Winther, Oscar O.: *Via Western Express & Stagecoach,* Stanford University Press, Palo Alto, 1945.

RECORDS AND MANUSCRIPTS

Wells, Fargo and Company Records. Excerpts from minutes of the Board of Directors, Annual Statements, etc. New York offices of Wells, Fargo and Wells Fargo Museum in Wells Fargo Bank and Union Trust Company, San Francisco, Calif.

Wells, Fargo and Company Letter to W. B. Latham, April 27, 1855. Wells Fargo Museum in Wells Fargo Bank and Union Trust Company Building, San Francisco, Calif.

Schaffer, John G.: *The Early History of the Wells Fargo Express,* unpublished Master's thesis in University of California Library, 1922.

Hume, J. B.: *Scrap-Books,* Wells Fargo Museum in Wells Fargo Bank and Union Trust Company Building, San Francisco, Calif. (Robbery material.)

Todd, Alexander H.: *Statement,* dictated 1878, Bancroft Library, University of California, Berkeley, Calif.

McConnell, W. J.: *The Idaho Inferno,* dictated 1873, Bancroft Library, University of California, Berkeley, Calif.

Index

264

266